A Wanderer in the Perfect City

About the Author

Lawrence Weschler is the author of twelve books, including *Mr. Wilson's Cabinet of Wonder,* short-listed for both the Pulitzer Prize and the National Book Critics Circle Award and, most recently, *Vermeer in Bosnia* and *Everything That Rises: A Book of Convergences.* Weschler's "Passions and Wonders" series also includes *Seeing is Forgetting the Name of the Thing One Sees* (a life of contemporary artist Robert Irwin), *David Hockney's Cameraworks,* and *Boggs: A Comedy of Values.* His books of political reportage include *The Passion of Poland; A Miracle, A Universe: Settling Accounts with Torturers;* and *Calamities of Exile.* A graduate of Cowell College of the University of California at Santa Cruz, Weschler has taught there as well as at Princeton, Bard, Vassar, and Sarah Lawrence. Following twenty years as a staff writer at *The New Yorker,* he is currently the director of the New York Institute for the Humanities at NYU. He is a widely honored political and cultural journalist and a regular contributor to such publications as *McSweeny's, Harper's, The Atlantic Monthly, The Three-penny Review,* and National Public Radio.

LAWRENCE WESCHLER

A Wanderer in
SELECTED PASSION PIECES
the Perfect City

The University of Chicago Press
Chicago and London

The University of Chicago Press, Chicago, 60637

First published in 1998 by Hungry Mind Press
University of Chicago Press edition 2006

Printed in the United States of America

10 09 08 07 06   1 2 3 4 5

ISBN: 0-226-89390-1

Grateful acknowledgment is extended to the publishers of earlier versions of these essays: the *New Yorker* for "Shapinsky's Karma," "Jensen's Shangra-La," "Slominsky's Failure," "Katchor's Knipl, Knipl's Katchor," and "Gary's Trajectory"; *Artforum* for the postscript to "Jensen's Shangra-La"; *Rolling Stone* for "Art's Father, Vladek's Son"; *L.A. Reader* for "Lennie's Illustion"; and *Interview* for "Miller's Gambit."

Portions of this work previously appeared in a slightly different version in *Shapinsky's Karma, Bogg's Bills and Other True-Life Tales,* published by North Point Press, 1988, and Penguin Books, 1990.

Weschler, Lawrence.
   A wanderer in the perfect city : selected passions pieces / Lawrence Weschler ; with a new foreword by Pico Iyer.—University of Chicago Press ed.
      p. cm.
   Originally published: St. Paul, MN : Hungary Mind Press, © 1998.
   ISBN: 0-226-89390-1 (pbk. : acid-free paper)
   I. Title.
   AC8.W415   2005
   081—dc22
                                                                2005023241

For Joanna, as ever,
my heart's true home

Contents

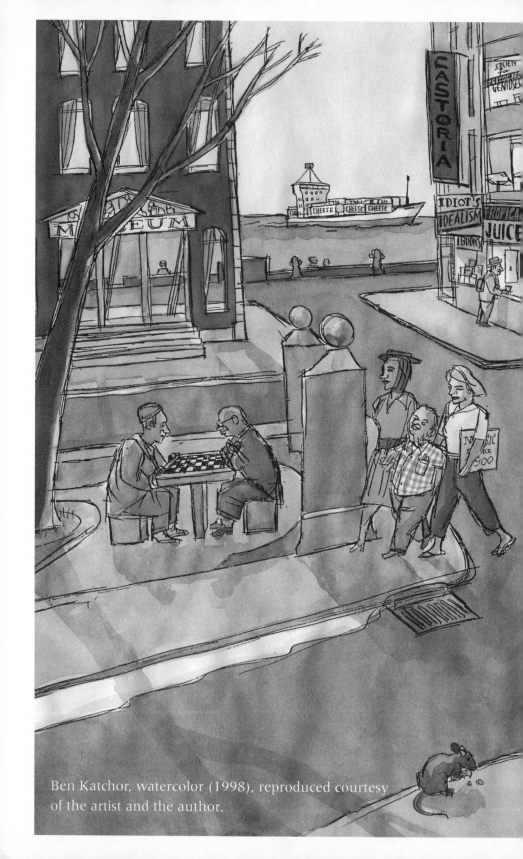

Ben Katchor, watercolor (1998), reproduced courtesy
of the artist and the author.

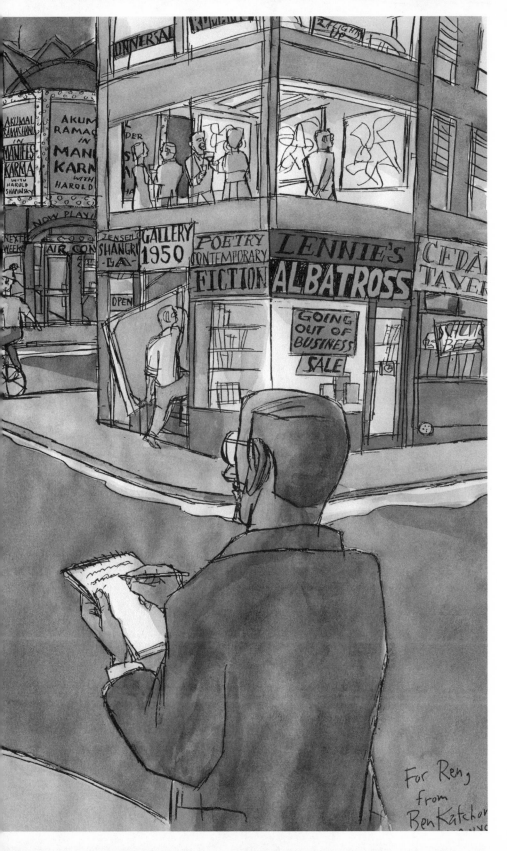

The Depths of the Curious
Foreword to *A Wanderer in the Perfect City*

Curiosity is the engine that drives a traveler out into the world, and the true traveler is the one who see that the world points in two directions. He is fired by his eagerness, his interest in the world, but what it gives back to him in turn is often a strangeness, a confoundingness that is the other half of what we mean by curiosity. The "wanderer in the perfect city," as the book you're holding in your hand commemorates, is a flaneur who finds perfection in the very act of roaming, or rummaging, browsing the streets as if they were dog-eared manuscripts in some eccentric's library. Everyone, he knows, if opened up with patience, contains a fabulous story, as barely credible as truth.

The propulsive force, in other words, is enthusiasm, which means (or meant, in the original Greek) "possessed by the gods," a term generous enough to take in gods that were as venal and fragile and mixed-up as ourselves. If the traveler is one who goes out in search of oddity, the things that remind him how much in the world exists beyond his understanding— "around the bend"—the writer, ideally, is one who passes that spirit of excited enquiry on to the reader with a gusto that becomes contagious. Curiosity + enthusiasm = wonder.

I thought these curious thoughts while reading, for the sixth or seventh time, Lawrence Weschler's tales of rambles in the world. I'd grown up, in all senses, reading Weschler in *The New Yorker,* been moved by his constant, cheerful worrying at the places where dark realities meet a born-again American spirit of optimism (Kafka in the cartoon version, you could say), and then been swept up by the man himself, met for the first time in the amnesiac sunshine of Los Angeles, where he was eager to whisk me off to a Museum of Jurassic Technology consecrated to the uncanny (immortalized in his book *Mr. Wilson's Cabinet of Wonder*). He was about to interview the magician-scholar-performer Ricky Jay onstage at the time, had just been writing about photographs—convergences—was talking about one of his regular radio broadcasts (shared on this occasion with his daughter) and had four books coming out imminently. Clearly the term "Renaissance man" needed an upgrade if it were to comprehend all of Mr. Weschler, who was also running an Institute for the Humanities, editing a magazine called *The Omnivore*, sponsoring a whole new school of writers and about to visit a museum in North Dakota that was mounting an exhibition about those who "disappeared" during the dirty war in Argentina. No other writer I know has managed to bridge the gap—as wide as the culture—between William Shawn's *New Yorker* and Dave Eggers's *Mc-Sweeney's*. Between the formalism of the historical and artistic, in short, and the heartfelt, ironic spirit of tomorrow.

But what I remembered more, reading this book again, was how Weschler had written of David Hockney, repeatedly over the decades, as a chronicler of light, able to find a brightness in an L.A. that many of us had given up on or never taken the trouble to look at closely in the first place. The most memorable piece I'd read in *The New Yorker* in recent years was Weschler's own investigation into light in Los Angeles—the incongruous hope amidst the smog—in which, with characteristic unexpectedness, he had sought out the golden-voiced baseball announcer Vin Scully to hymn the raptures of the late-afternoon light above Dodger Stadium. And then I'd come upon another piece by him about driving with Hockney through the hills of L.A., the artist's senses ever more alert as his ears began to fail him. It was as if the vagrant writer had found a kindred spirit in the one figure from the Old World who could see the real promise offered by California's spacey vistas and sense of suspended time.

I carried this image of Weschler—a Hockney on the page at times, finding light in forgotten places—back into the book you're reading now. And I saw how, from the very first sentence, he speaks for a spirit of possibility that too many of us have forgotten existed. A call comes from a stranger at 11:30 P.M. while our author is deep in an esoteric tome. Unlike anyone eager to hang onto his equilibrium, our author picks up the phone, schedules a meeting with the enthusiast and clearly is ready to follow him deep into the farthest reaches of human extravagance. Here is a character happy to be stood on his head and to get lost inside another's obsession, wandering through the mazy, endlessly divergent passageways of the unconscious, collective and very much otherwise.

The adventure that follows is, in classical Weschler fashion, given life and weird electricity by a wildly exuberant, hopelessly polymathic, surreptitiously poignant Indian who (if truth be told) catches the spirit of my ancestral homeland, always at least as energizing and engaging as it is exhausting, as well as anything I've read. Weschler's subject, you come to see, is art and ambition and failure and loneliness, but most of all the human condition, seen at an angle and inspected as closely as if a scientist's face were pressed up against a test-tube. The distinguishing feature of *homo Weschleris* is that he is voluble, extreme, the very opposite of jaded. "Authentically dazzled by the particulate density" of fate.

The method ("particulate," like the "metastable" he uses elsewhere, seems to go off in many directions at once) is unorthodox: Weschler holds you as the Ancient Mariner does the Wedding-Guest in Coleridge's poem, to involve you in what comes to seem an investigation, really, into magic. He uses a highly measured, precisely detailed, information-rich style out of the old *New Yorker,* but in search of the new; underneath the pose of "benign befuddlement," he is, like the Knud Jensen he evokes so vividly, a "masterly organizer." The result is a trip, in both the old and the new sense, which reminds you that the traveler who really engages us is not one who just moves himself, but one who knows how to move his listeners. Down the spiral staircase of the imagination, past all the bric-a-brac collected over decades, into the basement of the soul.

And there, where we least expect it, we are brought back to something essential that reminds us that we've been carried back in an elegant circle to our original state, but transformed. People retreat into themselves, one sees, and come out with something universal. Weschler, meanwhile, seems so hungry for life that the rest of us become hungry for him. There's little of himself in these pieces, except insofar as every portrait is a depiction of its maker. I first met him—I said this before, didn't I?—talking to a magician, a performer and a scholar. All in one.

—Pico Iyer

Santa Barbara, May 2005

Pico Iyer was born to Indian parents in Oxford, raised in California and lives now in Japan. He spends much of his life somewhere in-between, visiting North Korea, Bhutan, Easter Island, Iceland and many other places whose features he describes in such books as *Video Night in Kathmandu, Falling Off the Map, The Global Soul* and, most recently, *Sun After Dark.*

Of course I am a wanderer, a pilgrim on this earth.
But can you say that you are anything more?

—Goethe *(The Sorrows of Young Werther)*

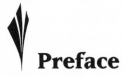

Preface

The pieces collected in this volume generally began betwixt and be-tween. That is to say that over the years, especially after I joined the staff of the *New Yorker* in 1981, I developed a pattern of shuttling back and forth between heavy political themes and more lighthearted cul-tural ones. Or so, anyway, did I come to explain myself to myself. I used to imagine that these cultural forays cleared the palate, as it were, between courses of heartier political fare. They were recreations—occasions for re-creation. Thus, for example, I might parse the comic adventures of a frantic Indian schemer at the highest reaches of the contemporary art world between stints of reporting on martial law in Poland and torture in Brazil. I'd flee to these brighter cultural venues as temporary respite from the darker political topics, which neverthe-less continued to exercise a deep pull on my concerns.

But in rereading many of these cultural pieces in preparation for the original version of this volume,* I came to see that such simple dichotomies just wouldn't do; they explained neither what I nor what my writing had been about. To begin with, these cultural pieces are

---

Shapinsky's Karma, Boggs's Bills, and Other True-Life Tales, North Point Press, 1988. The current volume differs from that earlier version in that the last of its six pieces, about J. S. G. Boggs, the money artist, has been peeled off for expanded separate publication as a book in its own right (*Boggs: A Comedy of Values*, Uni-versity of Chicago Press, 1999). The remaining five pieces from the original book have meanwhile been supplemented with three new ones—"Katchor's Knipl, Knipl's Katchor" "Miller's Gambit," and "Gary's Trajectory"—unique to this edition.

themselves often quite political: the story of the hell-bent Indian, for instance, opens out onto some fairly complex and subtle terrain involving the distribution of power in the art world. Beyond that, many of the central themes in my political reporting made their first appearance in these lighter venues, or else were recapitulated and refined there.

Thus, for example, the theme of passion. I used to speak loosely of these as my "passion pieces," without even noticing that I'd earlier titled my book on Solidarity *The Passion of Poland*. In all my writing, I guess, I have been concerned with people and places that were just moseying down the street one day, minding their own business, when suddenly and almost spontaneously they caught fire, they became obsessed, they became intensely focused and intensely alive—ending up, by day's end, somewhere altogether different from where they'd imagined they were setting out that morning. Many of the finest theorists and activists in Solidarity used to describe that movement as an expression of "the subjectivity of the Polish nation," by which, they'd explain, they meant its capacity to act as the subject rather than the object of history. Such transformations are, at root, grammatical—an entity that was content to receive the action of its sentences now suddenly demands itself to initiate such actions—and are, of course, metastable. They are perpetually up for grabs and under siege (indeed, in the political realm, states of siege are launched precisely to upend them), but once they've occurred, the field of play is forever changed.

Similarly, these passion pieces are punctuated with grace notes, and this mysterious working of grace is something I've likewise often considered in my political reporting: grace in its original sense as *gratis*, for free. One works and works and works at something, which then happens of its own accord: it would not have happened without all the prior work, true, but its happening cannot be said to have resulted from all that work, the way effects are said to result from a series of causes. There is all that work, which is preparation, preparation for receptivity, but then there is something beyond that which is *gratis*, for free. August 1980 in Gdansk, Poland, would never have happened without the years and years of tenuous labor by a small band of seemingly marginal activists—no one denies this—but when that strike suddenly happened, it seemed to come out of nowhere, to happen all by itself. Everyone still talks about this (particularly the activists), talks about and wonders at the sudden overwhelming sense of rightness that descended on the place at that moment.

The descent of grace, like the upwelling of passion, occurs in the lives of individuals as well as in the lives of polities, and though such occurrences are often fraught with significance, they can also be quite comical as well. There is something both marvelous and hilarious in watching the humdrum suddenly take flight. This is, in part, a collection of such launchings.

Most of these pieces first appeared in the *New Yorker*, in the old *New Yorker*, which is to say William Shawn's *New Yorker*. Mr. Shawn encouraged and supported and in a sense even inspired them: his generous concern for both the writer and the subject suffuses them. And I happily acknowledge that debt here.

On a more day-to-day basis at the magazine, it was generally either John Bennet or Pat Crow who watched over the conception and gestation of these pieces and then oversaw their passage into print. Their uncanny sense of tone and unfailingly wry reserve saved me and the reader from many an infelicity; those that remain simply testify to my own stubbornness in the face of wiser counsel.

North Point Press, the splendid small and independent Berkeley publishing house, "got" this book when no one else, certainly no one in New York, seemed quite willing or able to. ("What? A collection of nonfiction tales? Wouldn't ever sell. Impossible.") It was a joy working with them all the way through, especially with Jack Shoemaker and Tom Christensen, the editors who not only got it but saw it—and helped me to see it—clear.

Alas, North Point, for all its splendors, failed to survive into the nineties. Its example, however, lives on in the many similar ventures it helped to inspire, including the marvelous folk at the Hungry Mind Press of St. Paul, Minnesota, notably Dallas Crow, who saw fit to give this collection a second life.

None of these pieces would have been possible without the open-hearted cooperation of their subjects—Akumal Ramachander, Harold and Kate and David Shapinsky, Knud and Vivi Jensen, Art Spiegelman and Françoise Mouly, Nicolas Slonimsky and Electra Yourke, Leonard Durso, Ben Katchor, Jeff Miller, and Gary Isaacs—and I once again warmly thank them here for their forbearance in letting me into their lives.

Into my own life, these last many years, has come my heart's true home, my bride Joanna, and this remains, as ever, Joanna's book.

1988/1998

A Wanderer in the Perfect City

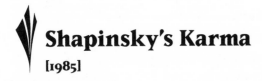

Shapinsky's Karma
[1985]

I was up late one night last fall, absorbed in Serge Guilbaut's provocative revisionist tract *How New York Stole the Idea of Modern Art,* when, at eleven-thirty, the phone rang. A stranger on the line introduced himself as Akumal Ramachander, from Bangalore, India. He was calling from Washington, D.C., he informed me in a spirited voice. He'd just been in Warsaw a few weeks earlier, where he'd had many fascinating experiences. He'd read a book I'd written on Poland, and could see that I'd given the situation there much thought. He was going to be in New York City later in the week, and would it be all right if we got together? It all sounded mildly diverting, so we set a rendezvous.

A few days later, on schedule, Ramachander appeared in my office—a youngish, fairly slight gentleman with short-cropped black hair and a round face. His conversation caromed all over the place (Gdansk, Reagan, Sri Lanka, Lech Walesa, Indira Gandhi, the Sikhs, Margaret Thatcher, Satyajit Ray, London); he told me that he was some sort of part-time correspondent for the local paper of one of those Indian towns almost no one in America has ever heard of. He'd taught English at an agricultural college but had generally been something of a drifter, he explained—that is, until recently, for he'd just discovered his true calling. "My destiny!" he insisted. "We Indians believe in karma, in destiny, in discovering the true calling for our lives. It has nothing to do with making money, this 'making a living' you have here in America. No, it is the spirit calling, and we answer. Not in some silly mystical way but as if the purpose of life were revealed—sometimes, as in my case, all-of-a-suddenly, like that! And this is what has now happened."

And what calling, I asked him, had he suddenly uncovered?

"Shapinsky!"

And who, or what, I hazarded, was Shapinsky?

"Harold Shapinsky," he replied. "Abstract Expressionist painter, generation of de Kooning and Rothko, an undiscovered marvel, an absolute genius, completely unknown, utterly unappreciated. He lives here in New York City, with his wife, in a tiny one-bedroom apartment, where he continues to paint, as he has been doing for over forty years, *like an angel*." Ramachander scribbled an address and a phone number on a scrap of paper, shoved it at me, and continued, "You *must* visit this Shapinsky fellow. He's a true find, a major discovery. It is my destiny to bring him to the attention of the world."

I was somewhat speechless.

Ramachander was not: "You will see—this is an extraordinary discovery. As I say, I don't care about money. What's money? I do it because of my destiny."

Well, at length Ramachander departed. (He was, he told me, headed for Europe a few days hence.) I tacked Shapinsky's address and phone number to my bulletin board but didn't get around to calling him right away, and then one thing led to another, and I pretty much forgot about the whole incident.

A few weeks later, at seven in the morning, the phone in my apartment rang me awake. "Hello, Mr. Weschler. Akumal here. In Utrecht, Holland. You won't believe the good news! I took slides of Shapinsky's work to the Stedelijk Museum in Amsterdam, and the curator there was amazed. He told me that I'd brought him the work of a great artist, that Shapinsky is a major find. I must tell you, I'm beginning to believe this is one of the great discoveries of the last five years. The curator was extremely supportive, and eager to see how things develop."

Myself, I wasn't really eager to believe any of it. I hung up and went back to sleep.

A few days later, the phone rang again—at ten in the morning this time. "Akumal again here, Mr. Weschler! Only, in London today. More good news! I visited the Tate this morning. Just walked in with no appointment, demanded to see the curator of modern art, refused to leave the waiting room until he finally came out—to humor me, I suppose, this silly little Indian fellow, you know—but presently he was *blown away*. He bows to me and says, 'Mr. Ramachander, you are right. Shapinsky is a terrific discovery.' I'm becoming more and more convinced myself that he's the discovery of the decade. Anyway, he gave me the name of a gallery—the Mayor Gallery. James Mayor, one of the top dealers in London, Cork Street—Warhol, Lichtenstein, Rauschenberg, first-rate. I went over there, and he, too, was flabbergasted. He's thinking about scheduling a show for the spring."

I still didn't know quite what to make of any of this; I assumed that it was all a bit daft, some elaborate fantastication, and, anyway, I remained too busy with other projects to take time to call and visit Shapinsky, if Shapinsky actually existed.

A few days later, the phone rang, again at seven in the morning, and, used to the pattern by now, I managed to preempt my new friend with a "Hello, Akumal."

"British television!" Ramachander exclaimed, utterly unimpressed by my prescience. "I showed the slides to some people over at British Channel 4 and they loved them, and right on the spot they committed themselves to doing a special, an hour-long documentary, to be ready in time for the show at the Mayor Gallery. Did I tell you? A one-man show to open on May twenty-first, Shapinsky's sixtieth birthday. They love the story, the idea of this unknown genius Abstract Expressionist and of the little Indian fellow and his destiny. They'll be flying me back to New York in several weeks with a camera crew to re-create our meeting—Shapinsky and myself—and then the following month they're going to fly Shapinsky and his wife and me to Bangalore, in India, so I can show them around my digs. This meeting of East and West, you see—that's the ticket. So maybe I'll see you in New York, yes?"

I set the phone back in its cradle, resolving to give the whole matter a bit more thorough consideration once I'd reawakened at some more decent hour. But just as I was nodding back off the phone rang again.

"The Ludwig Museum! I forgot to tell you. Just before Channel 4, I went to Cologne and showed the slides to the excellent lady in charge of the Ludwig Museum there. She couldn't get over them. She can't wait to see the show at the Mayor Gallery. Everyone agrees.

"I'm beginning to see it clearly now: Shapinsky is one of the top finds of the century!"

Several weeks later (I'd anticipated the visitation with a notation in my desk diary), the phone rang at my office, and of course it was Akumal, this time in New York, in Shapinsky's apartment—I simply had to drop whatever I was doing immediately, he told me, and come see for myself.

So I did. The address on Seventieth Street, east of Second Avenue, turned out to be a Japanese restaurant. Off to one side was a dark entry passage behind a glass door. I pushed a doorbell and was buzzed in—a five-story walk-up; steep stairs and dim, narrow corridors. I could hear something of a commotion upstairs as I approached. Rounding the corner onto the fifth-floor landing, I was momentarily blinded by a panning klieg light: the tiny apartment was indeed overflowing with a bustling film crew. I craned my neck into the bustle. The foyer was almost entirely taken up by a single bed (the only bed in the apartment, I later discovered), which was covered with coats and equipment; the next room was an almost equally crammed kitchen; and just beyond that I could see into a tiny bedroom, which was serving as the studio. A very dignified and dapper-looking English gentleman had spread several paintings about the floor of the studio and was crouched down making a careful selection as the television crew peered over his shoulder. I managed to step in. In the far corner I spotted Akumal, who was beaming. Next to him stood a soft, slightly stooped, fairly rumpled, gray-bearded old man, wrapped in a moth-eaten wool sweater and puffing cherry-sweet tobacco smoke into the air from the bowl of a well-chewed pipe.

"Ah!" Akumal exclaimed, suddenly catching sight of me. "Mr. Weschler! I want you to meet Harold Shapinsky."

Shapinsky looked up, mildly (understandably) dazed.

The dapper Englishman got up off his haunches, wiped his hands, gave one last approving glance at the paintings arrayed before him, and then looked over at Shapinsky, smiling. "Yes," he said. "I think that will do. That will do superbly."

"Cut!" shouted the film director. "Good. Very good." The kliegs went dark.

"James Mayor," Akumal said, introducing the distinguished-looking Englishman, whose identity I'd already surmised.

Shapinsky puffed on his pipe and nodded.

The cameraman asked if he could have Shapinsky and his wife stand by the window for a moment, and Mayor walked over beside me. "Most amazing story," he said. "I mean, an artist of this calibre living like this, dirt poor, completely unknown—*living in a virtual garret* five stories above a Japanese restaurant I've been to literally dozens of times. Quite good Japanese restaurant, by the way, that." Mayor is in his late thirties, trim, conventionally handsome, with a shock of black hair cresting to a peak over his forehead. "I must say, when Akumal brought me in those slides I was astonished," he continued. "I mean, this art business can get one pretty jaded after a while. One gets to feeling one's seen it all. You begin to despair of ever again encountering anything original, powerful, real. I haven't felt a buzz like this in a long time."

Akumal and the director of the film, Greg Lanning, joined us. Lanning explained that he'd now like to shoot a sequence of Mayor and Shapinsky talking together. Everything really was intolerably cramped. I asked Akumal if he'd like to join me for a little walk, and he agreed.

"Well," I told Akumal outside, "you've certainly gone and caught my attention. But do you think we might slow down and wind this tape back a bit? First of all, seriously, *who are you?*"

"Ah, yes." He laughed. "It's been just as I predicted, hasn't it? Wonderful destiny! Manifest destiny—isn't that one of your expressions here in America? Manifest *karma*, if you'll allow me. As I told you, I am a lowly professor of elementary English at the College of Agricultural Sciences in Bangalore. I am there every day from eight to three, teaching my classes of forty students grammar, spelling, sentence structure, conversational skills—only, I'm on leave just now, as you can see."

He was born in Bombay on the tenth of July, 1949, and his family presently moved to Calcutta. His father was a clerk in the army. His family was lower middle class, struggling to advance slightly higher, into the middle class proper. When his father and mother were married, they were so poor they couldn't afford a single night in the fanciest hotel in Bombay—they couldn't even afford tea there—so they went over and just rode up and down in the lifts. "That was their sort of honeymoon celebration. When I was growing up, there were six of us in two rooms."

Walking and talking at a brisk clip, Akumal continued, "My parents are both polyglots—they speak five Indian languages each, I speak seven—and they would encourage my reading. Especially my mother: I remember coming upon her in my room one day; she was reading my copy of *Death of a Salesman* and she was weeping. I was very bookish. I almost went blind with all my reading. There was no electricity, and to save my eyes my father made a huge clamor and got electricity for the entire block. He was not able to complete his schooling himself, so he sacrificed enormously so that his children would be able to: he sent me to a fine school where I perfected my English. Eventually, I even managed to teach English for many years before ever going to England my first time, which was in 1980.

"I was especially in love with beauty. In India, even the poorest will adorn themselves with colorful saris or simple jewelry—you may be economically deprived, we say, but God has given you eyes in your head to see—and from a very early age I was entranced, mesmerized by the flowing movements of all those intense colors. One of my earliest memories in Calcutta was going to the fields not far from Fort William, along the banks of the Hooghly River. This was my art school. Because there, each summer, thousands—no, hundreds of thousands—of butterflies would gather, and I would run among them, chasing them, all those brilliant hues floating about. I never actually tried to catch any. It was just the swarming of all that color. And that was my initial association when I saw the slides of Shapinsky's paintings for the first time. They reminded me of the butterflies back in Calcutta, and the rhythms of classical Indian dance, too—another great passion of mine. I knew I must be in the presence of a profound art if it could inspire associations like that."

Akumal went on to relate that his family had moved to Bangalore when he was sixteen. He received his bachelor's degree in physics and chemistry *and* mathematics from the National College in Bangalore in 1968, shifted fields and campuses and attained a master's degree from Bangalore's Central College in 1971. In addition to teaching, he wrote poetry in Hindi and fiction in English. In 1973, an early draft of an antiwar play of his somehow got him an invitation to Weimar, East Germany—his first trip abroad—and there he was "bowled over by Brecht." I say "somehow": Akumal was actually very specific—exhaustively so—about the circumstances, but my concentration had begun to buckle under the weight of his relentlessly detailed recapitulations. All of Akumal's accounts are exhaustive: it's not so much that he is incapable of compression as that he seems authentically dazzled by the particulate density of every aspect of his fate. Anyway, he returned to India and became something of a gadfly in Bangalore, one of the fastest-growing provincial cities in India, endlessly exhorting the editors of the local papers to expand their cultural coverage, especially of international film and literature. He haunted the British Council Library. He arranged for the first translation of Darwin's *Origin of Species* into Kannada, the local language. He acted as a literary agent on behalf of various local poets and essayists. He managed to finagle a special four-page supplement on the films of the Polish director Krzysztof Zanussi during a

Bangalore film festival in 1979. Zanussi eventually saw the supplement, and had Akumal invited to the 1980 Gdansk film festival, at the height of the Solidarity period—the first of several trips Akumal took to Poland. Somewhere along the line, he met Lelah Dushkin, a sociology professor at Kansas State University, who managed to arrange an invitation for Akumal to come to Kansas to lecture on Indian politics and cinema, so that early in the fall of 1984 Akumal found himself in Chicago, fresh from Poland (where he had just attended another film festival), en route to Manhattan, Kansas.

This is where the story proper begins—a story that Akumal has now told hundreds of times, each time the same way, with the same formulaic cadences and ritualized digressions, except for the addition, at the end of each new telling, of the name and reaction of the person he told it to the immediately prior time. It's like one of those Borges fictions, in which to hear the story is to become part of it. And the story always begins with Akumal's fresh astonishment, his sheer amazement at the wondrous coincidence of it all. Because, as he points out, if he hadn't been on his way to Kansas he would never have been in Chicago, and if he hadn't been in Chicago he would never have accompanied his host, the distinguished Indian poet (and MacArthur Fellowship recipient) A. K. Ramanujan, to a retirement party for Maureen Patterson, the South Asia bibliographer at the University of Chicago, and in that case he would never have had an impulse "to befriend one young man who was standing somewhat shyly in the corner"—an impulse that arose "because the man had an interesting, kind face"—and then he would never have met one of Maureen Patterson's graduate assistants, who proved to be David, the twenty-four-year-old son of Harold and Kate Shapinsky. "It could all easily never have happened," Akumal invariably points out here. "It was all built on the most precarious of coincidences. But, then again, it had to happen, because it was my karma to discover Harold Shapinsky, and it was Shapinsky's karma to be discovered by me."

David Shapinsky was in Chicago doing graduate work in American diplomatic history, so their conversation initially revolved around international relations, alighting on the subject of Poland, and thence on to the subject of a young Polish artist whose work Akumal had taken to promoting since his most recent trip to Gdansk, and some of whose etchings he had back in his suitcase at Ramanujan's. (He had bought them in Poland to assist the poor artist, and was now reselling them as he went along to finance his trip; beyond that, he was virtually without funds.)

"David didn't mention anything about his father that night," Akumal explained to me as we completed perhaps our twelfth lap of the block the afternoon he recounted the whole story to me for the first time. "That took another coincidence—the next day, we just happened to run into each other at the University of Chicago library, and he asked me if I'd mind going with him for coffee. Presently, he told me about his father and invited me up to his room to look at some slides of his father's paintings and see if I might be willing to promote his father's work as well. He is a loving son, and he was pained by the oblivion into which his father had fallen. I was interested, but I really didn't know much about Abstract Expressionism—I mean, I of course had Alvarez's anthology of twentieth-century English poetry, which has a Pollock on the cover, and I'd read a piece in the *Economist* for June 1978, a review of a book about ancient Indian popular painting in which the writer suggested that these artists must have unconsciously anticipated Pollock. So I knew about Pollock, though I'd never heard of de Kooning. And I had no idea how I would react to this work of David's father. In David's room, though, looking at the slides, I got butterflies—the butterflies of my Calcutta youth!

"Over the next few days, I got very excited. I told David to call his parents and tell them to sit tight just a big longer—that a crazy Indian from Bangalore was on his way to promote Harold's paintings. And I made David a two-part bet. I bet him that within a year I would secure a show for his father's paintings at a major world-class gallery— possibly not in America, possibly in Europe. I wasn't sure about New

York—they're funny in New York, you can never tell. And, secondly, we would force the *Encyclopedia Britannica* to revise its entry on Abstract Expressionism to establish the name Shapinsky in its rightful place among de Kooning, Pollock, Rothko, and the others. We bet a dinner at the fanciest restaurant we could think of, and then I was off to Kansas.

"From Kansas, I called a friend of mine in New Jersey, an Indian fellow named Sudhir Vaikkattil. An exceptional photographer, he was an earlier discovery of mine. I told him not to ask any questions but to call the Shapinskys right away, go over there, and take new slides of the work and of them. I'd be joining up with him in a few weeks. I told him not to worry, that somehow I'd find money to pay for the materials—although at that moment I was, frankly, penniless. I called Harold—this was our first conversation—and told him about Sudhir and the need for the new slides. And—this was fantastic—you know what he said? He said, 'Well, I hope he gets in touch with me.' This was a wonderful omen. In India, we have a proverb—'The thirsty man goes to the well, the well doesn't go to the thirsty man.' As I suspected, this confirmed that Shapinsky was a well, not a thirsty man. He is incredibly serene. He is *siddhipurush*—this is a Sanskrit expression meaning a wise man, self-actualized, unflappable, unfazed."

Akumal soon completed his lectures in Kansas and flew on, for some reason (he told me why; I just got lost somewhere in here), to Los Angeles and then to Washington, D.C. There, as elsewhere, he managed to find some Indian patrons. "I sing for them," Akumal explained to me matter-of-factly. "Oh, I didn't tell you? Yes, I am a great fan of Indian semiclassical music, and I can sing unaccompanied. Homesick Indians all over the world love to have me stay with them in their homes as long as I sing for my keep." He now launched his siege of the Smithsonian, armed with David's slides. There was a whole series of coincidences here as well, including a fellow named Asman ("This was a wonderful omen, because, you see, *asman* in Hindustani means the sky, and, of course, I was reaching for the sky, and also, in Bangalore, I am known as Chander, the Moon, so the Asman-Chander—you get the idea"), whom Akumal encountered somewhere along the way toward Dean Anderson, "the number two man at the Smithsonian." Anderson was impressed by the slides and dumbfounded that Shapinsky wasn't listed in any of the reference books on his extensive shelf. He promised to pass the slides on to the curators over at the Hirshhorn and get back to Akumal with their response as quickly as possible. On one of the days in here, Akumal happened upon a copy of my book on Poland in a bookstore and noted, from the jacket copy, that I'd also occasionally written on art ("another wonderful omen"), which is why he called me later (very much later) that night. As he pointed out, admiring his own tactical acumen, he'd limited his conversation in that first phone call to the subject of Poland. This was partly, he now told me, because he'd spent much of the interim that afternoon calling New York galleries. "I must tell you I've made a major discovery," he'd told one receptionist after another, "an extraordinary Abstract Expressionist of the genera-tion of Pollock, Rothko, and de Kooning, and I would like to make an appointment to come in and show you some slides." In a few cases, he managed to get past the flak-catchers, but it didn't much help. "Harold *who?*" was a common response. One prominent dealer, Ivan Karp, went as far as to assert, "He couldn't be very major if I've never heard of him." Akumal called thirty-two galleries and got not one appointment. A few days later, on October thirtieth, undaunted, he boarded a bus for Manhattan. He immediately called on the Shapinskys. They became fast friends, and later that very afternoon he showed up in my office, making his subtle (as it developed, almost too subtle) pitch.

The next day, Akumal called Anderson at the Smithsonian. "The people here are amazed," Akumal recalls Anderson's telling him. "They say either Shapinsky is an outstanding genius of twentieth-century art or he is a first-class derivative artist. They want more time." Akumal pointed out that all Western art was derivative of the East, if you wanted to get picky about things, and anyway art history was not a relay race. He asked whether Anderson would mind if he began show-ing the slides to art people in Europe. Anderson said of course not, and shortly thereafter Akumal boarded a flight to Amsterdam on the first leg of his prebooked, prepaid return to Bangalore.

We'd now accomplished a half-dozen more laps of the block, and we decided to peer in and see how the TV shoot was going. It was going like most such things—at a snail's pace—and Akumal would not be needed for a bit longer, so we decided to head out for a few more rounds.

"The next coincidence occurred on the plane," Akumal continued. "The KLM in-flight magazine happened to include an article about the Stedelijk Museum, mentioning a curator named Alexander van Gravenstein, so once I arrived in Holland I immediately took to calling him, and eventually obtained an appointment. When I arrived at his office, he invited me down to the museum cafeteria, and I was momentarily alarmed, because I literally didn't have a cent in my pocket and, you know, there is this phrase 'going Dutch,' and, this being Amsterdam and everything, I figured I might be expected to pay for my own coffee. But he was very generous—another good omen—and he just picked up the tab. And after he looked at the slides, he said, 'You have brought me the work of a great artist. The work of the late forties and fifties is especially original.' He gave me the name of Xavier Fourcade, a dealer in New York City, but I decided not to tell him how I'd already called the thirty-two New York galleries, all to no avail."

Buoyed by that exchange, Akumal borrowed money from some Dutch friends and took the boat to England, arriving in London early in the morning and being met by an Indian friend who was studying at Cambridge. Over dinner, their conversation turned to the Booker Prize for fiction and the fact that it had recently been won by Anita Brookner, who happened to be a professor of art. "I took this as an omen," Akumal recounted. "And I excused myself momentarily from the table. I went over to the pay phone and looked up her number in the phone book. It was listed—*another* good omen. And since it wasn't too late—before ten, anyway—I placed the call. She answered herself, and I quickly explained my situation and she was very gracious, at the end suggesting that the man to get in touch with was her friend Alan Bowness, the director of the Tate." When Akumal returned to the dining table, his Cambridge friend was aghast that he'd actually called Miss Brookner, but "once in a while you just have to be bold."

The next morning, Akumal presented himself at the reception desk at the Tate, insisting on seeing the director. No, he did not have an appointment, but he did have urgent business. Bowness, it turned out, was not in, but Akumal would not be budged. Finally, the receptionist managed to get Ronald Alley, the keeper of the modern art collection, to come down and attend to this immovable Indian. "I pulled out the slides, and as he looked through them he almost immediately said, 'You have made a major discovery.' I said yes. He suggested that what Shapinsky needed now was a first-class gallery, and asked if I'd like a referral. Of course, I said yes again. He went over to his phone and called James Mayor and told him he'd be sending over someone with some very interesting work. I thanked him, left the building, flagged a cab, and immediately proceeded to the Mayor Gallery."

Salman Rushdie, the best-selling author of *Midnight's Children* and *Shame,* who was to become another student and chronicler of this affair, has pointed out, correctly, that this was the turning point in Akumal's Shapinsky quest. As Rushdie says, "Now, for the first time, Akumal had become that most *pukka* of persons, a man who has been properly introduced." (*Pukka* is Hindustani for "complete," "whole," "together.")

Mayor had hardly had time to put his phone back in its cradle when Akumal arrived at his door, pulling out his slides. And Mayor, too, was impressed. He asked for a couple of weeks to think it over, but a few days later, on December fourth, he told Akumal that he would like to schedule a Shapinsky retrospective for the spring. Akumal asked him to frame his request as a letter. Mayor did, and the next evening Akumal told the whole story to Salman Rushdie, whom he'd met a few years earlier when a lecture tour brought the writer to Bangalore.

Akumal now took a boat back to Holland, made his quick and highly successful side trip to the Ludwig Museum in Cologne, and then prepared to resume his flight back to Bangalore, again virtually out of funds. Dutch television had become interested in his story and wanted to scoop the world with news of the Shapinsky discovery. Unfortunately, the sole slot it had available was for a few days after Akumal's prepaid and nonchangeable flight back. Akumal called Rushdie to ask what he should do.

Rushdie offered some tentative advice, but the real import of this call in terms of the saga was that it served to remind Rushdie of the whole affair. This was important, because that evening it just happened— "another incredible coincidence"—that Rushdie was going to be dining with his friend Tariq Ali. Ali, who comes from an area of pre-Partition India that is now in Pakistan, had been one of the foremost student activists in Europe during the Vietnam War period; he'd been instrumental in establishing the Bertrand Russell–Jean-Paul Sartre war-crimes tribunal in Stockholm; and he'd gone on to become a prolific and highly regarded political writer. Ali had also recently been named one of the executive producers of a documentary-film company named Bandung Productions, which was loosely affiliated with Britain's new television network, Channel 4. One of Ali's colleagues from Channel 4 was at the dinner, and Rushdie naturally regaled the group with his improbable tale of Akumal and Shapinsky. As he did so, he warmed to his subject, finally insisting that Bandung and Channel 4 commit themselves on the spot to doing a documentary on Akumal's discovery—or else, he assured them, he'd go to the BBC with the tale the very next morning. He made one proviso—that whoever took the project should take on Akumal's expenses for the interim as well. He was tired of seeing his friend ricocheting around the world so precariously close to bankruptcy. The dinner reconvened as an instant committee of the whole, they all agreed to Rushdie's proposal and his terms, and Akumal was called the next morning.

And now, a scant three months later, here we were. Akumal and I, negotiating loops around the real-life set of the resultant movie. We decided to go back upstairs, and this time Akumal's services were required. I spoke briefly with the Shapinskys, arranged for a meeting a few days later, when things would have quieted a bit, and took my leave.

Akumal telephoned me the next morning at my office to tell me that he and the film crew would be off to Chicago later that day to shoot a re-creation of the meeting with David ("We're going to reassemble the en-tire party," he said enthusiastically. "Miss Patterson is going to get to retire all over again"), but first he was going to the Museum of Modern Art to talk to William Rubin, the formidable director of the museum's Department of Painting and Sculpture.

"Do you have an appointment?" I asked.

"Of course not," Akumal shot back. "But, then, I haven't had ap-pointments most other places, either. I'll drop by afterward to tell you how things went."

Twenty minutes later, someone stepped into my office to tell me that there was a Mr. Ramachander asking for me in the lobby. "Well," I said sympathetically as I guided Akumal back to my office a few mo-ments later, "it must have been a short meeting."

"Ah," Akumal replied sheepishly. "It's Wednesday. I forgot. The museum is closed on Wednesdays. But"—he brightened—"I've made a wonderful new discovery." He reached into his satchel and pulled out a bag. "Croissants! Sort of like French flaky breakfast rolls. You can just go in and buy them at a place right around the corner. Very tasty. Here." He offered me one and then reached again into his satchel, this time pulling out a folder.

"I wanted to show you all the letters," he explained. He had appar-ently been collecting testimonials as he went along.

"Dear Mr. Akumal," the one from Ronald Alley began, under the Tate Gallery letterhead. "Thank you for showing me the slides of Harold Shapinsky's paintings. I am sorry to say he was completely unknown to me, but he is clearly an Abstract Expressionist artist of real interest whose work deserves to be widely known. His pictures have great freshness and beautiful colour, and I think people are going to be very surprised that an artist of this quality could have slipped into total obscurity."

There was one from Dr. Partha Mitter, the eminent Asian Studies scholar from the University of Sussex: "I was deeply moved by [Shapinsky's] immensely joyous paintings which appeared to celebrate life and its manifold creations. They exude power and dynamism, and their range of primary colours and sinuous lines evokes striking impressions of organic forms."

It must have been by way of Mitter that Akumal was able to get to Norbert Lynton, the celebrated historian of twentieth-century art who is also a professor at Sussex. (Lynton's *The Story of Modern Art* was conceived of, and is currently used in classrooms throughout the world, as an adjunct volume to E. H. Gombrich's classic *The Story of Art*.) "I write to thank you for coming in and showing me your slides of the work of Shapinsky," Lynton's letter began. "Some days have passed since then: and though I had intended to write to you sooner the delay has not been without value, in that I find my recollection of many of Shapinsky's works crystal clear, a sure sign (I know from past experience) of artistic significance. He is certainly a painter of outstanding quality. . . . The slides suggest a rare quality of fresh and vivid (as opposed to mournfully soulful) Abstract Expressionism, a marvelous sense of colour, and also a rare feel for positioning marks and areas of colour on the canvas or paper. When you see Shapinsky, please . . . bring him respectful, admiring greetings from me."

There were several other letters in the file as well, and Akumal beamed as I read them. "It's all quite fantastic, isn't it?" he said. "So, don't you think you should come to the opening?"

I told him that I might try to make it to London for the opening, which was two months away. We left it at that.

Then he asked me if I would mind writing a letter, just to say that I, too, had now seen the slides, and that I might be coming to the opening.

I told him I'd try to remember to.

He said it was okay; he could wait—he had a few minutes before he had to go catch the airport bus.

So far, I really hadn't had a chance to talk with Shapinsky, or, for that matter, to get a good look at his work, but now that the traveling documentary show had hit the road and quiet had returned to East Seventieth Street I went over for a chat the next day. Actually, several such visits were necessary: Shapinsky turned out to be as reserved and measured and withdrawn as Akumal was voluble and extravagant and outgoing. He was always gentle and polite, but he was subdued; indeed, at times his restraint verged on the spooky. He answered questions in a flat, becalmed voice with simple sentences often consisting of just one or two words ("Yes, marvelous," "Truly gratifying"). Though his answers eventually got longer, they often seemed preset—not that he was being evasive or had adopted some sort of party line but, rather, that his life seemed to hold little curiosity for him, few fresh surprises, no new vantages. His accounts had none of the free-associative, scattershot unpredictability that characterized Akumal's. I could see what Akumal had meant when he spoke of Shapinsky's serenity, but it seemed clearly a serenity that had a cost—there seemed to be a certain exhaustion behind the equanimity.

I was struck on each new visit to the Shapinskys by the extraordinary spareness of their circumstances. One day, there happened to be three dirty cups in the kitchen sink, and there were not enough clean ones to go around until Kate had washed one of them. Another time, I took along a couple of friends, and there were not enough chairs in the apartment for all of us to sit on until Shapinsky lifted an ancient stereo off a rickety stool, set the stereo on the floor, and brought the stool over to the table. At night, I learned, they pulled a rolled-up thin mattress out of the closet and spread it across the floor to sleep on. During my visits, Kate would occasionally sit with us in the kitchen, knitting (she was always more spry and animated than he); other times, she would repair to the little foyer, on the other side of the thin wall, and operate her sewing machine, using the single bed as a layout table, while tossing anecdotes and amplifications back into the kitchen.

Harold Shapinsky was born in Brooklyn in 1925, which is to say that, contrary to Akumal's telescoped version, he was a good fifteen years younger than most of the first-generation Abstract Expressionists. (For that matter, he was younger than many of the second-generation New York School painters as well.) His parents were first-generation Russian-Jewish immigrants, and his father worked as a designer in the garment industry. Harold was the third of four boys. Music was highly prized in the family—one of his older brothers became a classical cellist, and the other played double bass—but the visual arts were encouraged hardly at all. Indeed, as Harold's precocious drawing talent started garnering notice it began to be actively discouraged. A musician, after all, could always gain employment somewhere, but what possible livelihood could there be for a painter?

Nevertheless, from an early age Shapinsky inhabited a highly visual universe. As a small boy, he was always attracted to the museums—especially the Brooklyn Museum, where he was particularly taken with ancient figurines, Egyptian friezes, and Coptic reliefs. But he also found visual stimulation in contexts other than the formally artistic. For example, he was fascinated by the patterns chalked out across the swatches of fabric his father brought home from his work in the garment industry—"the complex jumble of shapes," he recalls, "and especially the spaces in between." He also spent hours poring over weather maps in the newspaper, his imagination stirred by what he calls "the compression of distances and scale, the layering, the sense of pressures building and spilling into winds, the gracefully sweeping front lines, the three-dimensional density expressed through the simplest of abstract graphic means." He says that the fabric swatches and the maps influenced his later work.

When Shapinsky was in his early teens, his parents divorced, and his home life, which he seldom discusses directly, appears to have become quite strained and unhappy. His mother would find his paintings and throw them out; even more distressing, his stepfather—after she re-married—would find his paintings and paint right over them, in an act of not even thinly veiled jealousy. Shapinsky persevered. He became fascinated by modern European painting—especially Cézanne and Picasso—and he says that by the age of fifteen, in 1940, he had resolved to become a painter. By that time, he had been out of school a year—he had been forced to drop out of junior high to help support his family. He worked at a succession of jobs, and continued to draw and paint in the evenings. His early portraits were highly influenced by the neo-classical Picasso. In 1945, he received some sort of scholarship to the Art Students League, where he studied with Harry Sternberg and Cameron Booth. (I derive this fact from a photostat of a handwritten two-page "résumé," the only documentation the Shapinskys were able to muster when James Mayor requested a curriculum vitae to be used in preparing the show.) That year, at twenty, Shapinsky moved to Manhattan—to an unheated three-room, five-flight walk-up on the lower East Side, for which he paid twelve dollars and fifty cents a month. (Forty years later, he and his wife share a space almost as small in a similar walk-up, although it's in a somewhat nicer neighborhood and costs a lot more.)

These were to be the high good times of Shapinsky's life—in many ways, its only good times, at least up until October of 1984. He got a job in a ceramics factory and gradually rose to become head of its deco-rating department. But that was just part-time. All the rest of his time, his energy, and whatever little money he was able to save were poured into his painting. "It was a wonderful period," he recalls. "There was a tremendous camaraderie among the artists. We were putting our all into painting, into the activity of painting itself. We'd get together at the old Waldorf Cafeteria at Sixth Avenue and Eighth Street, and we'd talk about the mission of painting. Nobody gave a thought to money, or to exhibiting, or even to selling the work. It was a pure scene."

The first-generation Abstract Expressionists were just making their breakthroughs—one-two-three, one after the other, like that! And

Shapinsky watched as it was happening all about him. "I saw my first Gorky show at the Julien Levy Gallery in 1946, right around the time I was myself turning decidedly toward abstraction," he says. "Although I never met him, Gorky was a great encouragement: he had a beautiful touch—such a warm feeling to him. I met and became friends with Franz Kline around 1947. I saw my first Jackson Pollock show in 1948, at Betty Parsons. Although I saw de Kooning himself a good deal on the street and about town, I didn't see my first de Kooning painting till 1950 or so. But the point is, everybody was painting. We weren't Abstract Expressionists—that designation would only come later. We were just *painters*."

Shapinsky met Kate Peters at an all-night New Year's Eve party as 1947 became 1948. She was, she says, "a dancer and a shiksa." She was the renegade bohemian offshoot of an established New England family. Her father was an architect and had a bit of the artist in him. But her parents, too, had divorced. Her mother had remarried, and her step-father was Hugh Lofting, the author of the Doctor Dolittle stories, though he didn't seem to like children very much, or at any rate had little use for her. Her insistence on becoming a dancer received little support from her family, but she kept at it, studying with Doris Humphrey and José Limón, among others. Like many dancers, she hung around the artists. She *had* met Gorky, baby-sitting for his children not long before his suicide. "He'd walk me home afterward to the Sixteenth Street Y," she says. "He was angry at the world. He had a great big dog. His little girls called his paintings 'broken toys.'" At that party, Kate says, she was immediately attracted to Harold—"He was so thin and gaunt, he had a face like El Greco's Jesus Christ"—but she didn't think she had a chance, because of her New England background. She was wrong. ("She had marvelous form," Shapinsky recalls of his first impression.)

A few weeks later, he tracked her down: she was nude, modeling on a dais at the Art Students League. He borrowed a large drawing pad, scrawled in big letters MEET ME IN THE CAFETERIA, and held the pad up before her. The class broke into applause. And after class she did meet him in the cafeteria. They went off to a pizza joint ("No," she corrects him, "it was a health-food place"), and the dinner cost two dollars, cleaning him out completely. "It was worth it, worth every penny," he says now, smiling over at her fondly. Their courtship was gradual, proceeding by fits and starts, and, like many affairs among artists of the period, it took a long time to formalize. They weren't officially married until 1955, and David, their only child, didn't arrive until 1960.

Shapinsky continued to scramble, hoarding whatever time he could for his painting, though he never seemed to have enough. A great break came when he happened to hear, in the fall of 1948, that a school named Subjects of the Artist was being established on Eighth Street by the painters William Baziotes, David Hare, Mark Rothko, and Robert Motherwell. (They were subsequently joined by Barnett Newman.) After work one evening, he went over to see about the possibility of a scholarship—he certainly couldn't afford the tuition. Baziotes happened to be there, and they had a long talk before class. "Finally," Shapinsky recalls, "Bill said to me, 'Well, let's see what you can do.' So I ran downstairs, found a paint shop, bought some black and white enamel and a board, hauled the things back up, squatted on the floor, and set to work. A while later, Bill came over, and he liked it and said he thought I had a good chance. A few minutes later, Motherwell came over and started watching. Something went wrong, though, and I became dissatisfied and began scraping the paint away, gouging it and starting over. Motherwell liked how I treated the painting as a process. So they offered me a tuition scholarship on the spot. It was worth thousands— or anyway, it was worth thousands *to me* at that time. I began hanging out there morning, noon, and night. There weren't very many students, actually—maybe about a dozen—and my work received a lot of attention, caused a lot of talk. David Smith liked it. Bradley Tomlin liked it. Sometimes I would draw with chalk directly on the wall—I liked its hardness, the challenge of opening up a space. One time, Mark Rothko, who was terribly nearsighted, was talking to the class, and he began to speak appreciatively about one of my wall drawings as an example. He reached up to get a better look and tried to pull it off the wall—only, it *was* the wall. It was very embarrassing. Baziotes meant the most to me as a teacher, although they all had an impact. He was warm and enthusiastic—the others were more intellectual—and he helped encourage me to continue dealing with issues in my painting that were just beginning to be formulated. That sense of painting as a process. There were Friday-night lectures—Jean Arp came and spoke, Adolph Gottlieb, others."

The school closed toward the end of the winter of 1949. Shapinsky dragged his stuff back to his cramped cold-water flat and continued working. He was pouring all his money into paint and brushes and boards. He was literally living on peanuts, consuming a packet a day. Finally, it all became too much. "I collapsed," Shapinsky recalls. "One day, I couldn't get out of bed in the morning. I couldn't move. It was terrible. If my brother hadn't come a few days later to see what had become of me, I don't know, I might have . . . Anyway, he came, he saw my condition and bundled me up and brought me back out to Long Island for the summer, where they pampered me, fattened me up, let me lie out on the beach, and I slowly recovered."

His brother, however, forgot to pay the rent on the cold-water flat— the twelve dollars and fifty cents a month. It may be that it didn't even occur to him. In the first of a series of terrible setbacks for Shapinsky, the landlord simply came up and cleared out the apartment, tossing several years' worth of work into the garbage. Although almost everything was lost, including all the large paintings, a few smaller pieces were salvaged at the last minute. (Some of them would eventually be slated for inclusion in the Mayor show.) Shapinsky was devastated by the news.

Had Akumal been with us the afternoon that Shapinsky related this sad incident, he might (good student of karma that he is) have noted the date—the summer of 1949. Karma metes out mysterious compensations, uncanny reincarnations: somewhere on the other side of the globe, Akumal Ramachander was being born.

Shapinsky returned to the city around Christmastime of 1949 to take a job as extra help at the post office. Around New Year's, he learned that Motherwell had founded a school in his own studio, on Fourth Avenue, as a sort of follow-up to Subjects of the Artist, and Shapinsky began attending the sessions. He returned to full strength, poured himself into the work once again. At the end of the year, Motherwell selected one of Shapinsky's paintings for an invitational show at the Kootz Gallery.

Samuel Kootz had five artists in his stable and eight slots on his annual calendar, so he was always having to come up with creative ways to fill the extra spaces while not unduly favoring any one or three particular artists. That December of 1950, he invited the five artists themselves—Baziotes, Hare, Hans Hofmann, Gottlieb, and Motherwell— to select three artists each for a "Fifteen Unknowns" show. During one of my visits, Shapinsky foraged from deep within a kitchen drawer a flyer for the show. Most of the unknowns have returned to oblivion, but there are some surprises. Hofmann selected John Grillo. Gottlieb included Clement Greenberg, in his sometime role as a painter, and Helen Frankenthaler—a year before her first one-woman show, at Tibor de Nagy. The Kootz invitational received some good notices, and Shapinsky was among those singled out. In the *Times,* for example, Stuart Preston cited his "deft profiling of creamy shapes, waving like flames in a crossbreeze."

As second-generation Abstract Expressionists go, Shapinsky had staked his claim early. Indeed, in a sense he could have been conceived of as a transitional figure, too young for the first generation but so thoroughly identified with it in terms of ambitions and conceptions of the activity of painting as to be more of a precursor than a simple member of the second generation. But all this speculation soon proved moot. A few months before the opening of the Kootz show came the outbreak of hostilities in Korea, and Shapinsky was drafted. He got a night's leave to attend the opening but had to be back in barracks the next morning. He wasn't sent abroad—in fact, he logged most of his hitch in Fort Dix, New Jersey—but he was effectively sequestered from the scene just as it was beginning to catch fire, or, rather, at the very moment that the torch was being passed from the first generation to the second. Thus, he missed the celebrated Ninth Street Exhibition, in 1951, in which several charter members of the Artists Club invited sixty-one artists to install one work each in an empty storefront in the Village. According to Irving Sandler, one of the period's premier chroniclers, in his book *The New York School,* the show included at least thirteen of the younger artists—Frankenthaler, Robert Goodnough, Grace Hartigan, Alfred Leslie, Joan Mitchell, and Milton Resnick among them. It is not inconceivable that Shapinsky would have been included had he been around. He might, at any rate, have been able to capitalize on his Kootz exposure, to insure that he would be part of the transition.

Instead, he was discharged, in the summer of 1952, into what he experienced as a radically altered environment. "The whole spirit had changed," he says, with something between a shudder and a sigh. "Money was beginning to flow in, and it was ruining everything. Politics was setting in. Everything was breaking apart. It was all becoming who you know, cliques, kowtowing, bootlicking. There was a mad scramble for galleries. It just got worse and worse." And Shapinsky began to fall inexorably away. "I couldn't stand all those cocktail parties," he recalls. He and Kate became more and more reclusive. "I tried to do my own work as quietly as possible, enjoy my family, my friends, visit the museums, study the masters, return to my studio, paint." He'd show once in a long while—a single painting or two in an obscure exhibition at some out-of-the-way gallery. But these shows were marginal, peripheral, in a scene, on an island, where centrality was everything. He looked on, aghast, as the art scene was transmogrified. "Painting became a business," he says. "The painters became like factories. Their product was the new—something new for each season. Most of it nowadays is like newspaper headlines. That's what the galleries seem to want—it creates a big splash, but then it doesn't mean anything. The work can be quite competent technically, but it's dead. You don't feel the artist's hand. It's all superficial. It's launching bandwagons and chasing after them. Nobody is concerned about *feeling* anymore, about the journey."

One day, he finally took me into his little bedroom studio to show me some paintings. "Look," he said. "*Feeling is everything.*" One after another, he pulled out works from 1946, 1958, 1963, 1982, 1970, 1948 . . . It was amazing: isolated, utterly alone, working for no one but himself, unconcerned about wider acceptance, not kowtowing to any gallery or potential moneyed patrons, Shapinsky had almost managed to make time stand still. The paintings *were* quite lovely. The ones he showed me (like all those slated for the Mayor Gallery show) were small, and many of them were on paper. Shapinsky explained that he would have loved to work on large canvases, but he could never afford the canvas or the paint; he never had the room to stretch any large canvases, or the space to store the resultant paintings. So he condensed his art, working in what the Abstract Expressionists would have considered a miniature format—eighteen by twenty-four inches. Remarkably, however, he seemed able to compress a great deal of energy into those limited spaces, so that there is occasionally an almost epic quality to the small images—or, rather, they start out lyric and seem to hover, to modulate toward the epic.

But the main thing about them was this sense of their being frozen in time. Perhaps, ironically, one of the functions of occasional gallery shows for an artist is to force him or her to focus and summarize and then to push forward to the next thing. Shapinsky never seemed to feel that pressure. In 1953, Robert Rauschenberg was erasing his de Kooning. Color-field painting, Pop Art, Op Art, Minimalism—they would all now come and go, and none of them would be in any way reflected in Shapinsky's stubborn, obliviously resolute passion. For almost forty years, Shapinsky would continue to do 1946–50 New York Abstract Expressionist painting. And Shapinsky's words, as he now spoke about his paintings, also seemed to come barreling out of some sort of time warp. "It's all a struggle with fluidity and spontaneity," he told me that day. "It's a journey—when you start, you don't know where it will take you, how it will all come out, how *you* will come out." *Now* he was becoming animated. "Sometimes I just start by throwing the brush at the blank surface. Then I try to respond to that mark. I enter into a dialogue with the surface. Then I try to deal with the surface tension. With enough tension, the piece comes alive, it begins to breathe, it swells, there's a fullness. I try to *puncture* the surface, to go deep inside, to build up the layers. I love to listen to music as I work—Mahler, for example, Bach, jazz—and, as they say, painting becomes a sort of visual music. It's abstract, but there's a sense of the world in it. I love to take walks in the park, see the way the branches intersect and sway, the swooping of the birds. I love looking down on the city from rooftops—the clean verticals and horizontals, the movement of traffic. All that gets filtered in. But, above all, it's *feeling*—feeling that is then carefully composed and constructed and integrated. Feeling that breaks apart and then comes together again. It's feeling, and a human touch, an existential trace."

Time passed. Shapinsky became a father. He held various jobs. For a while, he was an antiquarian bookseller. He taught art to children, ran an arts workshop with his dancer wife. He became a neighborhood activist, organizing the Sixth Street Block Association in the East Village. He continued to paint. And his health broke again. A back injury from his army days gave him chronic problems. He contracted a severe, lingering case of pneumonia, was bedridden literally for years during the late sixties and early seventies. He suffered from hypoglycemia. For a period, he almost went blind: much of his work from the seventies is even more miniature than usual—intricate murals on sheafs of eight-and-a-half-by-eleven-inch paper. He trembled. It was thought that he might have multiple sclerosis. Perhaps it was partly a physical manifestation of his frustration and despair at having been left behind as the train pulled out of the station—that, and the perversity of somehow being condemned to continue living right there inside the station amid all the noise and bustle of the new trains as they came and left: to wait there, eternally cordoned off.

The family was poor. One evening, David Shapinsky recounted for me over the phone how for long stretches he and his parents had lived below the poverty line. "It wasn't the lack of material comforts," he said, "but rather, the recurrent anxiety that come the end of the month there wouldn't be enough money to pay the rent and we might end up being thrown out on the street."

"I learned very early that sometimes you buy things just to make yourself feel better—and they don't," Kate told me one day. "Things you can buy usually don't matter." Kate began knitting sweaters and sewing patchwork quilt vests and jackets, and selling her wares to Henri Bendel. What with one thing and another, they got by. And Shapinsky continued to paint. Time passed—everywhere but in his painting world, where it seemed to stay 1948. He'd become like one of those tribes secreted deep in the jungle by the headwaters of some lush, narrow New Guinean stream, a little cusp of the world where the Stone Age still holds sway—and then, one day, over the godforsaken, fog-enshrouded pass, in stumbled Akumal.

In the ensuing weeks, I showed a set of transparencies of the twenty-two paintings selected for the Mayor Gallery show to various dealers around New York. A consensus quickly formed among those dealers. There was no question but that Shapinsky could paint. "This is the work of a real painter," André Emmerich, of the André Emmerich Gallery, told me. "Technically, these are very proficient, smart paintings. This one here"—he picked out the transparency of *Poe,* a black-and-white piece from 1949–50—"is excellent." Other dealers singled out other paintings as "charming," "beautiful," or "strong." "Really a very fine painter," I heard over and over. But almost everyone followed up such observations with a string of misgivings. For one thing, the paintings were too small. "You simply couldn't work this small and be a true Abstract Expressionist," Emmerich declared. "The whole point about Abstract Expressionism was that sense of Action painting, and that required scale." I started to point out Shapinsky's explanation for the small size of his works—the problem of storage, for example—but Emmerich wasn't buying that. "Canvases roll up," he said. "I could probably store all of Morris Louis's lifework in this little room." (The room *was* little, but, in fairness, it was still larger than Shapinsky's entire apartment.)

The most frequent recurring misgiving, however, was some variation on the theme that Shapinsky's life work was very close, uncannily close—indeed, uncomfortably close—to that of Willem de Kooning. "It's funny," Emmerich commented. "Future art historians might well have been excused if they'd accidentally attributed these works to de Kooning. That wouldn't have surprised me at all." Sidney Janis, of the Sidney Janis Gallery, agreed—the works seemed enormously derivative. Over and over, dealers would reach for their de Kooning catalogues and track the parallel years. "Look," one said. "See, here de Kooning is doing that sort of thing six months before Shapinsky—and he's doing it better." Shapinsky faced something of a double bind with these comparisons, because on those occasions—and there were several—when it appeared that Shapinsky had anticipated de Kooning (some of his paintings from 1947, for example, displayed the loose, lazy, languid curves of the very late de Kooning; and one Shapinsky, dated 1955–56, seemed to radically simplify the complexities of prior work, indulging in wide swaths of luminous, uninterrupted color, a full year before de Kooning was doing the same thing), the dealers uniformly challenged the accuracy of Shapinsky's dating, suggesting that he had probably got it wrong, if only accidentally. Since Shapinsky was judged derivative as his work went into the analysis, all the work *had* to be derivative by definition, and certain dates therefore *had* to be mistaken, since de Kooning, the man whom Shapinsky was ipso facto deriving everything from, hadn't yet reached that point. Q.E.D.

Irving Blum and his partner, Joseph Helman, of the Blum Helman

Gallery, were the most blunt in their evaluation of Shapinsky's significance. "It's just too dicey!" Blum exclaimed. "The early paintings are
versions of de Kooning and the late paintings are versions of the early
paintings. There were dozens of guys like this. He's just another one of
those close-but-no-cigar cases."

"Look," Helman said, pulling the current copy of the magazine
Flash Art from a nearby shelf and flipping through the pages quickly.
"Look at all these neo-Expressionist surrealists operating today. Dozens
of painters with virtually identical imagery. Look, look, here, this one,
this other one—a whole page of them here. Now, if one of these guys
goes on and develops, if he keeps pushing, if he breaks through, if he
can demonstrate his power and strength over and over again, if he can
keep it up—well, then you're talking about someone worth considering.
But by itself—nothing. You can go back and look through some issues
of *Art News* from the late forties and early fifties, and I'm sure you'd
find the same sort of things—dozens of Shapinskys. De Kooning had a
lot of clones—he was an enormously influential figure, an overpower-
ing presence; he exerted a tremendous force field, warping all sorts of
careers around him—but *he* moved on. He changed over the years
across a sustained career of dazzling inventiveness. Just because somebody was painting like him at one particular point in time doesn't
make him his equal, not by a long shot."

I pointed out that they had both agreed that some of the Shapinskys
were good paintings. Didn't that count for anything?

"You can't separate the issue of being derivative from the issue of
being good," Helman replied. "They're deft, they're flashy, but . . ."

What about the European museum people and art writers who had
vouched for the work?

"They never understood Abstract Expressionism in the first place,"
Blum said.

Helman agreed. "Most of the Europeans missed it when it was happening, and now they're misreading it in retrospect."

Blum asked me how much Mayor was going to be charging, and I told him I'd heard between fifteen and thirty thousand a painting, average around twenty-five.

"Look," Blum said. "That's big stakes. And this could all just be a bubble, hype feeding on itself. It can be smashed flatter than a pancake in an instant—and it may well be. These paintings will not bear the weight." Blum paused for a moment, and then continued, "The scene today is enormously protected, enormously serious: too much money is at stake."

Outside the office, as I left, the gallery walls were graced by a gorgeous selection of recent paintings by the thirty-three-year-old Donald Sultan—so recent, in fact, that you could smell some of the panels as they dried. Blum Helman had sold the show out before it had even opened, at sixty thousand dollars a pop. The whole question of art and money has become terribly vexed this past decade—we are living through a period of cultural inflation—but it seemed to me that some of these dealers were being a bit harsh. Given that a painting's true value bears almost no relation to its financial worth, its financial worth may just be whatever the market will bear. It had yet to be seen what the market would bear in Shapinsky's case. Hype, at any rate, is always the other gallery's publicity. As far as Shapinsky goes, as he nears the end of his career—in many ways a noble career, which has produced certain paintings of merit, of beauty—I couldn't see what was so terribly offensive about his finally being rewarded.

The questions of Shapinsky's relationship to de Kooning and of his true historical place in the transition between the early generations of Abstract Expressionism in New York were interesting ones in their own right, however, completely independent of any implications they might have for the market in Shapinsky's paintings. They were difficult questions to research, however, partly because there was virtually no history of exhibitions or critical commentary on Shapinsky's case to refer to. And now many of the principal witnesses were dead or unavailable for comment. De Kooning, in particular, has for many years maintained a policy of refusing to be interviewed.

I did reach William Baziotes's widow, Ethel. It turned out that she had barely met Shapinsky while Baziotes was alive, but she well recalls her husband's talking about his young colleague during the years before his death, in 1963. "The teachers and fellow artists liked him enormously," she recalls. "They felt his gifts were evident, so much so that Franz Kline gave him several works—and there is no higher praise a painter can give a fellow artist than that. They thought of him as a younger brother. They trusted him. They knew he would not confuse the issues or choose the easy way. Bill felt that Shapinsky had a grave mind. It had known many hells, he used to say—he seemed to need to fight alone, to be terribly singular. His dark, painful youth, Bill felt, had conditioned him to move obliquely. Bill felt that Shapinsky would take a sober course at great cost but that he would stay the course. He used to say that once in a while he had come upon a student like that, and that had made it all worthwhile."

I then called Robert Motherwell, at his home in Connecticut. I summed up the recent developments and asked him if he remembered Shapinsky.

"Oh, yes," he said, but hesitantly, seeming to reach far back. "Extraordinary, the way things like that return on you. Yes, yes. Harold Shapinsky: big horn glasses, very pale, thin." He paused. "There was no question with him that the talent and the dedication were real. There were a lot of students moving through those schools, and many of them were just passing through, but Shapinsky was clearly the real McCoy. However, the main thing I remember about him was how terribly intense he was—a combination of extreme intensity and shyness. He'd tremble; he'd quiver with all that intensity. It was too bad, because whereas that sort of temperament might have worked ten years earlier—many of those first-generation people were loners, they were into profound psychological and existential self-exploration—that just wasn't the way things were developing after 1950. By then, people were becoming looser, more optimistic, more sunny, more social."

Our conversation turned to how Shapinsky had fallen away. I mentioned his having been drafted.

"That's odd," Motherwell said. "He must have been registered with some other draft board than the one in Greenwich Village. The draft board in the Village, if they heard you were an artist they assumed you must be some sort of Communist—or, at any rate, you were manifestly unreliable—and they had no use for the likes of you in their army, so it meant an almost automatic deferment." (I subsequently asked Shapinsky about this, and it was true: he had been registered in Brooklyn, at his mother's address.) Motherwell agreed that Shapinsky's forced absence from the scene couldn't have helped his career. "But he would probably have been temperamentally unsuited in any case," he said. "He was so wound up. He couldn't have been one of the boys; it would have been like asking Kafka to be one of the boys. That second generation, they loved to party. I can't imagine Shapinsky enjoying a party or talking for hours at a time on the phone. I was married to one of them, Helen Frankenthaler, for twelve years, and I used to marvel at how much time she and her fellow artists spent on the phone. That first generation—there wasn't a single phone person. No, I take that back. Barnett Newman used to love talking on the phone. But Shapinsky just never could have been made to fit into the way things developed through the fifties."

I also visited with Irving Sandler, the chronicler of the history of the New York art scene since the war, at his apartment, in New York University faculty housing. "In my own work, I have a zillion loose threads," he said, smiling, as I laid out the basic contours of my Shapinsky subject. "Graduate students are going to be picking them up for years." Sandler had never heard of Shapinsky but seemed delighted at the prospect of widening his horizon. "What I love about the Shapinsky story as you've told it to me is that it manages to fulfill two of the most prevalent art-world fantasies of the time," he said. "One of them we all used to talk about was the fantasy of the late discovery at the very end of a career, after years and years of unsung labor. And the other one was the fantasy of the lonely secret master, slaving away somewhere completely apart: that here all of us were, expecting Master to emerge from our midst—we were, after all, the center—but in fact he was patiently working off in some barn or up in some garret, far away from it all." Sandler, however, was less than overwhelmed by the transparencies I now began to show him. "They're good paintings," he said. "Some of them are very good. But they're de Kooning. There were a lot of artists like this, but this one is almost the most de Kooning-like of any of them." Sandler then spoke for a little while about de Kooning's impact on the second generation. He read me a passage from a recent monograph he had written on Al Held, about the way de Kooning had labored heroically to create a new language, one that the second generation could now take for granted, could simply pick up and *start making sentences with*. Shapinsky fitted in there somewhere. Sandler continued to riffle through the transparencies, marveling at the dates. "His uniqueness is that he's still doing it. The conviction carries all the way through: the later ones are as fresh as the early ones. *He still believes it*."

Weeks were passing quickly now, and the London opening was less than a month away. I went over to the Shapinskys' apartment once again. (They had ended up not joining the film crew on its transit to Bangalore to film Akumal in situ.) I wanted to get a clearer focus on Shapinsky's own sense of his relationship to de Kooning.

Shapinsky was in his subdued mode again, puffing on his cherry-scented tobacco. It was difficult to narrow in on the issue—or, rather, Shapinsky's statements remained calmly consistent with his earlier claim that he had seen virtually no de Kooning work before 1950 or so. "I knew we were working in the same general terrain," he explained. "People kept telling me so. So I guess I bent over backward not to see his work. One time, he and Noguchi came by the Subjects of the Artist, and they were walking around looking at some of the students' work when they came upon one of my canvases—I happened to be on the other side of the room at the moment—and they spent a long time talking about it very intently with each other. That kind of thing didn't happen very often; it was sort of embarrassing. Later, de Kooning would call down to me from the window of his studio, inviting me up, but I intentionally made excuses, because I didn't want to be worried about the overlap."

He paused, and then said, "No, I really don't see de Kooning's having been that big an influence. Gorky, perhaps, a bit more. And several of the Europeans, definitely—Cézanne, Kandinsky, Miró. And above all Picasso. We were all of us drawing on the same sources, but Picasso was paramount. Everything you tried to do, Picasso had already done. It drove some people crazy, and they tried to reject Picasso. But I thought he was fantastic, and he was most important."

I decided to leave things at that and asked him and Kate if they were getting excited about the coming weeks.

"Oh, yes," Shapinsky said, with about as little excitement as I suspect it's possible for a human being to muster. "It is all very gratifying." He was silent for a moment. "The work will be seen."

"I can't get over it myself," Kate said, with more than enough animation for both of them. "I find myself on the phone talking to London— me, London!—and I can't believe this is really happening. At first, it was really scary—the prospect of life's becoming a little easier came as quite a shock. I have a rich fantasy life. I wrote whole novels in my head about what was going on, entire scenarios of calamities playing themselves out. But it looks as if everything is going to be all right."

I asked them how they'd imagined that things might go in the days before Akumal.

"I always had the feeling that something like this would occur sooner or later," Shapinsky said. "That the work would someday be seen."

Kate said, "I used to cry at night. I'd pray and pray to my grandfather, who was a minister. It was so unfair, so terrible to live with this man who was creating so much beauty, and not have anyone know about it. The worst came about a year ago. I heard about an old artist who died; all his lifework was just tossed out onto the street, stray people passing by were picking at it . . . That really got to me. I prayed all the harder. Akumal was like the answer to my prayers. Seriously, I think he's an angel." She said that Akumal had at first refused to accept any reward for all his labors but that she and Harold had insisted, during his most recent trip, and he'd finally agreed to accept a percentage of whatever they would be realizing from Harold's art from now on.

We made arrangements to meet in London. (This was going to be their first trip to Europe.) "Yes," Shapinsky said in his monotone. "It should be a big event."

"He's not like this all the time," Kate confided, smiling lovingly over at him. "Sometimes, lately, he just starts dancing. Sometimes he turns the radio to a disco station and suddenly he's *dancing.*"

I had just arrived at my London hotel and was emptying the contents of my bags into the drawers and closets, and absentmindedly listening to a television program called "The Antiques Road Show." It was apparently part of a series of such programs, and it essentially played out endless permutations on the same basic formula. Doughty plebian matrons of one sort or another would bring in examples of antique bric-a-brac, describe how they'd happened to come by them ("Oh, it were up in me attic, sir, just lying about for years"), and the supercilious experts, dressed to the nines in the most distinguished Bond Street finery, would then lavish their silken expertise upon the proffered objects—a tea set, a china bowl, a pewter jug, a dresser, a pocket watch—in ostentatious displays of virtuoso discernment. At first, I thought it was a Monty Python skit, but it was all in dead earnest—these were real people. The show generally proceeded as a sort of morality play: those who came on too confidently were obviously destined for a fall. One woman stood before a large early-nineteenth-century English landscape painting and smugly predicted that it was a Constable, offering as proof positive a letter of evaluation she'd procured from a putative expert named Thomas Keating. The television expert, however, was not impressed: he evaluated not only the painting but the prior expert's letter as well. "Really, very typical late Keating letter, this. Because he goes on to conclude it to be 'possibly a sketch by Constable' and in fact he gives you every reason to believe that it is an extremely important painting. Now, you know, Tom Keating during his lifetime was a likeable rogue—really, frightfully sad about the heart attack and all—but I can tell you without the shadow of a doubt that this painting has nothing to do with John Constable. Were it a Constable—three million pounds plus. But no, madam, it's not a Constable. It's not an F. W. Watts. *It's not even a John Paul.* Maybe it's a *Paul.*" The most humble of all the petitioners—a squat farm woman who could barely mumble her own name, so awestruck did she seem in the presence of her tuxedoed expert—had somehow managed to cart in an antique chest of drawers the size of a prize bull. The expert was beside himself: "This is the most important piece of furniture we've had on the 'Road Show,' and doubtless the most valuable. It's a commode—that's the official term, French term. French shape, English built. To begin with, note the exquisite construction, and how it's been covered over with the most extraordinary collection of veneers. How ever did you come by it?" The woman's tongue remained hopelessly tied. "This is—please, madam, pray, sit down here, yes—this is a piece of national, no of *international* stature. It was made between 1770 and 1785 by one of three or four people, maybe even by Pierre Langlois himself before he went back to France in 1773. Should you choose to put this commode up for sale— naturally very carefully, with a great deal of expert advice—you ought easily to realize forty thousand pounds, and soon it should be worth twice that." The farm woman started to cry.

The phone rang. "Welcome! I've got wonderful news. The *Observer* Sunday magazine is going to be featuring a full-color spread on the discovery with an article by Salman Rushdie. In addition, *Time Out* will be running a major story by Tariq Ali. And that's not all. Chatto &

Windus, the top-class publishers, will be bringing out a big illustrated autobiography of Shapinsky."

"Hi, Akumal," I said. "I didn't know Shapinsky could write."

"No, no. *I'm* going to write it."

"Well, sounds as if you've been keeping yourself busy and productive."

"Yes, everybody's talking about the discovery. I'd come over to visit with you right now, except that I'm afraid I must head over to the airport. I've got three friends coming in from India for the opening. It will be quite an international affair. There will also be six friends from Holland, three from West Germany, and one from America."

A couple of days later, on May twenty-first, Shapinsky's sixtieth birthday (and not even seven months since Akumal phoned me that first morning), I set out for Mayor's. Cork Street is a short nub of a thoroughfare, teeming with fashionable art establishments. Leslie Waddington seems to own most of them—four or five bear his name—and this May they were showing, among other artists, Alexander Calder, Sam Francis, David Hockney, Henry Moore, and Claes Oldenburg. John Kasmin runs another—the British outpost of Knoedler—right next door to Mayor's, and his current fare consisted of recent ceramic-and-steel wall constructions by Frank Stella. When I got to Mayor's, its large street window announced, in big white painted letters, HAROLD SHAPINSKY. Inside, Mayor and his partner, Andrew Murray, were making subtle adjustments to the lighting, and waiting for Akumal and the Shapinskys, who were going to drop by and give their final approval. The front two rooms contained the twenty-two Shapinsky paintings, framed and displayed to full advantage. Beyond the second room, a large, vaultlike space opened out and down (with a corkscrew stairway curling to the floor below), and that space was filled with Rauschenbergs, Lichtensteins, Twomblys, Rosenquists, and Warhols—remaining evidence of the preceding show, "A Tribute to Leo Castelli." Before long, Akumal and the Shapinskys arrived. This was the first time the Shapinskys had

seen the show, and Kate was thrilled. Harold took it all in calmly, puffing contemplatively on his pipe, admiring the work. "Very good painting, that one," he ventured, in his flat monotone, before moving on to
the next. "This one, too—fine painting. Nice sense of swell."

Akumal came over to me, flushed with freshly building excitement.
"I brought you advance copies of the texts of Salman's and Tariq's articles," he said. "And here." He reached over and pulled a catalogue of
the show out of a bulging box. "You'll want to have a look at this, too.
And, oh!" He riffled quickly through his folder. "Look at this." He produced another letter from Ronald Alley, this one handwritten on Tate
Gallery stationery. "Now that I have actually seen some originals of
Harold Shapinsky's work I feel I must congratulate you again on your
discovery," Alley had written Akumal some weeks earlier. "Colour
slides can be very misleading, and I had expected to find lyrical work
with glowing colours. Instead his pictures turn out to be much more
thickly painted—definitely paintings rather than drawings—and, above
all, much tougher and more dramatic. One senses a real drama and
tension, even anguish, behind the works, which though small are very
highly charged." As if in harmony with my reading, Shapinsky, on the
other side of the room, was commenting, "Nice tension in this one here.
Very gratifying."

David Shapinsky now entered the gallery, a surprisingly young
man with delicate features, blondish hair, wire-rim glasses, and, yes, a
very kind face. Kate greeted him warmly, and Harold came over as
well. I could see that in this slightly offbeat, mildly daft family, David
plays the role of the steady anchor, the responsible center, and had
probably been doing so for some time.

Akumal, Kate, Harold, and David presently set out to find a suit for
Harold for the opening; he didn't seem to own one. After they'd left,
James Mayor and I found ourselves talking about Akumal and his
mania for letters. "Did he have you write them, too?" Mayor asked me.
"Most extraordinary; every time we have a conversation, he seems to
want me to write it up as a letter—on the spot. I've got a title for your

piece. You should call it 'The Man of Few Words and the Man of Many Letters.'"

I left the gallery, intending to return to my hotel where I could look through the various texts Akumal had gathered for me in preparation for the evening's opening. But first I dropped in on the Stella exhibition next door. Kasmin was sitting the desk himself. "So," he asked, "what exactly is going on over there? Who is this Shapinsky fellow?" I gave him the quick capsule version: Shapinsky, forty years, Akumal, no interest in New York, the Tate, and now a big show. "How remarkable," Kasmin interjected. "That's the sort of thing that usually just happens to the widow. I've got a title for you. You should call your piece 'The Man Who Became His Own Widow.'"

Back at the hotel, I flipped through the various texts Akumal had gathered, beginning with the catalogue—a handsome, thirty-two-page booklet in square format with an elegant plain gray cover, twenty-two illustrations, four of them in color, a preface by Ronald Alley, and an extended essay by Marta Jakimowicz-Shah, a Polish artist friend of Akumal's who now lives in India. Alley's preface was laudatory in a careful, measured sort of way, concluding, "I am delighted that Shapinsky is at last beginning to get the recognition that he greatly deserves. Such a shame he has had to wait so long. As for Akumal, he amazes me more and more. Speaking for myself, it has usually been my experience when I try to help someone that the outcome is total disaster; but at least this time everything seems to have come out right." Well, not quite everything, I soon realized. Ms. Jakimowicz-Shah's catalogue essay, anyway, was, well, problematic: absolutely without any critical distance as it celebrated Shapinsky's virtually unparalleled importance.

Rushdie's and Ali's articles likewise tended to go a bit overboard in proclaiming Shapinsky's significance, but neither of them claimed any expertise in art. Both were mainly enthralled by the saga of the discovery itself. The circumstance of the discovery, the character of Shapinsky's art, his reticent nature—all seemed to act as a sort of

Rorschach inkblot, with each of the various writers projecting his own rich themes of signification upon the material. For example, Tariq Ali, a formidable political pamphleteer, discerned a moral in the Marxist tradition: "It is almost a truism these days to suggest that Art is big business. Late capitalism has completed the transformation of works of art into commodities. Most art galleries in the West function as ruthless business enterprises." Shapinsky in this version came off as a sort of martyr to the vagaries of art capitalism who through Akumal's fluky intervention may yet receive some measure of justice at the last moment. "One can safely assert," Ali concludes, "that there are many Shapinskys in different parts of the world (including Britain), most of whom will never be 'discovered'! It is only when the priorities of the existing social order are irreversibly altered that they will ever stand a chance."

Salman Rushdie, for his part, found a different moral in the story. He had recently been involved in a fairly heated exchange with, among others, Conor Cruise O'Brien, growing out of an article Rushdie published in the British literary quarterly *Granta.* In that article, entitled "Outside the Whale," he'd attacked the current spate of Raj fictions— the television serializations of *The Far Pavilions* and *The Jewel in the Crown,* and the films of *Gandhi* and *A Passage to India*—describing them as "only the latest in a very long line of fake portraits inflicted by the West on the East." It was not surprising, therefore, that the aspect of the Akumal-Shapinsky story that seemed to appeal most to Salman Rushdie was the theme of The Tables Turned. "For centuries now," he wrote in the last paragraph of his *Observer* piece, "it has been the fate of the peoples of the East to be 'discovered' by the West, with dramatic and usually unpleasant consequences. The story of Akumal and Shapinsky is one small instance in which the East has been able to replay the compliment, and with a happy ending, too."

Ronald Alley, in his catalogue preface, glancingly hinted at another Rorschach reading. He recounted how, early in the saga, Akumal had been taking his slides around to show to people. "He even telephoned about thirty galleries in New York and asked if he could bring the slides round, but not one said yes," Alley wrote. "I suppose they thought that the chances of a visiting Indian finding an unknown Abstract Expressionist painter in New York who was any good at all were so remote as to be not worth thinking about." His next paragraph began, "When I saw the slides I was amazed," and from the silent interstice between those two sentences welled up the theme of The Smug, Closed, and Self-Satisfied New York Art Scene, with its subtheme of Europe Still Open and Curious. Ironically, this theme received its fullest exposition in Rushdie's piece, his rage at the smugness of the Empire notwithstanding. "There has been a certain amount of gleeful hand-rubbing going on, because the Shapinsky case reflects so badly on the New York art scene," he reported. "New York has been ruling the roost for so long that this piece of European revenge must taste sweet indeed."

The shopping expedition had been a success: Shapinsky was decked out in a smart new suit when I finally caught sight of him in the midst of the throng at the Mayor opening—a debonair gray flannel outfit with sleek, fresh creases tapering down to a pair of blue canvas deck shoes. The cherry aroma from his pipe wafted about the assembly throughout the evening, which Shapinsky spent quietly enduring the sometimes effusive adulation of his new admirers. In the face of this onslaught, his composure attained almost epic proportions. As for Kate, she was wearing one of her patchwork vests, a lovely medley of black and white rectangles with an occasional highlight of bright, bright red. Toward the end of the evening, when the crowd had thinned, she pulled out a ball of wool and resumed her knitting. All the careful work that Mayor and Murray had put into modulating the lighting on the paintings went more or less unnoticed; in fact, this was one of those openings so crowded that the paintings themselves are virtually unseeable. In any case, this particular evening the lighting was drowned out by the roving television kliegs of the crew from Bandung Productions, capturing a few last shots for their documentary, which would be broadcast in a week.

"This is really more of a literary crowd than an art one," one of the guests told me. "But, then again, there really isn't much of an art scene here in London. The English like to look at words, not pictures."

"The whole thing is quite romantic in a shaggy-dog sort of way," I overheard one woman saying. "Aladdin's lamp and that sort of thing."

"But where has this fellow Shapinsky *been?*" her companion replied. "It all reminds me of those blind white fish swimming about deep in those underground caverns in Kentucky or wherever it is they do all that."

"Yes, look at him! He even *looks* like Rip Van Winkle, newly emerged from his sleep, his eyes still blinking in the glaring daylight."

"The Japanese soldier on that island outpost who's only just found out the war is over—say, what?"

At one point, I met Ronald Alley, who turned out to be a tall man in his late fifties, with a gentle, dignified bearing. "Originally," he recalled for me, "I went downstairs that morning simply to try and rescue my colleague from the siege of what she was describing to me as a very persistent Indian caller. I mean, you get people turning up like that from time to time, and I do try to go down and see them whenever I can, partly out of courtesy but partly in the hope that something like this might happen. It almost never does, but this"—he included the whole thronged room in his gesture—"sort of justifies the whole enterprise, doesn't it?"

For me, the opening provided an occasion to speak with several Indians who were able to offer me a much deeper understanding of Akumal's passion. (That passion appeared all the more remarkable to me when I learned, as I did in passing, that Akumal was suddenly deep in debt again, pending the eventual success of the show, because he had paid for part of the travel fares and lodging for several members of his Indian, Dutch, German, and American contingents.) Up to that evening, I'd seen Akumal's quest as by turns comic, resourceful, vaguely frenzied, but always inspired. Through these new conversations, I began to get a sense of some of the darker imperatives underlying his intensity. One of his group from Bangalore, a beautiful woman draped in a luminous blue-and-green sari, noted that Akumal had always been like this, that it was sometimes exhausting to be with him for more than fifteen minutes at a stretch, but that to understand him "one has to realize how stultifying, for example, is his daily regimen at the school where he teaches, as is the case in most Indian academic settings." She continued, "You also must try to imagine how incredibly hard it is in India for someone from the lower middle class just to survive, let alone rise. I think Akumal derives a lot of his energy from this being betwixt and between."

A few moments later, Salman Rushdie amplified on this theme. "I think with Akumal there is a sort of desperation in part of his makeup," he said. "To describe him as a teacher of English at an agricultural college is gravely to diminish him—but that is his status in Bangalore. It is a terrible thing when someone's picture of himself does not coincide with the world's. You have to realize that the gulf between the classes is much greater in India, and for Akumal to have pulled himself up by his own bootstraps, as he has done, has all along required the continuous projection of the kind of frenetic energy he's now been demonstrating in this affair."

I asked Rushdie how Akumal had got access to him in the first place.

"Well, I was in Bangalore briefly during a lecture tour a few years ago," Rushdie said. "My hosts had escorted me to my hotel and had just left the room when there was an immediate knocking on the door. I figured that it was my hosts returning with one last bit of instruction, or something; when I opened the door, I was instead confronted by the hugest garland of flowers I'd ever seen, deep inside which, barely visible, stood Akumal. He barged into the room in this overwhelming, unstoppable frenzy of vast smiles and flashing eyes, proclaiming that he was my 'number one fan in Bangalore,' and describing how he'd been pestering the editors of all the local papers for weeks, demanding that they include features and supplements on my coming visit, so that now, here, this was the result—whereupon he thrust a bunch of news-papers at me, all with big photographs and long stories. It was a unique and fairly winning sort of approach. I would then see him occasionally on his visits to Europe, although I must say I was a bit incredulous when he launched into this story about his discovery of an American painter. I mean, Akumal sometimes strikes one as a bit of an operator. But it's impossible not to warm to his evident enthusiasm for life, his disarming openness, and his obviously genuine devotion to the arts. And he's pulled it off. Well, I hope that maybe this success will bring him a measure of peace."

A few minutes later, I was talking with Tariq Ali, an expansive and friendly man, with none of the archness of his occasionally polemical prose. "When Akumal first told Salman the story about Shapinsky, Salman says, he thought Akumal was making this artist up," Ali re-ported. "Well, when Salman subsequently told me about Akumal, I thought *he* was making *Akumal* up—I mean, I figured he'd gone a bit over the top. Akumal sounded so much like a character in one of his own fictions. But I eventually saw the slides and met the man. It was all true, and the story seemed a natural for Bandung."

We watched for a few minutes as Akumal buzzed about the room, bringing his contingents over to meet James Mayor or Ronald Alley or Salman Rushdie. "The thing about India," Ali continued, "is that this synthesis of almost two hundred years of British rule and native tradi-tion means that there are a lot of people like Akumal—people with this very wide range of worldly, cosmopolitan interests who are con-demned to live fairly narrow, constricted, provincial lives. I think part of his nervous energy comes from this being between classes, between cultures. It was a very moving experience going to Bangalore with the film crew to shoot that part of the documentary. People would come up to us and ask what we were doing. We'd tell the story, and they'd be quite dumbfounded. 'Are you serious?' they would ask. 'All this is happening because of our Akumal?' Or his students in the English class: 'Our Professor Ramachander has accomplished this?' I mean,

Bangalore is a large and growing city, but in many ways it's like a Chekhovian small town, with Akumal as the village eccentric, the character from the local coffeehouse scene who suddenly makes good in the world. I mean, he's been doing this sort of thing all along in Bangalore, but everybody there is just amazed by the *scale* this time around."

Akumal had gone over to talk with Shapinsky. "A character from Naipaul meets a character from Bellow," Ali said.

On the evening the Shapinsky show was opening at the Mayor Gallery, a couple of miles away, at the Aldwych Theatre, Paul Eddington was starring in a revival of Tom Stoppard's metaphysical farce *Jumpers*. About halfway through the first act, Eddington, playing the role of a second-rate philosophy professor, delivers himself of the following contention: "Of the five proofs of God's existence put forward by St. Thomas Aquinas, three depended on the simple idea that if an apparently endless line of dominoes is knocking itself over one by one then somewhere there is a domino which was *nudged*." It occurred to me on several occasions during the next few days, as I kept returning for visits to a teeming Mayor Gallery, that in the case of Akumal's discovery of Shapinsky *two* lines of dominoes had needed to be nudged. For this was a story of how the lifelines of two individuals—marginal, utterly peripheral figures in their own societies—had, most improbably, managed to intersect, and then of the entirely improbable chain reaction that their intersection had subsequently set off. Actually, *three* coincidental factors were playing themselves out in this story: Akumal, Shapinsky, and the specific, highly peculiar (one might use the word "marginal" here as well) situation of the art world itself in 1985. To shift metaphors, Akumal and Shapinsky were like two stray crystals dropped into a flask: it was only because of the special conditions obtaining inside the flask—the specific momentary chemical dynamics of the supersaturated medium—that these two crystals were able to conjoin and blossom in such a surprising way. I am convinced that had Akumal met Shapinsky in 1975, say, or even 1980, his quest would have gone nowhere.

There are two major reasons for this. The first involves a sea change that has been occurring in the dominant aesthetic sensibility over the last decade. Fifteen years ago, Minimalism was at its height. The past decade has seen a resurgence of interest in both figurative and expressive imagery. This has proved true both retrospectively (witness the sudden rediscovery of the late Picasso at the Guggenheim in 1984, a phase of the Master's career that had been almost entirely dismissed until just a couple of years before; and the considerable popularity of the de Kooning retrospective that was up at the Whitney at about the same time) and with regard to the most up-to-date in gallery fashions as well (witness the proliferation of neo-Expressionist imagery throughout the world over the past five years). It is hardly surprising that the time was ripe for a comprehensive reconsideration of the second generation of Abstract Expressionists, and, indeed, precisely that was beginning to happen: Completely unbeknownst to Akumal during that afternoon in September 1984, when he was first being exposed to Shapinsky's work via those primitive slides in David Shapinsky's apartment, a major traveling exhibition entitled "Action/Precision" and featuring work from the fifties by six of the second-generation luminaries—Norman Bluhm, Michael Goldberg, Grace Hartigan, Al Held, Alfred Leslie, and Joan Mitchell—was touring the country. (The exhibition was organized by the Newport Harbor Art Museum.) The show's unusually lovely catalogue features several excellent essays touching on this sea change in aesthetic sensibility—a change that, of course, has had a bearing on Shapinsky's reception as well. Robert Rosenblum, for example, recalls what it was like in the mid-fifties, as the tide began pulling out for interest in that sort of work: "For me and many of my contemporaries, Rauschenberg, Johns, Stella swiftly became the Holy Trinity that led us from the Old Testament to the New, liberating us from the burden of living under the oppressive yoke of the coarse and sweaty rhetoric of Action painting, whose supreme deity, de Kooning, suddenly loomed large for many younger spectators and artists as a conservative force, a tyrant of past authority who demanded the instant embalming of any youthful, liberated spirit . . . a suffocating father image." Paul Schimmel notes how "the rich and diverse paintings of [the six artists in this show] were relegated to obscurity because they embraced and expanded upon the revolutions of their predecessors rather than reacting against them." Rosenblum talks about how at the time he thought he could "write off most of the work by the six artists in this show as irritating anachronisms, the product of loyal but growingly irrelevant satellites." This "temporary blackout of visibility" for the second-generation Abstract Expressionists lasted almost thirty years. But suddenly they were back. "And now how do they look?" Rosenblum asks. "For one thing, they look surprisingly up-to-date, riding in unexpectedly as ancestral figures behind the latest neo-Expressionist wave from Germany, Italy, or our own shores, a wave that once more permits us to wallow and frolic in the primordial ooze of oil paint. Seen as a whole, these pictures have the tonic quality of sheer sensuous enjoyment. . . . For anyone who was getting chilled by the laboratory calibrations of so much Minimal and Conceptual art and by the puritanical ban on color and palpable textures, this is the perfect antidote, a drunkenly deep breath of visual oxygen."

Akumal was thus going to find himself hawking just the right sort of elixir for 1985: the atmosphere in which he would be moving stood a good chance of welcoming Shapinsky's sort of oxygen. But the previous decade had also seen a second transformation in the art world—one that would have an even more dramatic impact on Akumal's and Shapinsky's fortunes. This had to do with the changing character of the art market. Prices across the board, as I suggested earlier, had shot completely out of sight.

The explanation for this is extremely simple: the market for art had exploded in size—the number of players (collectors) in the game had multiplied many times over. The explanation for *that* is more complex. For one thing, the baby-boom generation had come of age, gone to college in record numbers, and been exposed to the humanities and, in particular, the contemporary arts; and now many of its members were becoming professionals and earning substantial incomes, with the result that collecting seemed worthwhile to them both as an avocation and, increasingly, as an investment. Sidney Janis recently observed, "More money is being spent these days because more money is being made." Around the same time, corporations began to enter the art market, building up vast company collections as exercises both in good public relations and in shrewd investment. There was a tremendous increase in the number of museums and a tremendous upsurge in museum attendance. According to a recent article in the Los Angeles *Times,* West Germany will witness the launching of thirty new museums by 1990; another article in *Progressive Architecture* cites similar figures for the United States. Japan is involved in a parallel frenzy. Each of these new museum projects features dozens of empty walls, a board of trustees, and a carefully tended hive of supporting collectors. The infrastructure of art commerce—the network of galleries, art journals, and auction houses—has developed great sophistication, including extremely supple engines of publicity. Literally tens, and perhaps hundreds, of thousands of potential consumers are being funneled into the system. At recent contemporary-art auctions of the sort that just five years ago were being attended by only a few hundred collectors, well over a thousand people are jammed into auditoriums filled to standing-room-only capacity—and that's not even counting many of the highest bidders who choose to avoid the crush by phoning in their entries.

A friend of mine, the director of one of Europe's finest small museums, recently told me, "There's simply not enough work of superior quality anymore to go around—work, that is, by the *grands maîtres*—so the prices, of course, go way up, and prices for the next layer of artists, the *petits maîtres,* rise up in turn, to answer the demand. Paintings by artists I had barely even heard of until a few months before are going for fifty thousand dollars at auction."

This situation was recently encapsulated in a succinct formula by the Paris-based art critic Souren Melikian. In an article entitled "The

Ten-Percent Law," which appeared in *Art & Auction,* he wrote, "Over the last twelve months a new law has been verified with increasing frequency in the Impressionist and Modern masters field. Artists regarded rightly or (not infrequently) wrongly as second fiddles to famous artists are worth one-tenth of those from whom they supposedly took their cue." This assertion might at first appear to knock the wind out of any enthusiasms the *petits maîtres* could have been expected to arouse; but, on second glance, when one recognizes that individual works by *grands maîtres* are now selling for many millions of dollars, ten percent looms back up as a figure worth reckoning with, or for. Melikian cited several examples in his article. A work by Charles Angrand (1854–1910), a neo-Impressionist artist who "greatly admired van Gogh, who returned the compliment," recently sold for two hundred thousand dollars—one-tenth of what a van Gogh with a similar composition would fetch. This ratio also obtains between the works of Roger de La Fresnaye (1855–1925) and those of Braque, as it does between the works of Paul Sérusier (1863–1927) and those of Gauguin.

Lucy Havelock-Allan, the director of contemporary art at Sotheby's auction house in New York, recently confirmed for me that a similar trend was beginning to be noticeable in the contemporary market—though not yet at quite the same percentage rate. She noted that artists like Esteban Vicente, Conrad Marca-Relli, and Joan Mitchell are all getting personal record prices for their works these days. "One reason people are looking at works by artists like these is that they can't afford de Kooning, especially the de Kooning of the late forties and the fifties, and they know they never will be able to," she explained. "Theodoros Stamos, for example, languished at around twenty thousand dollars for years, then last year a painting of his sold for forty thousand, and this year we saw a fine one go for over ninety thousand—this for a work that ten years ago would have been lucky to bring five thousand."

Almost in passing, Melikian includes the interesting observation that the ten-percent law "has nothing to do with beauty, as non-specialists would call it, or 'quality,' as the sophisticated professionals like to put it." He cites the example of a "stunning" 1892 landscape by Maurice Denis (1870–1943) that recently sold for $25,400, or roughly "one tenth of any Neo-Impressionist painting of similar size, even of third-rate quality, by Monet, of which the great man committed more than a few." Melikian concluded, "In art-market thinking, there is no such thing as a masterpiece by a painter who is not currently dubbed a great master."

This last proviso would not have bothered James Mayor, if he read the article. With the prices of de Koonings what they had come to be, he still had a lot of room to maneuver. I spoke earlier of the Rorschach responses that Shapinsky's story seemed to summon. To these must be added Mayor's own calculations. Mayor may well have been—indeed, no doubt he *was*—authentically taken with Shapinsky's work. But he must also have realized that if he could just get Shapinsky included in the lists of the *petits maîtres* working in de Kooning's wake, his prices would have a vast horizon. This was especially the case in Europe, for when Europeans began collecting American art in a serious fashion, in the sixties, they initially went after Warhol, Oldenburg, Stella, Rauschenberg, and Johns, and later, Pollock, but not so much after de Kooning, because, ironically, they saw him more as a transitional European figure, and *Americans* were what they wanted. By the time they realized their mistake, de Kooning's prices were out of reach for all but the wealthiest among them. Collectors with a speculative turn of mind would realize this, too: as long as the current bubble in *all* art prices lasted (and there was no particular reason to believe that it would burst anytime soon), and assuming Mayor was going to be successful in establishing Shapinsky's status as a second-generation Abstract Expressionist, Shapinsky's paintings at twenty thousand dollars each might prove a good investment. As Ronald Alley explained to me while we huddled together at the opening, "There's a tremendous interest in Abstract Expressionism now, and the prices of the famous names have gone straight through the ceiling. Here's a chap who's been producing work of enormous quality, and his prices are starting from scratch. I mean, it seems to me it's a dealer's dream, and a collector's dream."

I wasn't the least bit surprised, therefore, a few days later (I'd returned to New York in the meantime) to be awakened—at 8:00 A.M.—by a phone call from Akumal telling me, "Wonderful news! The show has already sold completely out." The review in the London *Times* by the redoubtable John Russell Taylor had been a rave. ("An extremely good and original abstract expressionist . . . his forms have an extraordinary interior energy . . . exquisitely subtle harmonies.") A few days afterward, however, the Shapinsky juggernaut had received a bit of a jolt when the *Guardian* published a scathing review by its critic, Waldemar Januszczak, not so much on Shapinsky (whose paintings apparently left the critic fairly unmoved either way) as on Akumal and Tariq Ali and Salman Rushdie, and all their hype. All three of them immediately dispatched letters to the editor, and all three letters were published two days later, *along with a cartoon.* "It didn't really bother us," Akumal told me. "I was a little surprised, the fellow being of Polish stock and all, but even the Poles once in a while . . . And, anyway, it just doubled the ratings for the documentary on Channel 4 the next evening. The folks *there* were very pleased. And the BBC have invited the *Guardian* critic and Tariq to square off in a live televised debate next Sunday, and that should be interesting." The screening of the documentary had gone extremely well, and now Akumal was being stopped on the street, at bus stops, and so forth—especially by fellow Indians who were eager to congratulate him on his discovery.

I called up the gallery to see how things were going there. Andrew Murray answered the phone in the gallery's basement storeroom. "James and I are holed up down here, I'm afraid," he said. "It's the only place where there's any room. It's like a railway station up there—all chockablock. The limousines are queued up around the corner!"

Mayor picked up another extension. "There's a waiting list for Shapinsky! The last several purchases went to big world-class collectors, your household names. I've never seen anything like it. The press is all over Shapinsky. We had Greek television in here yesterday morning, Canadian national radio in the afternoon, the Jerusalem *Post,* two of the biggest German art periodicals. This morning, Shapinsky was being interviewed by a pair of Chinese reporters. Not Hong Kong–Beijing!"

I asked them how Shapinsky was holding up under all this. "He's starting to talk," Murray reported. "It's bizarre—he's turned positively loquacious."

Mayor confirmed this improbable finding: "He seems to think he's back in the Waldorf Cafeteria or something."

The following week, I got another call from Akumal. "You'll never guess what happened to me." I didn't even try. "I met a man from California who'd read about the controversy in the *Guardian* and went to see the show. He'd just been over to the gallery and the paintings had bowled him over, and now he wants me to fly to Hollywood to meet a producer friend of his, so we can talk about the possibility of making a movie." Akumal seemed even more excited, however, by the fact that two of India's leading weekly magazines were going to be doing major stories on the discovery. "And I have another important bit of news," he added. "Norbert Lynton was in the gallery again yesterday, and he inscribed a copy of his book, *The Story of Modern Art.* Listen to the inscription. I have it right here: 'All good wishes to Akumal, who is doing his best to force us all to rewrite our art histories.' So, you see, I think it's a good omen. I may yet win the second half of my bet with David." It occurred to me that whether or not Akumal succeeded in forcing Shapinsky into the *Encyclopedia Britannica,* he himself stood a good chance of transmigrating one of these days straight into the *Oxford English Dictionary:* "Akumal: *n.* A genie, a fairy godfather, a doer of good deeds, esp. with regard to artists who regard him as a sort of patron saint, *e.g.,* 'Marcel had been slaving away at his easel for years, all to no avail; he was beginning to wonder if he'd ever meet his *Akumal.*'"

"You know what the moral of the story is?" Akumal asked me. All the others had given me theirs. I wondered what Akumal's would be. "That sometimes the good can win," he said.

"Yeats—the poet I admire much more than Eliot—he wrote a poem called 'The Second Coming,' and two lines of that poem go, 'The best lack all conviction, while the worst are full of passionate intensity.' There is pure motive and there is impure motive. I see it as my mission to give the best some passionate intensity. And, you see, this is a story that celebrates the unity of the human race. Think about it: there are Dutchmen, Americans, Englishmen, Poles, Germans, Indians, Pakistanis—all united by a karma to bring a little good into this world. Don't you think it's wonderful? No matter what happens now, Harold will have a few years to paint in peace. He'll be having a big show at a gallery in Cologne—did I tell you? Fifteen paintings at increased prices, later this year—it's all arranged. But it doesn't matter anymore if not a single other one of his paintings sells, because now Harold and Kate will have a little comfort. They're even talking about moving here to England."

Akumal was silent for a moment, seeming to bask in the light of his good works. "With me, you see," he concluded, finally, "it was always *pure motive.*"

Postscript (1988)

Shortly after the events described in these pages, Akumal returned to India, to Bangalore, to his parents' home, where he subsided into a sixteen-hour-a-day sleeping depression. I can picture him there, the talk of his neighborhood, children huddled in the shade outside the house gossiping about the guy inside who sleeps all day long and about the rumors of his earlier worldly adventures.

He slept for weeks on end, and then he roused himself, and a few months later my phone was ringing at 7:00 A.M. and it was of course Akumal, who had just arrived back in town—in fact, he was still at the airport.

"Gee, Akumal," I said groggily. "You must be suffering from jet lag."

"No," Akumal replied, laughing. "Are you kidding? Me? The *jet* has lag. I never get lag."

We arranged to meet a few days later at my office, and there he regaled me with a new saga, one that was barely more probable than the first. It turned out he'd made another discovery. He'd received dozens of calls and letters following the Shapinsky opening, he explained, young artists likewise eager to have themselves revealed to a thirsting world, but most of them he'd let slide. "This thing of discovering people is quite taxing," he explained. One inquiry, however, had for some reason held his attention (for several reasons, actually, all of which he rehearsed at length for me and none of which I can any longer remember). This was the plea of another son on behalf of his painter-father—in this case, a father who'd been dead for some years. Patrick Carr invited Akumal out to his mother's place to have a look at the paintings of his late father, David Carr.

Now, David Carr *had* been known in the British art world, but principally as a collector and an enthusiast—his own production (faux-naïf renditions of Irish peasants and fishmongers and more complex, neo-cubist studies of factory workers and their machines) had been virtually private. Akumal was thunderstruck ("completely floored") by these paintings, and he immediately set to work. By the time he returned to New York, he'd already managed to arrange for a major retrospective at the Mayor Gallery; the publication by the well-regarded firm of Quartet Books of a full-color, hardbound, coffee-table volume, with an introduction by Ronald Alley; and, of course, a full-length television documentary (this time with BBC-2 rather than Channel 4). All of these events have since come off flawlessly, and Carr's revival seems well assured.

The Shapinskys, for their part, did indeed prosper following the success of Harold's London show. They transposed themselves to England for about half a year but eventually returned to New York City, abandoning their East Side garret for somewhat more commodious circumstances in the Chelsea district. Somewhat nonplussed by his sudden success, Shapinsky himself seemed to retreat for a time into the fabrication of dozens and presently hundreds of miniature paper-and-tinfoil sculptures—this mad progeny came to occupy virtually all the shelves and then all the floor space as well in his new apartment. After a while, though, Shapinsky returned to his painting, which he now seemed to tackle with renewed vigor and zest.

Akumal and James Mayor, however, were still having trouble cracking the New York City gallery scene. Most dealers remained dubious (the eerie stasis of Shapinsky's style, its proximity to de Kooning's, etc.), and not a few of them continued to resent the London provenance of this whole Shapinsky renaissance (or, rather, naissance).

Following his triumph with Carr, Akumal therefore decided that it was time to give his Shapinsky discovery another push. Here I get a little foggy as to the exact chronology (and chutzpahlogy), but somehow Akumal managed to befriend Kathy Ford, the wife of automobile tycoon Henry Ford II, and to enlist her support in the cause. At one point he was even talking about the possibility of having a Shapinsky show in the living room of her own Palm Beach, Florida, mansion—so that they could display Shapinsky's marvelous canvases directly to the potential buyers in that elite community, bypassing the hopelessly hidebound New York art scene altogether. As things actually developed, Shapinsky had a one-man show at Bruce Helander's Palm Beach gallery, which is how it came to pass that on a January 1987 evening, Akumal and Harold Shapinsky found themselves being celebrated at the gala opening of their new show by over eight hundred of the upper crustiest of *le tout Palm Beach,* including the Fords, Peter and Sandy Brant (owners of the White Birch Polo Farms and publisher of *Art in America,* respectively), and Hector and Susan Barrantes (the well-known Argentine polo player and his wife, the mother of Sarah Ferguson, the recently endowed Duchess of York). Another vision well worth conjuring.

By the time of the Helander show, Shapinsky canvases were fetching as much as $34,000 each—and once again the show proved a financial success (it had been half sold out before it even opened, partly on the strength of Mrs. Ford's contacts). The reviews were mixed to good, but the most remarkable of all was a rave by Kenworth Moffett, the former curator of contemporary art at the Boston Museum of Fine Arts, who now publishes a newsletter of his own, entitled *Moffett's Artletter* ($150 for ten issues, artists half price). In discussing Shapinsky with his subscribers, Moffett went *way* out on a limb. He characterized the objection of most New York dealers, the similarity between Shapinsky's and de Kooning's work, as "beside the main point, which is that Shapinsky is better than de Kooning. I think if a show were hung with alternating pairs of the best pictures of Shapinsky and de Kooning, Shapinsky would win every time. He is simply a much more talented artist. His pictures have more movement and intensity. They have better color and drawing. They have more life." And then, further on: "Maybe Shapinsky's presence will help people finally see de Kooning's work for what it is. In any event, Shapinsky, despite his modesty, has been unusually good from the start and has been consistently good for forty years. He has known how to sustain his intensity. If de Kooning first invented the style, Shapinsky is the one who filled it up with feeling."

Mr. and Mrs. Murry Robinson, who purchased a Shapinsky from Helander, proceeded to donate it to the National Gallery of Art in Washington, D.C. On one of his subsequent visits to New York, Akumal handed me a copy of the letter with which the National Gallery's director, the redoubtable J. Carter Brown, accepted the gift:

> I am happy to report that at today's meeting, the Board of Trustees of the National Gallery of Art accepted with pleasure your gift of *Untitled*, 1948, by Harold Shapinsky.
>
> The story of the discovery of Shapinsky is fascinating and having now seen *Untitled*, I must say that the discovery is long overdue. In fact, this work will make an important addition to our twentieth-century holdings. The art of the Abstract Expres-

sionists is a crucial strength of our collection, and Shapinsky's splendid painting will fit in exceedingly well.

Thank you very much for your generous gift to the National Gallery. It is always a particular pleasure for us when collectors become involved with the Gallery, and I hope that in the coming months members of our curatorial staff can visit you either in Providence or in Palm Beach to view your collection and to discuss present and future projects.

To a skeptic this letter might reveal J. Carter Brown to be not only an erudite connoisseur but also a suave diplomat.

Helander now contacted his New York colleague Nathan Shippee, who runs a gallery in the prestigious Fuller Building at the corner of Madison and Fifty-seventh. Shippee, like many who read my piece when it first ran in the *New Yorker* in December 1985, had imagined the whole story to be an elaborate fiction. He was now pleased to discover otherwise, and after seeing some slides and canvases, he scheduled a New York opening for Shapinsky at his gallery in the fall of 1988. Ironically (although Akumal would surely begrudge the concept, he'd insist it had simply been fate, karma, all along), the opening will occur three stories directly below the room into which André Emmerich had earlier insisted to me that he'd have been able to fit Morris Louis's entire life production.

Having righted and relaunched the Shapinsky juggernaut, Akumal set himself to other tasks. One day, a few months later, he barged in on me at my office, bearing a medium-smallish white cube carton that came flying out of his arms as he entered the room, smashing against my filing cabinet and then rolling onto the floor. "Oh dear," he said, picking up the box, which he then proceeded to drop—indeed, almost to spike—all over again. After a few more elaborate stumbles and fumbles, Akumal triumphantly opened his little package: a package that turned out to contain in its hollow—otherwise utterly unprotected—a single, entirely undamaged, not even pockmarked, egg. I surmised that the egg must be hard-boiled. But Akumal proceeded to take a nearby coffee mug, crack the egg, and pour out its liquid (though completely scrambled) contents. "My newest discovery!" Akumal announced enthusiastically.

It turned out that Patrick Carr, the painter's son, was some sort of inventor in his own right, and this particular product of his laboratory, a virtually weightless ingeniously molded polystyrene-like packing box that could be mass-produced and sold in flats "so easy to assemble that any grandmother could do it," or so Akumal insisted, was going to "revolutionize the packaging industry." This was going to be Akumal's new project—this, and the career of that Polish graphic designer—Stasys Eidrigevicius—whose work Akumal had already been flogging when first we'd met. In fact, he was heading back to Warsaw to bring himself up to date on Eidrigevicius.

The next time he was back in New York, Akumal brought me up to date. He'd managed to secure a one-man show for Eidrigevicius in the very heart of New York's Soho, something I had never for a minute doubted he would. I asked him how things were going with the box. "Superbly!" Akumal exulted. As karma would have it, his friend Shippee, before turning to art dealing, had been in the packaging business himself and retained all sorts of contacts. "So we've now been able to show the box to the president of one of the top companies in the country, and he was completely high on it, totally sold out!"

If the box takes off, I commented to Akumal, he'd be able to retire. "Are you kidding?" he said. "I'll be even more busy."

I've decided that "akumal" would never work as a noun. It is going to have to be a verb.

Post-Postscript (1998)

If I'm not sure what became of that box scheme, it's only because, as the years passed, there were so many others. While the Shapinskys settled into a relatively comfortable life of middling late-career success

(Kate herself even achieved a certain renown displaying her own abstract geometric miniature quilt tapestries), Akumal was hardly one to rest on his laurels. He discovered a young black American opera singer in Warsaw and promoted the living daylights out of the poor lucky man. He composed and had himself recorded singing a sort of jazz sutra. And he even created a book of his own—an improbable children's story pitched somewhere between *Charlotte's Web* and *The Gulag Archipelago,* the tale (lavishly illustrated by Stasys) of a little girl on a pig farm who rescues the runt of the litter, raises it to full thriving health, and then, under enormous pressure from her father, gives it up for transport to the slaughterhouse. That night, wracked by guilt, the girl dreams that she herself is turning into a pig, and by morning she has indeed become one, at which point, at story's end, she's being hauled off to the slaughterhouse. Good night and sweet dreams! Owing to the strength of Stasys's startlingly vivid imagery and Akumal's indefatigable promotions, the vegetarian tract eventually made it into numerous foreign editions. Akumal even turned it into a musical which achieved a full-fledged Warsaw production.

I haven't heard from Akumal in a while, but the other day I received a flyer announcing a major Stasys retrospective in Bangalore, India. So I have to assume all's right with the world.

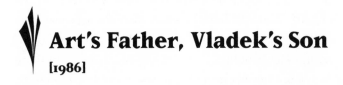

Art's Father, Vladek's Son
[1986]

A good way to study the many possible furrowings of the human brow is by telling a succession of friends and strangers, as I've taken to doing lately, that the best book you've read in a long time is a comic-strip history of the Holocaust. Brows positively curdle, foreheads arch, faces blanch and stiffen as if to say, "If this is one of your jokes, it's not very funny." Only it's not one of my jokes—it's the truth. The book is *Maus* (published by Pantheon), and its author—the perpetrator of my perplex—is Art Spiegelman.

Actually, the fans of *Maus* have been following its development for some time in installment form. Each new episode has been tucked inside successive issues of *RAW*, the semiannual journal of avant-garde cartooning (The Graphix Magazine of Abstract Depressionism, as its cover once proclaimed) that Spiegelman and his wife, Françoise Mouly, have been editing and publishing out of their Soho loft, in New York City, since 1980. Jules Feiffer has described *Maus* as "a remarkable work, awesome in its conception and execution," and David Levine has characterized its effect on the reader as "on a par with Kafka" and its mastery of tone as "reminiscent of Balzac."

"A comic-strip history of the Holocaust" isn't quite right: such a characterization is begging for trouble—or for misunderstanding, anyway. This is no Classics Illustrated/Cliffs Notes digest of the despicable schemings of Hitler and Himmler and their whole nefarious crew. Hitler and Himmler hardly appear at all. Rather, *Maus* is at once a novel, a documentary, a memoir, an intimate retelling of the Holocaust story as it was experienced by a single family—Spiegelman's own. Or rather, as it was experienced by Spiegelman's father, Vladek, who recounts the story to his son, Art, who was born in 1948, after the war was over, after everything was over, including the possibility of any sort of normal upbringing. The conditions of survivorship skew everything: Vladek's first son, a brother Art never knew, was an early victim of the Final Solution; Vladek and his wife, Art's mother Anja, somehow survived their separate fates in concentration camps, emerging hollowed out and cratered; years later, Anja would take her own life, just as Art was leaving the nest. Art's relationship with his father is a continual torment, a mutual purgatory of disappointment, guilt, and recrimination. This relationship is as much the focus of Art's story as is his father's reminiscence. The elegant back jacket of the Pantheon edition features a map of World War II Poland and, inset, a street map of the Rego Park, Queens, neighborhood where that war continued into the present in the mangled graspings and grapplings of father and son. *Maus* is subtitled *A Survivor's Tale,* but the question of *which* survivor is left to hover.

Maus is all this—and then again, it's just an animal story. For Spiegelman has recast his tale in the eerily familiar visual language of the traditional comic book—animals in human clothing and in a distinctly human environment—thereby playing off all our childhood associations and expectations. Art, Vladek, Anja, Art's stepmother Mala, and all the other Jews are mice. The Germans are cats, the Poles pigs, the Americans dogs. Spiegelman's draftsmanship is clean and direct, his characterizations are charming and disarming—the imagery leads us on, invitingly, reassuringly, until suddenly the horrible story has us gripped and pinioned. Midway through, we hardly notice how strange it is that we're having such strong reactions to these animal doings.

And then it all stops: the volume is truncated in midtale. Vladek and Anja's desperate progress from prosperity into the ghetto and beyond, from one hiding hovel to the next, ends abruptly with their arrival at Mauschwitz. To learn what happened to them there, how on earth they survived—and whether or not this father and his son ever do achieve a measure of reconciliation—we are invited to await a second volume.

The man greeting me at the entrance to the fourth-floor walk-up apartment in Soho looked far younger than his almost forty years. He also looked considerably more clean cut and less threatening than the intense, long-haired, mustachioed, scrungy, Zappaesque character he had contrived as his own stand-in in some of the existentialist underground comic strips he'd produced during the seventies.

The apartment, too, was more spacious than I was expecting, and it was bustling. In fact, the Spiegelmans occupy the entire floor, which they've divided in two: the front half consists of the staging area for *RAW*, while the back half provides them with living quarters. After seeing me in, Spiegelman excused himself to go confer with Françoise, a strikingly lovely French woman with high cheekbones and a luxuriant overflow of wavy brown hair. The next issue of *RAW* was about to go to press, and Françoise was on her way out to consult with the printers. The production values of *RAW* are exceptionally high—"neurotically precious" is how R. Crumb, the legendary underground-comics master and an occasional contributor to the magazine, once described them to me.

Spiegelman and Mouly launched *RAW* with the twin intentions of raising the status of cartoon graphics to an art form and introducing an American audience to the sort of high-level comic-strip art that has thrived for many years in Europe and Japan. Mouly, as the publisher, is famous for the painstaking attention she lavishes on all technical aspects of the production process.

The two of them had a certain amount to discuss before she left, and they stood together for a few moments huddled over the proof sheets, chainsmoking filtered Camels. Meanwhile, several assistants sat hunched over flatbed tables, monkeying with galleys. The room was surrounded on all sides by bookshelves, which were sagging under the weight of the most extensive library of comic books and anthologies anyone could ever imagine. After a while, Mouly took off, and Spiegelman invited me into the back half of his loft, the living quarters.

"The whole next issue is ready," Spiegelman confessed anxiously. "Everything's now waiting on me, because I still have to finish the next installment of *Maus*. And it's taking forever." He escorted me to the far back of the loft, to his Maushole, as he calls it, where a worktable was covered with a neat clutter. Notebooks bulging with transcripts and preliminary sketches were piled to one side; dozens of little packets of papers were scattered about on the other—each bundle representing the successive workings and reworkings of a single panel. "Comics offer a very concentrated and efficient medium for telling a story," he said. "And in this case it's like trying to tell an epic novel in telegraph form. In a way, it's a lot more challenging than trying to simply tell a story. In a prose story, I could just write, 'Then they dragged my father through the gate and into the camp.' But here I have to live those words, to assimilate them, to turn them into finished business—so that I end up *seeing* them and am then able to convey that vision. Were there tufts of grass, ruts in the path, puddles in the ruts? How tall were the buildings, how many windows, any bars, any lights in the windows, any people? What time of day was it? What was the horizon like? Every panel requires that I interrogate my material like that over and over again. And it's terribly time-consuming.

"It's strange," he continued. "The parts of my father's story which I've finished drawing are clear to me. The parts I haven't gotten to yet are still a blur—even though I know the story, know the words. I've got everything blocked out in abstract, except the ending. In Part Two, the question of my father's veracity starts coming into play. Not so much whether he was telling the truth, but rather, just what had he actually lived through—what did he understand of what he experienced, what did he tell of what he understood, what did I understand of what he told, and what do I tell? The layers begin to multiply, like pane upon pane of glass.

"I still don't know how I'm going to end it," he said, pointing over at the notebooks. "I don't *see* most of it yet. I'm only just beginning to see Mauschwitz."

I asked him why he'd decided to publish the book version of *Maus* in its current truncated form.

"Funny you should ask," he replied. He suggested we go up on the roof, where he'd installed a rudimentary sun deck. We sat on some garden furniture and surveyed the Soho skyline, the tar-roof line. He lit up a Camel, took a deep drag, and resumed: "I'd never really had any intention of publishing the book version in two parts. But then, about a year ago, I read in an interview with Steven Spielberg that he was producing an animated feature film entitled *An American Tail,* involving a family of Jewish mice living in Russia a hundred years ago named the Mousekawitzes, who were being persecuted by Katsacks, and how eventually they fled to America for shelter. He was planning to have it out in time for the Statue of Liberty centennial celebrations.

"I was appalled, shattered," Spiegelman continued with a shudder. "For about a month I went into a frenzy. I'd spent my life on this, and now here, along was coming this Goliath, the most powerful man in Hollywood, just casually trampling everything underfoot. I dashed off a letter, which was returned, unopened. I went sleepless for nights on end, and then, when I finally did sleep, I began confusing our names in my dreams: Spiegelberg, Spielman . . . I contacted lawyers. I mean, the similarities were so obvious, right down to the title—their *American Tail* simply being a more blatant, pandering-to-the-mob version of my *Survivor's Tale* subtitle. Their lawyers argued that the idea of anthropomorphizing mice wasn't unique to either of us, and they, of course, cited Mickey Mouse and other Disney creations. But no one was denying that—indeed, I'd self-consciously been playing off Disney all the while. If you wanted to get technical about it, the idea of anthropomorphizing animals goes all the way back to Aesop. No, what I was saying was that the specific use of mice to sympathetically portray Jews combined with the concept of cats as anti-Semitic oppressors in a story that compares life in the Old World of

Europe with life in America *was* unique—and it was called *Maus: A Survivor's Tale.*

"I didn't want any money from them—I just wanted them to cease and desist. What made me so angry was that when *Maus* was eventually going to be completed, people were naturally going to see my version as a slightly psychotic recasting of Spielberg's idea instead of the way it was—Spielberg's being an utter domestication and trivialization of *Maus.* And then there was a further infuriating irony: theirs supposedly took place in 1886, and what with the Statue of Liberty tie-in, they were going to be swathing the story in all this mindless, fashionable, self-congratulatory patriotic fervor—whereas, if you were being true to the initial metaphor, in depicting the way things actually were in 1940, you would have had to strand my mice people off the coast of Cuba, *drowning,* because it is precisely the case that at that point, the time of their greatest need, mice people were being denied entry into the U.S."

Spiegelman started to calm down. His cigarette had gone out; he lit up another. "Well, anyway, it's over for the time being. My lawyers told me that while I had a very strong moral case, my legal one wasn't so hot. It'd be hard to prove anything one way or the other, certainly not enough to justify a prior injunction against release of the movie, which is the only thing I really wanted. Some of my friends couldn't understand why I was getting so worked up. One editor told me 'Look, all the guy stole was your concept, and frankly, it's a terrible concept.'" (The redoubtable R. Crumb was likewise bemused by Spiegelman's desperate churnings. "He's such an egomaniac," Crumb told me, laughing. "I mean, who the hell cares? I've seen some of the previews for Spielberg's film. Those mice are cute." R. Crumb has the most devastatingly prurient way of pronouncing the word *cute.*)

Spiegelman may have been calming down, but he was still obsessing: "I mean, if Samuel Beckett had stolen the idea, I'd be depressed, but I'd be *impressed* as well. But Steven Spielberg! Oy! I just read where they've now licensed off the *doll rights* for the Mousekawitzes to Sears, and McDonald's is going to get the beverage-cup rights!"

So, Spiegelman continued, he decided that if he couldn't stop Spielberg, he might nevertheless beat him to the turnstiles, immediately publishing as much of the story as he'd already completed (he explained how all along he'd seen the arrival at Mauschwitz as the narrative's halfway point) and thereby at least establishing primacy. Pantheon was happy to go along, and Spielberg's production company obliged by running into difficulties and having to delay the film's release until around Thanksgiving. As Spiegelman observed, "It was actually a great idea. You see, in Europe there's a real tradition, in serious cartooning as well as in high literature, of multivolume projects—just think of that supreme mouse writer, Proust, and all the volumes he was able to generate from that initial whiff of Camembert!"

When Art Spiegelman was about ten years old, in 1958 in Rego Park, Queens, he fell one day while roller-skating with some friends, who then skated on without him. Whimpering, he walked home to his father, who was out in the yard doing some carpentry repairs. Vladek inquired why his Artie was crying, and when Art told him about the fall and his friends, Vladek stopped his sawing, looked down at his son and said gruffly, "Friends? Your *friends?* If you lock them together in a room with no food for a week, then you could see what it is, friends!"

Spiegelman places this incident as the first episode in the book version of *Maus,* and it serves as a sort of overture, an intimation of one of the book's principal themes. For, at one level, Artie was an all-American boy, rollerskating, out goofing with his gang. Back home, though, life was haunted, darkly freighted and overcharged with parental concern.

Actually, Artie had been born in Stockholm in 1948, three years after his parents' miraculous reunion at the end of their separate camp fates. Two years after Artie's birth, the family was finally permitted to immigrate to America. Back in the old country, in Poland between the wars, Vladek had been a wealthy man, or rather Anja's father had been a wealthy man, and Vladek had married into that wealth. Art seems to leave intentionally ambiguous (although here, as elsewhere in *Maus,* the ambiguity is of an almost crystalline precision) whether or not he thinks Vladek initially married Anja for her money and her station. At any rate, Vladek managed important aspects of her family's textile business and attained substantial financial security for himself, his wife, and their beloved baby son, Richieu—until the war, that is, when both the wealth and the beloved son were snatched away. In America, in New York, Vladek worked in the garment trade and later in the diamond district, but he never recaptured the security of his earlier life. Though the Spiegelmans were basically middle-class, they lived below their means. Raising his first son, Vladek had been a young father with a buoyant sense of his future. Raising his second son—his second "only child"—he was an old man, fretting over his insecure present when he wasn't fixated on his desolate past. Art's parents *were* old. There were really two generations separating them from this American boy; on top of that, they were Old World; and on top of that, they'd aged well beyond their years owing to their experiences during the war. As Artie grew into young adulthood in America of the sixties, he would be facing generation gaps compounded one upon another.

And yet, for all that, Art remembers his childhood as remarkably normal. "I really didn't encounter serious problems," he recalled that afternoon on his sun deck, "until I went away to college and was able to match my experiences against those of others. I mean, for instance, the fact that my parents used to wake up in the middle of the night screaming didn't seem especially strange to me. I suppose I thought everybody's parents did. Or the fact that in the Spiegelman household, the regular birthday gift for my mother, year in and year out, was some sort of wide bracelet, so that she could cover over the number tattooed on her forearm. Sometimes when neighbor kids would come over and ask her what that stuff on her arm was, she'd say it was a telephone number she was trying not to forget.

"No," he continued, "I was a pretty normal kid, except that I was reading a lot too much Kafka for a fourteen-year-old. I knew I'd grow up to be neurotic, the way today I know I'll soon be losing my hair." He brushed back a thinning, brown wisp, further revealing his precipitously receding hairline. "It didn't, it doesn't bother me.

"By fourteen, too, I knew I'd be a cartoonist: I was obsessed with comics. I spent hours copying from comic books, especially the satirical ones, like *Mad* magazine, which was a terrific influence."

I asked Spiegelman whether any of that bothered his parents. "They encouraged me up to a point," he replied, "up to the point where it became clear that I was serious. A kind of panic set in as I turned fifteen and was still doing it. They were terribly upset because clearly there was no way one could make a living at cartooning, and my father especially was, perhaps understandably, obsessed about money. They wanted me to become a dentist. For them, dentist was halfway to doctor, I guess. And we'd have these long talks. They'd point out how if I became a dentist, I could always do the drawing on the side, whereas if I became a cartoonist, I couldn't very well pull people's teeth during my off hours. Their logic was impeccable, just irrelevant. I was hooked."

Young Spiegelman knew he wanted to be a cartoonist, but he wasn't sure what kind, so he tried everything. When he was twelve, he approached the editors of the Long Island *Post,* a local paper, seeking employment as a staff cartoonist. The *Post* ran a story about the incident, headlined, "Budding Artist Wants Attention." When he was fifteen, he was in fact appointed staff cartoonist of the *Post,* an unpaid position. Meanwhile he commuted by subway to the mid-Manhattan campus of the High School of Art and Design, where he edited the school paper, hung out after (and sometimes during) school at the nearby offices of *Mad* magazine, and, inspired, began turning out his own cartoon digests, one called *Wild,* and another *Blasé,* which "was printed with a process even cheaper than mimeo." He contributed to a

Cuban exile paper, and served a stint up in Harlem, disguised to the world as a hip black cartoonist ("Artie X").

In 1966, Art left home for Harpur College, the experimental sub-campus of the State University of New York at Binghamton, and there things began to come seriously unmoored. The underlying conflicts with his parents roiled to the surface now that he was no longer in their immediate presence. Furthermore, "Binghamton was one of the early capitals of psychedelics," he says, "and the drug culture definitely accelerated my decomposition beyond any containable point." His intensity became increasingly manic. He was living off campus, in a forest cabin. "And I made a strange discovery," he recalls. "I was just kind of holding court, people were coming out to visit, and I found that if I just said whatever came into my mind, the atmosphere would get incredibly charged—and if I kept it up, within half an hour, either my guests would run out, screaming, or else we'd approach this druglike high. It was like a primordial sensitivity session. And this was going on for days on end. I wasn't eating, I was laughing a lot, I was beginning to suffer from acute sleep deprivation. I was starting to experience these rampant delusions of grandeur. I was sure I was onto something, and sure enough, I was—a psychotic breakdown."

Eventually, they came to take him away (he informed the school shrink that the top of his head looked like a penis); he was dispatched by ambulance to a local mental ward (exaltedly he wailed in tune with the siren); they sedated him (it took three full-bore shots) and threw him into a padded cell. ("Waking up, my first thought was that I was God alone and that what I really needed to do now was invent me some people . . . Later, I began screaming for a nurse, and when this guy came in, I said, no, I wanted a *nurse*. He said he was a nurse—I'd never heard of such a thing as a male nurse—and I said, 'Gee, how do you people reproduce here on this planet?'") Gradually, they reeled him back in—or he reeled himself back in; they didn't seem to be of much help. One attendant, a conscientious objector doing alternative service, befriended him and advised him on how to get out. ("He told me to drink less water—they seemed to think I thought my brain was over-heating or something—to play Ping-Pong, *lots* of Ping-Pong, and to blame it all on LSD, which was a category they could understand; all of which I did, and within a month I was released.")

He was released on two conditions: first, that he start seeing a psychotherapist on the outside, and second, that he go back to living with his parents. "Living at home was exactly the wrong prescription," Spiegelman said, "since it was home that was driving me crazy. I said this quite emphatically to the shrink one day, and he asked me, 'So why don't you move out?' I told him about the condition. And he said, 'You really think they're going to throw you back in if you don't follow their conditions?' I said, 'Gee, thanks,' and immediately left both home and psychotherapy.

"The wonderful thing about the whole episode, though, is that it cut off all expectations. I'd been locked in a life-and-death struggle with my parents. Anything short of the nut house would have left things in-soluble. But now I could venture out on my own terms. Over the years, I have developed a terrific confidence in my own subconscious."

Art was out of the house, but the tormented Spiegelman family drama did not subside, and a few months after his release, his mother committed suicide.

Spiegelman becomes quiet and measured when he talks about this period. "The way she did it, I was the one who was supposed to dis-cover the body, only I was late coming by, as usual, so that by the time I arrived there was already this whole scene . . . Was my commitment to the mental ward the cause of her suicide? No. Was there a relation? Sure. After the war, she'd invested her whole life in me. I was more like a confidant to her than a son. She couldn't handle the separation. I didn't want to hurt her, to hurt them. But I had to break free."

He's silent for a moment, then resumes: "But talk about repression. For a while I had no feelings whatsoever. People would ask me, and I'd just say that she was a suicide, period. Nothing. I moved out to Califor-nia, submerged myself in the underground-comics scene, which was thriving out there, imagined myself unscathed. And then one day, four years later, it all suddenly came flooding back, all the memories re-surging. I threw myself into seclusion for a month, and in the end I emerged with *Prisoner of the Hell Planet*."

That four-page strip, which first appeared in San Francisco as part of the *Short Order Comix* series in 1972 was an astonishment—one of the most lacerating breakthroughs yet in an extraordinarily active scene. The strip opens with a drawn hand holding an actual photo-graph portraying a swimsuit-clad middle-aged woman and her smiling T-shirted boy; the photo is captioned "Trojan Lake, N.Y., 1958" (the same year as that of the roller-skating incident with which *Maus* opens). In the next frame, the mustachioed narrator peers out, framed by a fierce spotlight and decked out in prison (or is it concentration-camp?) garb. "In 1968, my mother killed herself," the narrator declares simply. "She left no note."

There follow four pages of vertiginous, expressionist draftsmanship and writing—part Caligari, part Munch. The story of the suicide is recounted, and the strip concludes with the narrator locked away in a vast prison vault: "Well, Mom, if you're listening, congratulations! You've committed the perfect crime. . . . You put me here, shorted my circuits, cut my nerve endings, and crossed my wires. . . . You murdered me, Mommy, and you left me here to take the rap." A voice bubble intrudes from out of frame: "Pipe down, Mac, some of us are trying to sleep."

A few months before *Hell Planet*, Spiegelman had composed an early version of *Maus*, a three-page rendition that he included as his contribution to an underground anthology called *Funny Aminals*. In that first version, the relationship between father and son is quieter, al-most pastoral. The cozy Father Mouse is telling his little boy Mickey a bedtime story. It's an adorable, cuddly scene (there's a Mickey Mouse lamp on the bedside table)—only the story is ghastly. Several of the in-cidents that were to be amplified years later in the book-length version appear here in concentrated form. But by the strip's end—as Daddy and

Mommy in the bedtime story are being herded into Mauschwitz—Daddy explains that that's all he can tell for now, he can tell no more, and Mickey has, in any case, already nodded off to sleep.

It's strange: Spiegelman's 1972 take on his parents—a warm, empathetic father and cruelly manipulative mother—was to undergo a complete reversal by the time he returned to these themes in the book version of *Maus*. As if to underscore this transformation, he contrived to include the entire *Hell Planet* strip within the body of the new *Maus*'s text, drawing on a true episode in which his father accidentally comes upon a copy of *Hell Planet* his son never intended for him to see.

The 1972 *Maus* and *Hell Planet* strips were representative of one channel in the distinctly bifurcated artistic program that Spiegelman was pursuing now that he'd launched his underground cartooning career. On the one hand, he was trying to push the comic-strip medium as far as he could in terms of wrenchingly confessional content. Simultaneously, although usually separately, he was testing the limits of the comic strip's formal requirements. In high deconstructionist style, he was questioning such things as how people read a strip; how many of the usual expectations one might subtract from a strip before it began to resemble an inchoate jumble of images on the page; whether that mattered. By 1977, he managed to unite examples of both his tendencies in a single anthology of his work, which he titled, with considerable punning cleverness, *Breakdowns* (besides its obvious confessional connotation, the word *breakdown* refers to the preliminary sketches that precede and block out a finished comic strip).

"*Breakdowns* came out as I was turning thirty," Spiegelman recalls, lighting up another cigarette, "and with some of the strips there, it was really like I'd taken things, particularly the formal questions, pretty much to the limit. So I was faced with a dilemma, 'Now what?'And after all my experiments, it was as if I finally said, 'All right, I give up, comics are there to tell *a story*.' But what story? Drawing really comes hard to me. I sweat these things out—one or two panels a day, a page maybe a week. And I was damned if I was going to put in all that work for a few chuckles. I hesitated for a while, but finally I decided that I had to go back and confront the thing that in a way I'd known all along I'd eventually have to face—this presence that had been hanging over my family's life, Auschwitz and what it had done to us."

With the first installment of that second version of *Maus,* which appeared in the December 1980 issue of *RAW,* Mickey, the little pajama-clad mouse boy of the initial version, had grown up. He was now a chain-smoking, somewhat alienated, somewhat disheveled, urban cartoonist mouse named Art. His father, too, had aged, become more stooped and crotchety, and their relationship had become far more complicated. "I went out to see my father in Rego Park," says Art, the narrator mouse, introducing his tale. "I hadn't seen him in a long time—we weren't that close."

"After I'd left home to go to college," Art, the real-life cartoonist, recalls, lighting up another cigarette, "my father and I could hardly get together without fighting, a situation that only worsened after Anja's suicide. Vladek remarried, this time to a kind woman named Mala, another camp survivor who'd been a childhood friend of Anja's back in her old town of Sosnowiec, but it was a sorry mismatch, and that relationship too seemed to devolve into endless kvetching and bickering. It was a classic case of victims victimizing each other—and I couldn't stand being around. And yet now, if I was going to tell the story, I knew I'd have to start visiting my father again, to get him to tell me his tale one more time. I'd heard everything countless times before, but it had all been background noise, part of the ambient blur; precisely because I'd been subjected to all of it so often before, I could barely recall any of it. So now I asked him if he'd allow me to tape-record his stories, and he was willing. So I began heading back out to Rego Park.

"From the book," Spiegelman continues after a pause, "a reader might get the impression that the conversations depicted in the narrative were just one small part, a facet of my relationship with my father. In fact, however, they *were* my relationship with my father. I was doing them *to have a relationship with my father.* Outside of them, we were still continually at loggerheads."

The Vladek portrayed in the present-tense sequences of *Maus* is petty, cheap, maddeningly manipulative, self-pitying, witheringly abusive to his second wife, neurotic as hell. But when he settles in and starts retelling his life story, you realize that, yes, precisely, he is a survivor of hell, a mangled and warped survivor. The present Vladek imbues his former self with life, but that former Vladek illuminates the present one as well. Spiegelman develops this theme overtly but then, too, in the subtlest details. At one point, for example, Vladek is recounting how when he was a Polish soldier in a Nazi POW camp, early on in the war, he and some fellow soldiers were billeted into a filthy stable, which they were ordered to render "spotlessly clean within an hour," a manifestly impossible task, the failure at which cost them their day's soup ration, "you lousy bastards." Suddenly Vladek interrupts his story and the scene shifts to the present, with Artie seated on the floor before his father, taking it all in. "But look, Artie, what you do!" Vladek cries. "Huh?" asks the absorbed Artie. "You're dropping on the carpet. You want it should be like a stable *here?*" Artie apologizes and hurries to pick up the cigarette ashes. "Clean it, yes?" Vladek will not relent. "Otherwise I have to do it. Mala could let it sit like this for a week and never touch it." And so forth: kvetch, kvetch, kvetch. And then, just as suddenly, we're back in Poland: "So, we lived and worked a few weeks in the stable . . . "

While many of the ways Vladek grates on his son amount to minor foibles and misdemeanors, he is capable of more substantial outrages as well. Perhaps the most mortifying (and unforgivable) of these atrocities emerges only gradually as the story unfolds: the fact that Vladek didn't just misplace the life history that Anja had written out years earlier to be given someday to their son, a folio Artie even remembers having seen somewhere around when he was growing up—that, actually, he destroyed it. "Murderer!" cries a flabbergasted Artie when Vladek finally confesses the callous immolation at the climax of Book 1. "Murderer," he mutters, walking away. Curtain falls.

"The fact that he'd destroyed that autobiographical journal of hers," Spiegelman says, "meant that the story forcibly became increasingly *his* story, which at first seemed like a terrible, almost fatal, problem. The absence of my mother left me with—well, not with an antihero, but at any rate not a pure hero. But in retrospect that now seems to me one of the strengths of *Maus*. If only admirable people were shown to have survived, then the implicit moral would have been that only admirable people deserved to survive, as opposed to the fact that people deserved to survive as people. Anyway, I'm left with the story I've got, my shoe-horn with which to squeeze myself back into history.

"I've tried to achieve an evenness of tone, a certain objectivity," Spiegelman continued, "because that made the story work better. But it also proved helpful—*is* proving helpful—in my coming to terms with my father. Rereading it, I marvel at how my father comes across, finally, as a sympathetic character—people keep telling me what a sympathetic portrait I've drawn. As I was actually drawing it, let me tell you, I was raging, boiling over with anger. But there must have been a deeper sympathy for him which I wasn't even aware of as I was doing it, an understanding I was getting in contact with. It's as if all his damn cantankerousness finally melted away."

I asked Spiegelman about the mouse metaphor, the very notion of telling the story in this animal-fabulist mode. It seems to me one of the most effective things about the book. There have been hundreds of Holocaust memoirs—horribly, we've become inured to the horror. People being gassed in showers and shoveled into ovens—it's a story we've already heard. But mice? The Mickey Mice of our childhood reveries? Having the story thus retold, with animals as the principals, freshly recaptures its terrible immediacy, its palpable urgency.

I asked Spiegelman how he'd hit upon the idea. "It goes back to that *Funny Aminals* comic anthology I told you about before," he explained. "Along with several of the other underground-comics people out in California, I had been invited to contribute a strip to this anthology of warped, revisionist animal comics. Initially, I was trying to do some sort of Grand Guignol horror strip, but it wasn't working. Then I remembered something an avant-garde filmmaker friend, Ken Jacobs, had pointed out back at Binghamton, how in the early animated cartoons, blacks and mice were often represented similarly. Early animated cartoon mice had 'darkie' rhythms and body language, and vice versa. So for a while I thought about doing an animal strip about the black experience in America—for about forty minutes. Because what did I know about the black experience in America? And then suddenly the idea of Jews as mice just hit me full force, full-blown. Almost as soon as it hit me, I began to recognize the obvious historical antecedents—how Nazis had spoken of Jews as 'vermin,' for example, and plotted their 'extermination.' And before that back to Kafka, whose story 'Josephine the Singer, or the Mouse Folk' was one of my favorites from back when I was a teenager and has always struck me as a dark parable and prophecy about the situation of the Jews and Jewishness.

"Having hit upon the metaphor, though, I wanted to subvert it, too," continued Spiegelman, the veteran deconstructionist, lighting up again. "I wanted it to become problematic, to have it confound and implicate the reader. I include all sorts of paradoxes in the text—for instance, the way in which Artie, the mouse cartoonist, draws the story of his mother's suicide, and in his strip (my own *Hell Planet* strip), all the characters are *human.* Or the moment when the mother and father are shown hiding in a cramped cellar and the mother shrieks with terror because there are 'Rats!' All those moments are meant to rupture the metaphor, to render its absurdity conspicuous, to force a kind of free fall. I always savored that sort of confusion when I was a child reading comic books: how, for instance, Donald would go over to Grandma Duck's for Thanksgiving and they'd be having turkey for dinner!

"But it's funny," Spiegelman continued, "a lot of those subtleties just pass people by. In fact, I remember how I was over at my father's one evening soon after I'd published the three-page version of *Maus.*

As usual, he had several of his card-playing buddies over—all fellow camp survivors—and at one point he passed the strip around. They all read it, and then they immediately set to trading anecdotes: 'Ah, yes, I remember that, only with me it happened like this,' and so forth. Not one of them seemed the least bit fazed by the mouse metaphor—not one of them even seemed to have noticed it! A few days later, I happened to be making a presentation of some of my work at this magazine. I was sitting out in the art editor's waiting room with a couple other cartoonists, old fellows, and I pulled out *Maus* and showed it to them. They looked it over for a while and began conferring: 'Kid's a good mouse man,' one of them said. 'Yeah, not bad on cats, either,' said the other. Utterly oblivious to the Holocaust subject matter."

I asked Spiegelman what his father had thought of the newer installments of *Maus,* as they began appearing in *RAW.* "He never really saw them," Art replied, snuffing out his cigarette. "Early in 1981 he and Mala moved down to Florida, and within a few months of that he was already beginning to lose it. He was past seventy-five years old, and he was pretty much incoherent throughout the last year before his death. We had to put him in an old-age home. He died on August 18, 1982."

Art paused for a moment, then continued: "I was less affected by his death than I thought I'd be, perhaps because he'd been a long time going, maybe because there was no room for that relationship to change. I went to his funeral, almost like a reporter trying to see how his story was going to end up. But my feelings were more inchoate than anything that would make a good anecdote.

"I'd already finished all my taping sessions with him before he'd begun to go senile, and I had the story pretty well blocked out, chapter by chapter, except for the ending. As I say, I still don't know how I'm going to end it. The last time I saw him, he was sitting there propped up in the nursing home. He may or may not have recognized me. The nurses were trying to stroke any last vestiges of memory in him. They were showing him these 'Romper Room' flashcards, you know, 'Dog,' 'Cat,' 'Dog,' 'Cat,' . . . 'Cat.'"

Spiegelman's voice trailed off. It seemed he might have come upon his ending after all.

Postscript (1988)

As things turned out, Spiegelman need not have worried about Spielberg's film. The film opened to middling reviews and middling success—no one, at any rate, was confusing it with *Maus,* which, for its part, was greeted with overwhelming critical acclaim and proved an unexpected best-seller. During its first year and a half, Spiegelman's book sold almost one hundred thousand copies in the United States, and arrangements were under way for no less than twelve foreign editions (including German, French, Hebrew, Finnish, and Japanese translations). Meanwhile, Spiegelman continued to eke out the subsequent chapters, slowly, laboriously . . . And a new character made a brief appearance in the eighth chapter, in a momentary flash-forward to the present: a baby girl mouse named Nadja, Vladek's sudden granddaughter.

Post-Postscript (1998)

Nadja was joined, in 1991, by another child, Vladek's first grandson, Dash—and that same year, the first volume of *Maus* was joined by a second and concluding one, which proved, if anything, an even greater critical and commercial success. The following year, the entire *Maus* series was honored with a "Special Pulitzer" ("'Special' as in Special Olympics," Spiegelman would subsequently quip)—and the books have gone on to sell millions of copies worldwide in now over twenty languages. (Spiegelman's second volume, incidentally, once again preceded Steven Spielberg's second whack at parallel material, this time of course in his much heralded 1993 film *Schindler's List.*)

For its part, Spiegelman's career continued to soar. The *Maus* drawings and documentation were the subject of exhibitions at the New York's Museum of Modern Art and in other venues around the world.

Art produced an exquisite illustrated edition of Joseph Moncure March's lost flapper-age classic, *The Wild Party,* and even tried his hand at children's books with the instant classic, *Open Me, I'm a Dog* (another tale of animal transformation, in this instance the story of a puppy transformed into a book—in fact this very book in the child reader's lap—by an evil wizard's terrible curse). Spiegelman became a regular contributor to the *New Yorker,* perpetrating many of the magazine's most striking and controversial recent covers, and a consulting editor at *Details* (where he's been unleashing the *RAW* menagerie on a new generation). And by decade's end, he'd even begun designing and composing the libretto for an original opera.

In 1998, Françoise asked Art what he might like for his fiftieth birthday and he replied: her hand in marriage. That is to say, not the grudging city hall green-card ceremony they'd shared twenty years earlier, but a real wedding bash. Which is how over a hundred well-wishers came to converge, one brisk winter night, on a festive Manhattan penthouse—floating in the spangled sky between the Empire State Building and the World Trade Center—where, between riffs of a small band led by R. Crumb, they got to hear Art and Françoise exchange fresh vows and then be celebrated, in turn, by Nadja, who serenaded them with a winning rendition of "When I'm Sixty-Four," and six-year-old Dash, who contributed an original epithalamonic offering, a poem extolling first his mom ("When I think of Françoise, I think of *flowers:* They are soft and gentle as she is.") and then his dear papa:

> When I think of Art, I think of *amazing:*
> It is amazing that he could make a book all by himself
> and the book is *Open Me: I'm a Dog.*

Over a half century after the Holocaust, Vladek's line had at last produced a blessedly oblivious survivor.

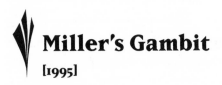

Miller's Gambit

[1995]

Chess is boring, but Jeff Miller is not. Or anyway, he's not *bored*—not anymore.

I had never heard of Jeff Miller until a while back, when I happened to be out in Berkeley, California, visiting some old friends, several of whom I found to have become mildly obsessed with a strange new game, a bizarre variation on chess. All of them told me that if I thought they were obsessed, I should meet Jeff Miller, the game's recent inventor and uncontested grandmaster. They warned me that Jeff was a bit odd himself, and had been even before he invented the game. He was described to me as a sporadically employed software designer—he'd helped to automate the fingerprint storage and retrieval system for the California Department of Justice and collaborated on the safety-assessment system for New York's Indian Point nuclear power plant—and as a frequenter of the area's legal poker parlors. ("He's one of those guys who's probably in the top single percentile of poker players in the country," one of his friends told me, "which is a dangerous place to be, since it's really only those in the top *half* percent who can make a concern of it.")

His game is actually quite captivating. It's played on a standard chessboard with standard chess pieces, each of which is allowed the standard moves. Chess itself, of course, always begins with each player's full panoply of pieces ranged in their rigidly fixed positions. Jeff's game, by contrast, starts *with an entirely empty board*. Each player—black and white—stares down on this blank expanse, with all sixteen of his pieces by his side, outside the playing field. As in standard chess, White moves first, and he can place any one of his pieces anywhere on the board. Black then does likewise. In his next move, White can either move the piece he's already placed on the board, or else he can put down his second piece, anywhere else on the board. And Black likewise. The pieces move exactly as they do in regular chess except that, at the outset, they aren't allowed to take an opponent's piece. The black queen, for example, can move horizontally, vertically, or diagonally; however, if, in so moving, she runs up against, say, a white pawn, she's blocked: she has to stop at the immediately prior square.

During its first phase, the game is thus almost entirely one of *positioning,* of tactical jockeying in anticipation of the carnage to come when the board becomes "activated." And the board becomes activated, for either player, the moment he puts down his own king. Once White's king is on the board, then (and not until then) White can start taking Black's pieces according to the standard chess rules. And likewise with Black. So both players have an incentive to get their king onto the board. On the other hand, they also have an incentive to keep their king off the board as long as possible, since in the end the point of the game is exactly the same as in regular chess, to mate the other player's king before one's own king can be mated (something that, of course, by definition can't happen if one hasn't even put one's king on the board yet).

One afternoon I was visiting some friends who were trying to acquaint me with the game's subtler intricacies when, sure enough, Jeff Miller himself happened to drop by. "Happened" is perhaps too strong a word, since these days he tends to make a regular circuit of those friends he's already managed to ensnare in the game's fascinational field. He's a slight fellow, in his mid-thirties. His face is like Kafka's as it might be reconceived by a caricaturist to bring out its most animalist features—high cheekbones set wide apart, small brownish eyes: a ferrety fox. I couldn't help but notice his hands (for he'd no sooner entered the room than he'd wedged his way into a game), and they were small and quick and agile, almost feminine: a raccoon's. His short-cropped black hair had retained the impress of his previous night's pillow well into the afternoon.

Within just a few moves, the game had become exquisitely convoluted. That's one of the nice things about Jeff's game—slam, bam, two or three moves and you're already in the thick of the action, threats being met by counterthreats, which in turn are being subverted by yet wilier stratagems. The game might well be dubbed "in media res."

As the knot of that particular game's action quickly tightened, I asked Jeff, who was playing white, why he didn't just place all his pawns on the seventh row, such that on the next move they could instantaneously get themselves queened. (In standard chess, on those rare occasions when a pawn manages to make it to that last row, it attains queenly powers.) For that matter, why not just beam the pawns directly onto that last (eighth) row? "That's an interesting point," Jeff explained, "and in fact it's the only other rule we had to make. We've arbitrarily decreed that pawns can only be introduced onto the board in second, third, or fourth rows—otherwise, as you say, everybody would be lining up all their pawns on the verge of queening, and the game would become completely distorted.

"But there are all kinds of paradoxical transformations that happen with this game," he continued. "In ordinary chess, the queen, of course, is the most powerful player. But here—at least until you put your king on the board, thereby activating all your pieces—the queen or any of the other major pieces can effectively be neutralized by a well-placed blocking pawn. In fact, it turns out that the really powerful piece in this game, at least at the outset, is the knight, of all things—because, as in standard chess, the knight is the only piece that is allowed to jump over otherwise blocking pieces. That gives the knight an awesome advantage in this game—that is, of course, until you put down your king and activate all your other pieces, thereby negating all those passive blocks."

He was silent for a moment, his countenance darkening. "There is one problem I've just discovered with the game, however. I was playing with this guy the other day—Larry." (Everybody in the room nodded; they all knew about Larry.) "And Larry did something really unnerving. Here, look." Jeff then cleared the current board in midgame—he was obviously far more interested at this stage in the exotic mysteries embedded in the game in general than in any particular instance of the game. "What Larry did is he . . ." And Jeff *began* by putting his king down on the board. "It's completely counterintuitive, but it turns out to be extremely effective. By activating its side of the board from the very start, White appears to gain a decided and perhaps insurmountable advantage. In which case, of course, the game is far less interesting than it otherwise might be." The players all stared—glumly, intently—at the lone white king on an otherwise empty board.

I explained that I was late for an appointment and had to be going, but not before making a date to meet up with Jeff a few hours later at a nearby cafe.

"False alarm," Jeff announced immediately, a smile spreading across his face, as I settled into the cafe banquette a few hours later. "It turns out that Larry's move isn't as insurmountable as all that. There are several ways to counter it."

He was relieved. I was relieved. I asked him about his background. He told me how he'd grown up, somewhat improbably, in Visalia, a small town outside Fresno, in rural central California—the son of a doctor whose family hailed from a White Russian shtetl by way of New York City. (I suddenly sensed where he might have come up with the idea of plopping solitary chess figures into the middle of empty boards.) In 1972, like many kids his age at the time (thirteen), he'd been transfixed by Bobby Fischer's performance at Reykjavík. At first he sharpened his skills against his father, but his father was "a really, really, really bad chess player," he claims, "ideologically opposed to trading queens, and what's more, the kind of player who'd just blow up and scream at you whenever you happened to make a good move, which gave him somewhat of an advantage." Jeff presently graduated from his father to local tournament play, traveling regularly to Los Angeles and once, by himself, to Chicago. He generally did quite well, regularly beating almost all the other kids in his neighborhood, with the exception of one boy "who was way better than me, a legitimately good player," he recalls, "until he started sniffing glue and completely lost it."

Eventually, though, Jeff seemed to achieve the limits of his competence, leveling out a little above a 2,000 rating, which is to say at the rank of expert. "Senior-master status starts at 2,400 and grand master at 2,600," he explained to me. "But those relatively small numerical differentials disguise huge differences in skill and capacity. I mean, me compared to a senior master is like a high school grad compared to a postdoc." He eventually attended UC San Diego, where he majored in mathematics, encountering another version of the same problem. ("It's all so rigorously objective: the best are simply the best, and if you're not the very best, that fact quickly makes itself evident.") He went on to his other careers but retained his social interest in chess—at parties, for example, he was not adverse to playing two opponents simultaneously, or either one blindfolded—an interest that, as time passed, increasingly gave way to annoyance.

"Because chess *is* boring," Jeff now insisted to me, "even at the highest levels—certainly for spectators. A good solid player playing white and playing defensively can almost always achieve at least a draw, which is why tournaments become so slow and dull: the minute one player gets ahead he has no incentive to risk a mistake. Beyond that, the game has been played for so long and has been so thoroughly explored that, what with the rigidity of its opening configuration, every single possible opening gambit has been exhaustively analyzed and evaluated through the first fifteen or twenty moves. There's a book of modern chess openings laying out all the possible permutations, and it's like *six inches thick!* So a huge amount of grand-master wisdom consists of rote memorization: if on move thirteen Black does X, then White should respond with Y.

"Bobby Fischer in particular was said to have an awesome capacity for instantaneous apprehension and memorization. They tell a story about him in Reykjavík, how he called somebody's home, got the guy's daughter, who didn't speak a word of English. She said a long sentence to him in Icelandic, of which he didn't speak a word. Nevertheless, he was able to turn to his hosts and repeat the girl's phrase verbatim so as to ask what she meant. I mean, that's incredible: Most people would find it impossible to repeat a sentence in an unknown language. It's like repeating the sound of shower water running. But he could do it, and he could do the same thing with that six-inch book. Which is fine; it just doesn't leave much room for surprise or chaotic improvisation. And, in fact, Bobby Fischer himself was said to feel the same way. He often advocated a variation called shuffle chess, in which the players lined up their pawns along the standard second row, but the first eight moves on either side then consisted of each player's arraying his major pieces, one at a time, in some novel configuration along the back row—say, king to one corner, bishop to the other, knight in the middle, queen next to rook, and so forth, precisely to upend all that rote prior knowledge—so as to make *something new* happen."

I asked him how he'd actually come up with his new game. "Obviously, this isn't the first time anyone's come up with a variation on chess," he conceded. "I already mentioned Fischer's shuffle chess. There are all sorts of other variants in which, for example, the pieces get assigned weird new hybrid moves, such that, for instance, a knight would be allowed to move like both a knight and a bishop. But to my mind the best of these chess variations is a game called bughouse chess, which required *four* players on two boards. I don't know whether it got its name because you had to have been insane to come up with it in the first place, or else because playing it too much is pretty certain to drive you well around the bend. But the idea is that you've got two games going on simultaneously, side by side, and the white player in one is partnered to the black player in the other. Let's say I'm White in the one game and you're Black in the other. As the game proceeds, I might find myself saying, or even just silently indicating, 'Gee, if I only had another rook, I could do such and such.' And that would be your cue. Because with you playing Black, if you could capture one of your opponent's white rooks, you could hand it to me, your partner, and I'd be allowed, on my next turn, to introduce it wherever I wanted to on the board in my game. Or vice versa. Or either of our opponents could do likewise—or both. Or all of these at once. The winning team being whichever one achieves mate first in either of the two games. You can imagine the strategic chaos such possibilities introduce into the game. In standard chess, a player will sometimes craftily sacrifice a queen for some greater advantage; but in bughouse chess, one of the team members could easily sacrifice virtually his entire game for the sake of his partner's need of a particular piece. It's great!

"And so, a few months ago, I was experiencing a hankering for a good game of bughouse chess," Jeff continued. "Only, I was having a hard time coming up with the necessary foursome. At some point I went to bed, wondering whether it would be possible to contrive a version of bughouse for two. And by morning I'd come up with this new game."

Jeff fell silent for a moment, contemplating his good works. "I mean, in standard chess there are—what?—twenty possible first moves and twenty possible first responses. With this game there are something like three hundred possible first moves! So just *try* to standardize it. And then, too, there's a sense in which it's like bringing chess into the twentieth century. Because for thousands of years the commanding metaphor in chess has been that of battle—and specifically the infantry battle. The king and queen surveying their troops on the eve of the engagement, the scramble for territorial advantage, all the tactical feints and strategic redeployments. And this game is just like that—only, *it's like chess with paratroopers!*"

He smiled. "Wanna play?" He reached into his satchel and pulled out a board, opened it up, pulled out a pouch, and started divvying up the pieces. The board lay open between us, glistening, pristine, empty—and you could tell that Jeff was already savoring all the possibilities.

Postscript (1998)

In the meantime, speaking of possibilities, Jeff has moved to New York, where he's taken up a new job as a computer programmer with a downtown investment bank. He's brought his game with him, and a small coterie has begun to experiment with its permutations there—as well as in Santiago, Chile, and Capetown, South Africa (to name just two venues)—and, inevitably, all along the internet, where one particular aficionado has even started running tournaments.

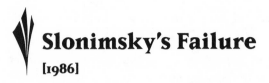

Slonimsky's Failure
[1986]

I.

Nicolas Slonimsky is continually driving his daughter crazy, and it's not just because he named her Electra, although that certainly didn't help. To hear Slonimsky tell it, he chose the name because it means "amber" in Greek, or because it contains "good hard letters" like *E* and *T* and *R* missing from his own name, or for some such reason. "But can you imagine what it was like growing up as a kid in Boston with a name like that?" his daughter asked me recently, seeming palpably to shudder at the memory of the experience, though it's over forty years past. "That name was a blight, a plague—it was like lugging around an extra leg, or having another eye sprouting out of the middle of my forehead. You know how terrifically cutting kids can be, and naturally they're going to grab on to something like that." But it's *not* that. Nor is it because of some of the other, well, peculiar aspects of her upbringing. For instance, the way her father insisted on conversing with her almost exclusively in Latin during the first five years of her life. This is one aspect of the enterprise that Slonimsky himself—a spry, animated, and exuberant ninety-two-year-old who is considered to be one of the foremost musical lexicographers in the world—seems particularly to savor to this day. "Yes, we'd have long conversations," he told me when I was visiting him a few months ago at his home in West Lost Angeles. "I'd imparted to her a vocabulary of several hundred words, and they were part of the lingua franca of our household: *auris, oculi, fenestra, nummi.* Visitors were always tremendously impressed by her precocity. Over time, she became somewhat ambivalent about it, I suppose. Once, she picked up a feather and held it out to me. I dutifully told her *'Pluma,'* and she countered, 'No, Daddy, the way Mommy would say it!' And then, one afternoon, she came home and angrily announced, 'Daddy, it's not true! *None* of the other daddies speak Latin to their kids at home.' After that, she'd simply stare at me blankly whenever I tried to revive our Latin conversations."

Electra is not charmed by the tale. "It was basically a trained-seal act," she says, dismissing her apparent precocity. "I mean, what does it take to teach a child what is basically the wrong word for something? In fact, if anything, it was a mild case of intellectual child abuse." Electra is likewise uncharmed by her father's delight in recounting his experiments to determine innate predisposition toward either consonance or dissonance in music. "I was curious whether people automatically start out by favoring consonant musical experience or whether it might be possible to pattern an infant toward a preference for dissonant experience through some sort of behavioral conditioning," Slonimsky recalls. "So, for a while, whenever I was home alone with her and she'd awaken crying for her bottle I'd immediately rush over to the piano and launch into some lovely Chopin nocturne, utterly ignoring her urgent entreaties, and continue to play like that for about a minute. Then I'd pause for a moment, pound out ten seconds of the densest Schönberg, at which point I'd immediately hand her her bottle." The experiment appears to have worked, though perhaps not as Slonimsky intended: Electra reports that today, notwithstanding her remarkable genetic inheritance from her father, she finds herself entirely unmusical. But none of that is what drives her crazy about her father; indeed, she reports that while she was growing up she generally found her eccentric dad vastly amusing and great fun to be around.

No, what exasperates her is her father's seeming inability to make anything of his career; his endless tendency to squander his immense talents; his ongoing failure to focus. That and his total lack of self-discipline. It's a surprising indictment, especially since on the surface her father appears a man of overwhelming accomplishment: his résumé, if he were any longer bothering to keep one, would include sterling achievements as a piano accompanist to several world-renowned singers during the twenties, as secretary and "piano pounder" to the conductor Serge Koussevitzky (first in Paris and then in Boston), as a professor of Slavic languages at Harvard University, as a composer of considerable distinction, and as a path-breaking conductor who introduced major compositions into the canon of avant-garde music—all this before, quite late in his career, he launched into his new vocation as musical lexicographer. The charge of indiscipline seems especially untenable. In the past couple of years alone, Nicolas Slonimsky has managed to bring out three new books: the seventh edition of *Baker's Biographical Dictionary of Musicians;* a supplement to his authoritative *Music Since 1900* (a day-by-day "descriptive chronology" of musical birth dates, death dates, premier dates, and all sorts of musical arcana); and his translation of a major Russian biography of Alexander Scriabin.

Most surprising of all, however, Electra's is an evaluation that Slonimsky himself shares, endorses, and even amplifies. "You see, I *am* a failure," he says bluntly. "It's true. My life has been an enormous disappointment." He reaches for a huge sheaf of typed pages stacked on a nearby table. "Here," he says, plopping the pile in my lap. "I've even acknowledged as much in the title of my forthcoming autobiography." "Failed Wunderkind," the manuscript's title page announces portentously, in boldface, and, beneath that, in a lighter typeface, the subtitle "A Rueful Autopsy." The cloud of seriousness has fled the room, and Slonimsky is beaming. "Autopsy, yes? That's precisely correct usage. Not the dissection of a body, of course. Rather, from the Greek: that's auto, 'self,' and ops, 'eye'—hence, self-observation. You can look it up.

The publishers are dubious, but I told them they could look it up, too."
(I subsequently did; the publishers may have a point.)*

With Slonimsky, it's hard to tell: he's cheerful and expansive almost all the time, and perhaps that facade indeed merely masks interior
desolation; on the other hand, his sense of the tragic undergirdings
of his life, whenever he does allow himself to show it, almost immediately melts away to reveal an antic humor, grounded in a yet wider
perspective. In any case, whether happy or sad, content or disillu-
sioned, he is continually and freshly open to the wondrous structure of
language itself—be it musical or verbal—and through the grace of this
linguistic fascination he is at all times momentarily on the verge of
transport.

"When I was six years old," Slonimsky's autobiographical manuscript
begins, "my mother told me I was a genius." Paragraph break. "This
revelation came as no surprise to me." Slonimsky's putative genius
had an air of inevitability. Indeed, he reports a few paragraphs down,
"So precocious was I that even before I was born and before my gender
was determined, I was named Newtonchik, a diminutive Newton."

As we sat talking in his living room, Slonimsky commented, "My
family, you see, had been a hotbed of geniuses for generations. All
my ancestors were intellectuals." As he spoke, I recalled the opening
sentence in Slonimsky's *Baker's* entry on himself: "Possessed by inor-
dinate ambition, aggravated by the endemic intellectuality of his family on both maternal and paternal branches (novelists, revolutionary
poets, literary critics, university professors, translators, chess masters,
economists, mathematicians, inventors of useless artificial languages,
Hebrew scholars, speculative philosophers), he became determined to
excel beyond all common decency in all these doctrines; as an adoles-

---

*The publishers, at any rate, retitled the book for publication. A failure even at
failure, Slonimsky had to make do with their dictate: *Perfect Pitch* (Oxford University Press, 1988).

cent, he wrote down his future autobiography accordingly, setting down his death date as 1967, but survived."

"In short," he now summarized, "my family were model specimens of that extraordinarily peculiar and uniquely pointless species, the Russian intelligentsia."

Los Angeles seems a long way from St. Petersburg, where Slonimsky was born, and 1986 a long way from 1894, the year of his birth. And yet he seems at ease here, and he certainly doesn't look—or behave—like a man of his years. "The other afternoon, I went to the movies, as I often do," he told me at one point, "and the cashier refused to give me a senior-citizen discount unless I produced some valid identification. I was so flattered I gladly paid full fare."

I asked him about his health in general. "Listen, I don't have *time* to be sick," he replied. "I could use a good nervous breakdown, or even a cold, but I can't work one in with all my deadlines. Actually, though, I seem to be in good shape. A while back, during a physical, my doctor wanted to test my hearing, so he put some earphones on my head, sat himself down behind some complicated-looking machinery, adjusted his dials, and then played two tones, asking me which of the two sounded higher. 'Well,' I told him, 'the first one was 3,520 cycles per second and the second was 3,680 cycles per second. Is that what you mean?' He rechecked his dials and then looked over at me, dumbfounded. But, I mean, that was just sheer exhibitionism of the worst kind—an ongoing problem with me. Anyway, the point is, though I may not be endurable, I *am* durable."

Slonimsky lives alone—as he has since his wife's death, in 1964, when he first moved to Los Angeles—but over the years he has enjoyed the companionship of a succession of devoted secretaries and oblivious cats. The secretaries are invariably beautiful young women, the more innocent of culture the better, as far as he's concerned—although the current pair, Laura Kuhn and Dina Klemm, arrived on the scene extremely well read and musically sophisticated. In the past, Slonimsky has particularly savored his role as mentor, guiding the cultural tutelage of these wards, whom he and everyone else (including the young women themselves) refer to as his "odalisques." Month by month, year by year, Slonimsky and his odalisques have compiled their files and piled their galleys while the cats have lounged indolently about. "First," as one of the odalisques recalls, "there came Mango and Papaya. They were then succeeded by Dorian Gray, a gray cat who was supposed to age and grow old in place of Nicolas—*and did!* And now his latest cat, a fluffy black-and-white, is named Grody-to-the-Max."

WARNING: HOUSE GUARDED BY ATTACK CAT, announces a scroll tacked to the white front door of Slonimsky's house, a light green bungalow, which is one of a series of such bungalows in a quiet residential-tract neighborhood about a half mile from the Santa Monica Freeway. But the door is usually ajar, and the only thing Grody appears to be guarding is his own languor. The front door opens into a living room with beige walls and a beige carpet, on which a wooden rocking chair is pulled up close to a rectangular glass-topped wrought iron work-table in the middle of the room. Over to the side is a fairly beat-up upright piano, and on top of the piano, occasionally (not always), is a blown-up photograph of a human skull. "That is the cranium of one J. S. Bach," Slonimsky will inform you, if you can't restrain yourself from asking (though he's also perfectly content to hold his peace and watch you eyeing the photograph nervously). "Don't even ask me how I managed to dig it up—we haven't got the time." The walls all around Slonimsky's worktable are festooned with a gallery of ghoulish nonsense—bizarre tabloid headlines, M. C. Escher conundrums, a reproduction of an 1853 painting by William Holman Hunt entitled *The Awakening Conscience,* which depicts a male pianist reaching seductively toward a young, demurely clothed female student. ("When I was growing up," Slonimsky volunteers, "that image represented the height, the very pinnacle, of depravity.") Beyond the piano is a plain, not terribly well inhabited kitchen; through another door is the file room, with the odalisques' desks and typewriters; off down a corridor is Slonimsky's austere bedroom, with a narrow single bed facing a framed copy of Richard Avedon's famous photograph of a naked Nastassja Kinski, reclining seductively, draped by a huge snake. One of Slonimsky's odalisques got it for him, to replace a poster he used to have there of a heavily bearded old man, recumbent and seemingly asleep: Brahms on his deathbed.

Slonimsky is clean shaven—a short man of odd shape. He has written of "the unfortunate lack of Grecian golden mean" between the parts of his body. He has the legs, shoulders, and arms of a slight man, and then, as he says, "where other people have abdominal cavities, I have an abominable convexity." His belly balloons—the buttons on his shirts (usually plaid flannel) strain to contain their unexpected bounty (any shirt that fits him at the shoulders will at best barely suffice to encompass his midriff). But then everything tapers precipitously from the waist down: I'm sure he hasn't seen his belt in years, not even in the mirror. I have read rave reviews of concerts in the twenties and thirties in which he was said to resemble a "young gentleman out of Pushkin's Byronic pages" or, in another context, "Napoleon at Marengo." Today, he resembles a skinny tenor trussed up with vast pillows for a stint as Falstaff. Walking, he pads along like a fat man, gingerly, carefully; talking, his arms and hands dart all over; seated, listening, he crosses his arms and rests them atop his belly as if on a bar counter.

His face is smooth, virtually without wrinkles, like a turtle's; it rests on a neck that is jowly, like a turtle's, too. He has a turtly beak nose, which swerves abruptly, halfway down, to his left, like a freeway on-ramp. It wasn't always thus: when he was a youth, his nose was beaky and *straight,* but in 1916, in Tallinn, the capital of Estonia, while serving as rehearsal pianist with a provincial opera company and walking across a darkened backstage area, he fell through an open trapdoor and landed on his back, entirely unscathed except by a chair he'd grabbed falling, whose leg now stabbed smack into the middle of his face. No blood, but a crooked nose forever after. His wide, smooth forehead is crowned with a thatch of gray hair, parted virtually down the middle and shagged to either side. Down below, the forehead ends in two incongruously black circumflex eyebrows, which are seldom still. Nowadays, his eyes are milky blue, with large, cloudy pupils. People who knew him years ago have described his eyes as beacon black, and perhaps they were darker then. They still seem to shine—indeed, they pierce.

His eyes pierce, but it's his voice that captures and holds. It is high and yet throaty, accented and yet clear and assured, somewhere between Dr. Ruth ("Good Sex") Westheimer and Clara ("Where's the Beef?") Peller. It is a voice that invites study—and, in fact, it has *been* studied, by one Charles Amirkhanian. Amirkhanian, the music director at KPFA, the Pacifica radio station in Berkeley, is also a poet and composer. He is one of the leading American proponents of text-sound composition; that is, the manipulation of taped word and phrase fragments into musical form through repetition, acceleration, deceleration, cross-tracking, and so forth—a battery of advanced techniques that result, in Amirkhanian's case, in a sort of restless minimalism. On several occasions, he has used taped interviews of Slonimsky as raw material for his compositional forays. Being a percussionist as well, Amirkhanian likes to think of words as percussive objects, and he finds Slonimsky's words particularly easy to think of in that way. "He's always speaking with a lot of energy, from the gut," Amirkhanian told me one afternoon when I asked him to describe Slonimsky's voice. "He's always aspirating, enunciating, trying to make himself clear. He can't manage an American accent for the life of him—consonants are always intruding at the beginning and end of words. I called one of the pieces in which I used his voice 'Heavy Aspirations.' But the contour of his voice is remarkable: he punches the words out, as distinct entities, in extraordinarily complex rhythms—rhythms that I think are related to his musical rhythms, his conducting and piano rhythms. And then there are those odd things—for instance, the way that when he's thinking, or gathering his words, instead of a typical flat 'uuunnnhhh,' his voice goes through amazing extended timbral changes, like what you get with a Tibetan monk. It's a high voice but with profound authority. The high energy of the voice relates to the high energy, the boundless energy, of his life. He centers on a story and becomes full of himself, but in an attractive way: he's giving himself over to the listener through his voice."

As Slonimsky and I sat talking in his living room, he was still giving himself over to stories of his family background, in St. Petersburg and before. "Our family was, if anything, *plus Russe que les Russes* in our passion to be seen as members of the intelligentsia, because in fact we were just passing," he said. "You see, we were Jewish—a fact which my mother, especially, regarded with horrendous shame and tried to keep hidden from us children for years. Indeed, in our family there were two great taboos. The first was sexuality. One time, a doctor friend of my parents was visiting and asked my mother how she was handling the topic of human sexuality with her three teenage sons. 'Sir,' she interrupted him severely, 'this is a *literary* family.' And, indeed, there was no instruction on the topic whatsoever, except for the persistent admonition that kissing would lead inexorably and inevitably to syphilis, a prospect before which I lived in continual terror, not so much for fear of the physical consequences—which, I assure you, my mother had rehearsed for us in morbid detail ad nauseam—as out of the dead certainty that were I ever to contract the disease she would immediately broadcast my dread condition to everyone within miles.

"The other taboo, as I say, was Jewishness. We had all been baptized in the Russian Orthodox Church. I mean, we weren't believers or anything; we were confirmed agnostics. I for one have always found transubstantiation difficult to swallow, figuratively speaking—not that I later felt any special reverence for the Jewish God Jehovah, either: for one thing, his punishments always seemed wildly out of proportion to the offense in question.

"Our baptisms were only part of a massive effort, especially on my mother's part, to render us as Russian as possible. For instance, she named my oldest brother Alexander, after the czar who had been assassinated just two months before his birth, and I was named Nicolas, after the czarevitch at the time, who became the last czar, Nicholas II. My mother used to account for our obviously Jewish physiognomies by reference to our 'noble Roman heritage'—whatever that meant. I was so protected from the horrible fact of our Jewishness that I used to imagine Jews were some ancient tribe, like the Sumerians or the Babylonians, and, in fact, one day, the story goes, I asked the poet Nicholas Minsky, who was married to my cousin (and after that to my aunt), whether any Jews were still alive. 'I wish I could see a real Jew,' I'm supposed to have said, to which he is said to have replied, 'Go look in the mirror.' Apparently, the hint didn't take, because it wasn't until I was fifteen that the traumatic revelation struck me with full force. I was looking my father's name up in the Russian encyclopedia, and the entry opened with 'Son of the preceding.' The preceding turned out to be one Chaim Selig Slonimsky, who was described as an eminent Hebrew scholar and scientist. So it was true after all."

Nicolas's father's *grandfather,* Abraham Jacob Stern, was one of the first eminent geniuses on the Polish branch of Nicolas's bountiful family tree. He was born in 1760 (just three generations separate Nicolas from the heart of the eighteenth century) and was renowned as the inventor of a sophisticated calculating machine—an early precursor of the computer or an awesome elaboration of the abacus, depending on how one chooses to look at it. "This device achieved such fame," Slonimsky told me, "that my great-grandfather was summoned to bring his machine for an audience before Czar Alexander I, Savior of the Russians, Victor over Napoleon, who was known to dabble in the sciences. He complied, and after he'd demonstrated the intricacies of the machine the czar challenged him and the machine to an arithmetic contest. The czar had previously instructed the court chamberlain to prepare a sequence of arithmetic computations—addition, subtraction, multiplication, division—and now the man read them out. My great-grandfather set to work at his machine; the czar dipped his quill into a nearby inkwell and was just completing his first calculation when already my great-grandfather announced the final result. The czar looked over at him, then at the chamberlain, who nodded confirmation as to the correctness of the announced result, and then pronounced solemnly, 'The machine is good, but the Jew is bad.'"

Stern's daughter Sarah presently married Chaim Selig Slonimsky, who was born in Bialystok in 1810. Chaim Selig had pursued rabbinical and Talmudic studies alongside some remarkably precocious—and remarkably secular—scientific investigations right up through his nineteenth year, when, marrying Sarah Stern, he moved in with his new father-in-law. In subsequent years, he perfected Stern's calculating machine, adding the capacity for extracting square roots. In 1862, he founded *Ha-Zephirah* (Daybreak), one of the first Hebrew-language periodicals, which continued publishing, in the spirit of the modern Jewish Enlightenment, until 1931. Chaim Selig Slonimsky has a prominent entry in the *Jewish Encylopœdia,* where he is credited with having popularized all manner of contemporary sciences for Polish and Russian Jews of the period. Nicolas had stories for me about this grandfather as well: "My mother used to say to me, 'He was a genius, but an impractical one. Don't follow in his footsteps.' For instance, she'd tell me how one day, while puzzling over the question of instant communication from a theological point of view, he'd invented a prototype for an advanced form of telegraphy. But the act of invention appears to have satisfied him; he felt no need to publicize or patent his invention. 'There, Sarah,' he said to his wife, folding the sheet of paper and placing it high above a cupboard. 'Let's see how long it takes *them* to figure it out.' And several years later, when word of the new invention was published, he reached for his sheet of paper, examined it, clucked contentedly, and announced, 'Well, they got it right.' Or, anyway, so my mother claimed. The amazing thing is that in more recent years the Soviets have taken to publicizing an identical claim on his behalf." Chaim Selig Slonimsky died in 1904, at the age of ninety-four. "So," his grandson concludes, "that means that I must still have a few years to go myself."

Chaim and Sarah Slonimsky had three sons, of whom two lived out their lives in Warsaw and the third—Leonid, Nicolas's father—eventually went to live in St. Petersburg. Leonid's brothers, Stanislaw and Josef, were themselves fairly remarkable. Stanislaw was a much-beloved doctor, and *his* son, Nicolas's first cousin, was Antoni Slonimski, one of the foremost poets and satirists in modern Polish literature. Antoni was continually in trouble with the Communist authorities in postwar Poland. (The Communist Party chairman Wladyslaw Gomulka had at one time been a personal friend of his. But one day Gomulka questioned him about his relations with acquaintances in the former wartime London government-in-exile, and Slonimski replied, "Friend Gomulka, I cannot stand physical pain, so please don't waste your time calling in your Star Chamber boys—just list my crimes and I'll sign the confession," whereupon the friendship came to an abrupt end.) "Something I learned just recently," Slonimsky told me, "is that Antoni's personal secretary in the years just before his death, in 1976, was Adam Michnik, this young fellow who went on to become such a leader in Solidarity. So nowadays when I'm being hounded by my publishers because of my perennial tardiness I plead with them, 'Yes, I admit it, I'm late, I admit to everything, but my cousin was like a godfather to Solidarity. Surely that must count for something!'"

Josef, the other brother who stayed in Warsaw, was "a linguist with a passionate obsession for completeness," his nephew recalls. "He knew every single European language fluently and passed his time composing phrase books for use by citizens of one country on their travels inside another one, covering just about every circumstance in every conceivable permutation. My personal favorite was the Norwegian-Yiddish booklet. Years later, Wanda Landowska, the Polish harpsichordist—now, *she* was some baby—told me a story about how one young man had approached my Uncle Josef inquiring whether he could enroll with him for six weeks of intensive Spanish lessons in preparation for an upcoming assignment in Brazil; my uncle complied with the request, the student progressed quite nicely, and on the last day, after the student left the apartment on his way to the train station, Uncle Josef turned to his wife and said, 'Boy, is that young man going to be surprised when he finds out it's *Portuguese* they speak in Brazil.' But, anyway, he is the one who devised that utterly forgotten, utterly forgettable language which he called Universal Romanic, which even lost out to Esperanto, the invention of a similarly obsessed contemporary of his in Warsaw, in that particular sweepstakes for futility."

The third brother, Leonid, moved to St. Petersburg, where he married Faina Vengerova, Nicolas's mother. Toward this bearded, fairly withdrawn, and remote but kindly father of his, Nicolas still harbors feelings of devotion and admiration, especially for his many scholarly publications, which, as a young boy, Nicolas imagined constituted the very pinnacle of worldly achievement. Leonid Slonimsky was the foreign affairs editor of the liberal St. Petersburg journal *Messenger of Europe*. He was also the author, in 1890, of *The Economic Doctrine of Karl Marx*, one of the first books on Marx ever published in Russia. "Tolstoy read the book and seems to have made extensive notes in the margins of his copy," Slonimsky says. "Lenin read it, too, and because of this my cousin Antoni years later told me—only half-facetiously, I'm afraid—that he held my side of the family responsible for the whole Bolshevik business. Lenin himself, however, had some pretty nasty things to say about my father. In a pamphlet published in 1894 in the Russian underground, he dismissed my father as 'an ordinary liberal, utterly incapable of understanding contemporary bourgeois society' and argued, for good measure, that my father's soft spot for the idea of peasant ownership of small plots of land simply revealed his 'reactionary utopianism.' I don't know: with us he was always a mild, fairly befuddled man, with his head in the clouds, and his status entirely overshadowed by the huge, overbearing presence of my mother."

Faina's family heritage, when her son was finally able to ferret it out, years later, turned out to stretch all the way back to the Maharal of

Prague (1525–1609), the great rabbi who was said to have fashioned the legendary Jewish robot known as the Golem. One of her second cousins was the renowned chess master Semyon Alapin. Faina's mother, Pauline Epstein, married a rich Jewish banker, Afanasy Vengerov, had four children, and lived to a ripe old age, at which time she published a book entitled *Memoirs of a Grandmother,* which became something of a Victorian best-seller. "In that book," Nicolas told me, she included a scathing denunciation of her children who'd lost their faith, allowing themselves to become baptized, and then of the third generation, who, she said, 'feared neither God nor the Devil.'" Nicolas paused and gulped melodramatically, his eyes widening. "That's us," he then continued, in almost reverentially hushed tones, "my generation, the ones who feared neither God nor the Devil—that's really something."

Faina's brother Semyon was renowned in Russia as a professor of Russian literature, a tireless editor of Pushkin, and the compiler of a celebrated critical-biographical *cartothéque* of Russian writers. Her younger sister Isabelle Vengerova was a superbly gifted pianist, who contributed a great deal to Slonimsky's early development and, years later, after moving to America and attaining a professorship at the Curtis Institute, in Philadelphia, contributed even more to the careers of Samuel Barber, Lukas Foss, Gary Graffman, and Leonard Bernstein (who called her his Beloved Tyranna).

Slonimsky's mother became one of the first women medical students in Russia, studying chemistry under the composer-scientist Alexander Borodin. But, to hear Nicolas tell it, she gradually abandoned that career so as better to be able to rechannel all of that inherited, imperative energy into wreaking domineering havoc on the lives of her children. The first of these, Alexander, born in 1881, became another noted Pushkin scholar; then came Julia, in 1884, also a future writer; there followed a decade-long hiatus—or rather, a series of perilous miscarriages—before Nicolas himself arrived, in April 1894. "My mother continually assured me—indeed, she never for a moment allowed me to forget—that she'd lain in bed for a full year so as to effect my safe delivery," Nicolas recalls. "The extra three months were my mother's poetic license, for dramatic effect, but she never tired of reciting all the sacrifices she'd made on my behalf and denigrating the sad, pathetic recompense she'd gotten in return."

"Clearly, she was some kind of monster," surmises Slonimsky's own daughter, Electra, who never really knew her. Slonimsky himself generally displays more equanimity—or, at least, resignation—when he is describing her; that is to say, when he describes her as a monster, he means it physically. "She was *huge*," he says. "Often, when we were kids, she'd call for us to come over to the bottom of the stairwell so as to help push her up the stairs."

After Nicolas, Faina gave birth to two more sons—Vladimir, in 1895, Nicolas's closest kindred spirit, who was to die of tuberculosis just after his twentieth birthday; and Michael, in 1897, who became a prolific and well admired Soviet novelist. "And all of them," Slonimsky now said with a sigh, after completing the inventory of his predecessors and the members of his own generation, "they're all now gone. I'm the last of the Mohicans."

The first of Michael Slonimsky's many books—he produced more than a dozen before his death, in 1972—was titled *Lavrovy*. Published in Russia in 1926, it was a model of Socialist Realist fiction, detailing the travails of a spoiled young bourgeois as he tried to adapt himself to the rigors of the Revolution. According to Gleb Struve's summary of the novel (in *Geschichte der Sowjet Literatur,* this passage translated by Robert Stevenson), to the hero "are opposed, on the one hand, the other members of his family—his vulgar domineering mother; his meek, henpecked father; his vain futile brother—and on the other, Fonna Kleshnyov, a true Bolshevik. "

"Yes," Nicolas said, after I read him that plot summary one day. "The vain and futile brother, that's me. A not altogether inaccurate portrait." He paused for a moment, then smiled broadly. "What's interesting there is that as the years have passed I've ended up having to write about Michael's son, Sergei, who has become a leading Soviet avant-garde composer whose work is every bit as far-out as the most outrageous stuff we've been able to produce here in the West."

After another pause, Slonimsky resumed. "My nephew Sergei is interesting for another reason. He illustrates a curious pattern in our family line. For, you see, in our family it appears that the musical gene is transmitted across a series of chess knight's moves. Aunt Isabelle was musical, her sister Faina, my mother, was not, but I was. My own daughter isn't, my brother Michael wasn't, but his son, my nephew Sergei, turned out to be. This may in part explain in some mysterious way the course my life has taken. For, you see, with that background, in that hothouse atmosphere of the St. Petersburg intelligentsia, and especially under the pressure cooker of my mother's expectations, I was going to have to be a genius at something. And perhaps this knight's gene dictated that it be in music."

Indeed, there was no special musical emphasis in Nicolas's immediate household. "We were a middle-class, bourgeois family, typical of the late nineteenth century," he continued. "So naturally we had a piano, just as part of the furniture. But this piano quickly became my favorite household beast. You see, I possessed perfect pitch, and from an extremely early age I used to dazzle any and all comers by simply reeling off the name of any note—indeed, any combination of notes—that would be played for me. It all started out with this aspect of simply showing off."

When Slonimsky is in his darker moods—that is, when he is playing the theme of his self-estimation in a minor key—he sometimes asserts that it all ended there as well, that throughout his remarkable career he has simply been locked into a compulsive pattern of infantile exhibitionism. (Electra has been known to venture similar thoughts about him.) Without doubt, he still relishes astounding. One time, for example, while he was briefly in another room, I meandered over to the piano and mindlessly klimpered out a fairly complex and utterly inchoate sequence of nonsense chords—about ten seconds' worth. He came back in, I returned to my chair, and he went over to the piano and reproduced my sequence exactly, concluding with an elegant harmonizing flourish. "Sometimes," he said, his eyes twinkling, "it's best not to leave things unresolved like that, don't you think? Now, where were we?"

We were at his musical youth. "Ah, yes," he continued. "From a very early age, I was completely fascinated by sounds. I was as receptive to sounds as I was to objects, to toys, to the letters of the Russian alphabet. I would sit by, rapt, as my Aunt Isabelle gave piano lessons to my mother and my older brother and sister, none of whom were particularly musical. I'd approach the keyboard afterward and poke out elementary versions of the melodies they'd been rehearsing. She gave me my first official lesson on November 6, 1900, by the old Russian calendar. I remember the calendar itself, the look of the numbers, the configuration of black dates and red holidays. Numbers and arithmetical patterns were quickly coming to fascinate me as well. I was six years old, and my aunt was only twenty-three."

He continued his lessons with his Aunt Isabelle for several years, and his mother became increasingly invested in his precocity. Years later, he wrote of his first day at grade school, "My mother addressed the class, cautioning my schoolmates against coming into close physical contact with me or indulging in rough games which might be harmful to my delicate pianistic fingers. This speech led to the expected results, but I was not badly maimed." By the time he reached age fourteen, his aunt determined to enroll him in the St. Petersburg Conservatory. He was paraded into the rehearsal room to audition before the conservatory's imposing director, Alexander Glazunov, who was at that time one of the reigning titans of Russian music. Glazunov was especially taken with the boy's virtuoso exhibition of perfect pitch, and at the end of the examination he announced that he was admitting him. At a subsequent exam, Glazunov recorded the top mark of five in his gradebook, with the parenthetical notation "Talent." "My mother immediately took to whispering the glory of this 'five (Talent)' to every visitor to our home, until it got to the point where the phrase itself began physically to repel me."

In school, Nicolas excelled in mathematics; he memorized vast swaths of Latin and recited them in exhibitionist extravaganzas. At the same time, he was attaining considerable pianistic heights: "I was able to get my 'Minute Waltz' down to forty-three seconds." But now—and this was the beginning of the major crisis of his youth, one of the defining crises of his life—he started to encounter kids as gifted as he, some even more so. "The truth was I didn't like practicing, I wasn't very good at it, and as I began to reach high levels I came to realize I simply didn't have the requisite technique. I could master expression—my aunt, on her deathbed, said that no one could play Schumann as expressively as I could. I had very good *touché,* as they call it—a sense of which notes should be brought to the fore, which ones left in shadow, how to shape the piece, bring out the internal contrasts, how to express the structure of the work. But I didn't have the technique. And, as I say, I couldn't help noticing, with a jealousy that verged on panic, that other boys did have it. With growing horror, I watched as boys my age rose past me to prominence. One, in particular, I remember to this day: Pepito Arriola. I ask you—how could one ever forget a name like that? A young Spanish child, still in knee socks, *on tour,* for heaven's sake— he was tan and chubby in a healthy, Mediterranean sort of way, I was skinny and pale in a neurotic, Russian sort of way. He dared to perform a recital of works I considered my own special province—Schumann, the Romantics—and he even got his name in the paper the next day! I'd never had my name in the paper."

Meaning itself began to desert Nicolas's existence. If he was not a prodigy, what identity could he claim? "Suicide was very much in vogue in St. Petersburg in the years before the war," Nicolas told me another afternoon, as we discussed this period of his life. "It had a certain aura. Russian romantic literature was strewn with convenient role models. And, as a stale nineteen-year-old wunderkind, I was in a fairly hopeless way. In addition, this business about sex and syphilis, all the terror associated with temptation, was becoming intense. Two of my classmates in fairly quick succession in fact succeeded in killing themselves, a circumstance that held me spellbound and which I took as some sort of omen or dictate. I conscientiously prepared, therefore, to hang myself in the bathroom, and, indeed, did so—only the hook in the ceiling gave way under my weight, and I collapsed ingloriously onto the floor, a wet, crumpled heap. So much for my pseudo-suicide, my fraudulent pendency. I guess I was just trying to call attention to myself."

Nicolas's parents proceeded to do what any members of the St. Petersburg bourgeois intelligentsia would have done if they had been faced with a like calamity: they bundled their son up and sent him straight to a sanatorium on the banks of the Rhine, where he could be cared for by specialists and cured by the fresh, clean air. I asked Nicolas about the results of the regimen of the ensuing months, and he answered, "Well, by age twenty I realized that I was not a genius, that it was no longer important whether I was a genius, and that what was important was to kiss girls."

One afternoon a few days later, I was talking about Slonimsky with Ana Daniel, a young writer and photographer who acted as one of his secretaries for seven years during the seventies, and at one point she commented, "When he realized that he wasn't a genius, he realized he wasn't the center of the world, and that led to a certain mock despair—in fact, a tremendous amount of mock despair—but I think it also came as a relief."

Slonimsky returned to Russia in the spring of 1914 and resumed his studies at St. Petersburg University, where he was concentrating on physics, astronomy, and mathematics, having abandoned hope of a pianistic career, although he was continuing to take private lessons in composition with Vasily Kalafati, who had been Stravinsky's first teacher. Within months, the First World War began.

In early 1916, Slonimsky was drafted. "When the czar had to recruit a soldier the likes of me," he said one evening, as our conversation turned to this phase of his life, "it was a plain indication—plain to me, anyway—that he was in serious trouble." Slonimsky was assigned to the music section of the Preobrazhensky regiment, which had been founded as Peter the Great's own. In the summer of 1916, the Preo-brazhensky orchestra was sent to the placid delta of the Don River, where Slonimsky helped safeguard the empire's southern flank by, among other things, serving as soloist in the orchestra's rendition of the first movement of Rachmaninoff's Second Piano Concerto. He and the regiment were called back to Petrograd—as St. Petersburg had been recast, to rid the capital's name of its Germanic connotations—toward the end of 1916, just in time to appear as featured players in the initial Russian Revolution in February the following year. To hear Slonimsky tell it, less than world-historical forces were at work. "Actually, all the trouble started because of a crazy rule about the electric trams," he insists. "Soldiers, because of their service in the war, were being allowed to ride free, but because of the way they tended to hog all the available space, preventing civilians from even getting on the trams, the number of soldiers permitted on board a tram was limited to six at a time. If a seventh soldier boarded, all seven were subject to immediate arrest, notwithstanding the manifest innocence of the first six. This led to increasing clashes between soldiers and military police, and one day in February some regular army troops were called in to back up the military police, but they refused to act against their buddies. So then, in an effort to stanch the deteriorating situation, the most loyal imperial regiment, my own Preobrazhensky, was called in to quell the mutiny—only, we refused, too. And within hours came word that the czar had abdicated. We'd had no idea! All over a silly, unenforceable regulation."

Slonimsky was swept up in the revolutionary fervor. In his auto-biography, he quotes a passage from the diary of a bohemian contem-porary: "Nicolas Slonimsky, a student, came to see us, full of the joy of the revolution. He even forgot all about his egocentrism." Things in Russia radicalized fairly quickly during 1917, and the parliamentary revolution that had brought the moderate Aleksandr Kerensky to the fore was soon superseded by the October Revolution of the Bolsheviks. "That second revolution actually took place during a night and early morning when I happened to be on a train returning from Moscow to Petrograd," Slonimsky recalls. "And the first indication I had that anything had happened was that the town of Petrograd seemed unusually quiet as I disembarked from the train. A few minutes later, on the tram, I was reading a newspaper which a few weeks earlier would have been thought quite radical but had overnight been transmogrified into a forum for reaction. A sailor seated next to me demanded, 'How can you read a rag like that, which supports that Jew Kerensky? Me, I endorse that true Russian, Trotsky!' Of course, Trotsky was the Jew—he was born Bronstein—and Kerensky was a pure Russian from the Volga region, but I decided that this might not be the appropriate moment to debunk this particular young man's misconceptions. He was carrying a bayonet."

Although Slonimsky was basically sympathetic to the initial goals of the Revolution, he was, like his father—perhaps like most members of the St. Petersburg intelligentsia—at best only vaguely political. He witnessed some remarkable things—he was present, for example, at the rally where Trotsky actually called for the formation of the Red Army and began taking volunteers—but he barely recognized their political import. Or, at least, in his autobiography and in his conversational recollections, he seldom frames matters in political terms. (He and John Reed, for example, seem to have inhabited two different revolutions.) Rather—but perhaps this is what it is actually like to have lived through such seminal events—Slonimsky's recollections quickly descend into a chaotic, almost anarchic swirl of shortages, pestilence, mobilizations, sieges, marauding armies, insuperable bureaucratic complications, and devastating famines. Slonimsky stayed on in Petrograd through the winter and spring of 1918. (Indeed, he was engaged for a brief period as a piano teacher to the children of the Grand Duke Michael, the brother of the deposed czar—a job for which he was regularly picked up in a splendid troika.) But in the summer and early fall of 1918 the situation in Petrograd deteriorated dramatically: with famine spreading, Slonimsky recalls, the city of his birth was turning into "a city of death." Hunger hallucinations were becoming commonplace, along with things that ought to have been hallucinations but weren't: one afternoon, gazing down a street, Slonimsky saw people pouring out of their houses, carving knives held at the ready in every upraised right arm, converging on an overworked horse that had just collapsed in the street. In mid-autumn of 1918, Slonimsky resolved to leave Petrograd.

Having been granted a three-month passport to organize concerts in the Ukraine, Slonimsky set out for Kiev. It was the beginning of a harrowing journey: the civil war was by then in full fever, and the landscape was overrun with shifting armies. "The terrible thing," Slonimsky recalls, "was that you never had any idea who was manning each new barricade, so you never had any idea which password to use, which documents to show, which loyalty to claim. And things weren't much better once you got to Kiev, because that city, too, seemed to be overrun by some new army every second week. In fact, between 1918 and 1920 Kiev changed hands seventeen times! So you went to bed in a city flying the white flag, or the green, and woke up in one flying the red, or that of some Ukrainian nationalist army or some other freelance outfit. One morning, we woke up and the town had been overrun by *Martians*—or people who might as well have been Martians for all we understood of their language, which certainly wasn't Russian or any Ukrainian dialect. These guys turned out to be elements of the Polish Army who'd simply boarded an empty train and ridden it a couple hundred miles east, since nobody seemed to be around on that particular day to stop them. But they had no particular reason to be there, either, and I guess they got bored, because a few days later they were gone, having taken the same train back."

During his time in Kiev, Slonimsky resided in the city's only skyscraper—a six-story building, owned by an industrialist friend of his family's, that was also serving as refuge for a remarkable collection of cultural figures, including the widow and children of the composer Scriabin, and the great religious philosopher Lev Shestov and his family. By late 1919, however, Slonimsky had launched out once again, heading south on a journey that proved even more harrowing. Eventually, he made it to the Crimea, to Chekhov's Yalta, which was in its final days of White Army rule. There, among other things, he saw the famous beach promenade transformed into an improvised gallows, with the bodies of young men and women strung up from telegraph poles and swinging in the breeze, signs reading RED draped across their chests.

At length, he managed to book passage aboard a small boat flying the Turkish flag and bound for British-occupied Constantinople, where he debarked, famished and virtually penniless, in late March 1920. As luck would have it, musicians were in great demand in the bars and restaurants and theaters and silent-movie houses of the Turkish capital. There, during the next year, and then briefly in Bulgaria as well, Slonimsky gradually recouped both his physical and his financial health; and, finally, in April of 1921, he set out for Paris, the great magnet for Russian émigrés.

The evening Slonimsky described this terrifying period of his life for me, I asked him whether he had ever got nostalgic for life before the Revolution, for the life he might have led if it had never happened.

"On the contrary," he said vehemently. "I was *saved* by the Revolution. Without the Revolution, I would have become obsessed with my vanity. I would have reverted to brooding over my supposed genius, I would have become subsumed into the pointless life of the St. Petersburg intelligentsia. The Revolution—and especially the civil war that followed it—reduced everything to its lowest common denominator: survival. It forced me, among other things, to go out and earn a living—me, from my family, in which any commercial undertaking had always been deemed a disgrace. It forced me out into the world."

Still, I asked him, hadn't all the horrors he'd experienced and witnessed somehow scarred him?

"History never drives anyone mad," Slonimsky replied. "History made *me* sane. I was unbalanced. These sorts of upheavals quickly deprive you of vanity, of egotism, of self-centeredness, *because nobody's interested.* If you simply have to save your physical self, your mental and psychological disturbances tend to vanish."

As it turned out, Slonimsky stayed in Paris less than two years, but they were eventful years. He was quickly caught up in the vigorous Franco-Russian cultural scene, with its concerts and recitals and parties. In his autobiographical manuscript, he reports one of his "most striking memories" of a party from that period:

> Among those present was a very tall, middle-aged woman with a rather small head which looked like an extension of a long slender neck, continued in an elongated torso, with the whole upper body reposing rather incongruously on a disproportionately large pelvis and fat legs. I asked the hostess who the woman was. "Why, she is Mademoiselle Eiffel" was the reply, "the daughter of the builder of the Eiffel Tower."

During this period, Slonimsky procured a great deal of work as piano accompanist for opera singers giving solo recitals—he could sight-read virtually anything. Occasionally, these concerts produced their share of problems: critics would praise the accompanist more than the featured soloist. But he continued to be in considerable demand. He also served a stint as a pianist with the Diaghilev ballet company.

His most important breakthrough in Paris, however, came when he was approached by Serge Koussevitzky, who asked whether he'd be willing to try out for a position as a rehearsal pianist. "I'd never heard of such a thing," Slonimsky explained, "but it appeared that Koussevitzky—who was independently wealthy by way of his wife and could therefore afford to do so—preferred to rehearse for his full-orchestra rehearsals by going over the score alone with a pianist. I'd play a piano arrangement of the orchestra score, and he'd be off to the side, keeping the beat and delivering elaborate cues to the phantom orchestra which—in his mind, anyway—he'd managed to crowd into the room with us. We'd rehearse thus over and over, until he felt ready to face the actual full orchestra."

Koussevitzky invited Slonimsky to join him for the summer of 1922 in Biarritz and help him prepare for an autumn performance of Stravinsky's *Le Sacre du Printemps*. "This proved my first experience at tackling a truly modern work," Slonimsky recalled. "The discords, the rhythmic fluctuations were all incredibly exciting to me. But, to my dismay, I began to realize that they were beyond Koussevitzky's grasp: in particular, he seemed unable to cope with the sudden metrical changes. For instance, where the score went from 3/16 to 2/8, he kept slowing down the sixteenth notes or else accelerating the eighths, dissolving everything into formless, neutral triplets. Or, at the very beginning of the most difficult section, the 'Danse Sacrale,' there's a sixteenth-note rest followed by a full-orchestra chord on an eighth note. Conductors often have trouble with this. Stravinsky himself, when he conducted *Le Sacre,* usually solved the problem by burping on the tacit downbeat. But Koussevitzky just couldn't get it. Then, one day, I noticed that the situation could be remedied, after a fashion, by rebarring the piece so that, for instance, a succession of bars of 3/16, 2/8, 1/16, and 4/8 could be integrated into a single bar of 4/4. This created certain problems with regard to the downbeat, but they could be compensated for. I sketched out some of these possible revisions for Koussevitzky, but he'd have none of it. 'We can't change Stravinsky's rhythms,' he insisted. Several weeks later, however, back in Paris, re-hearsals with the full orchestra were going badly, and at one point he came up to me and said, 'Show me that arrangement you made.' I ea-gerly explained the idea to him, pointing out examples in the score, but his eyes quickly glazed over. 'I don't understand a thing you say,' he declared. 'Just go over there and put in your bar lines in blue pencil.' Which I did, and the solution worked. Every performance thereafter, in Paris and subsequently in Boston, Koussevitzky worked from scores rebarred according to my arrangement.

"The story has a coda," Slonimsky now said, getting up for a mo-ment, heading down the hall, and returning with a large scrapbook. "Back in April 1984, on the occasion of my ninetieth birthday, there was a party, and various people sent notes, and—let's see, where is it? Ah, yes, this one here." He handed me a sheet of elegant, heavy beige paper, on which was inscribed the following handwritten message: "Dear Nicolas: Every time I conduct *Le Sacre,* as I did most recently two weeks ago (and always from Koussy's own score, with your rebarring), I admire and revere and honor you as I did the very first time. Bless you, and more power to you.—Lenny B."

In addition to serving as Koussevitzky's surrogate orchestra, Slonimsky increasingly took on responsibilities as his secretary. Between brief touring forays as an accompanist, he'd return to Paris and help order the Maestro's affairs. For example, he handled the negotiations when Koussevitzky commissioned Ravel to produce a full-orchestra version of Mussorgsky's *Pictures at an Exhibition.* And things would no doubt have continued along such lines had not Slonimsky, one day early in the fall of 1923, received a telegram from America.

Vladimir Rosing, one of the countless musicians with whom Slonimsky had toured Europe as an accompanist, was a somewhat eccentric, ostentatiously mannerist Russian tenor (and, incidentally, a great favorite of Ezra Pound's). Some months after their tour together, Rosing happened to be crossing the Atlantic aboard a luxury liner on which George Eastman, the millionaire inventor of the Kodak camera and lavish cultural philanthropist, was a passenger. After being introduced to Eastman, Rosing suggested, on the spur of the moment, that perhaps he ought to include an opera subdivision in the Eastman School of Music, which he'd recently founded in Rochester, New York; and, on the spur of the moment, Eastman agreed, appointing Rosing to head it. As a consequence, one morning in October 1923, Slonimsky found himself getting off a train in Rochester, to which he'd been summoned to take up the position of coach and rehearsal pianist with Rosing's newly formed American Opera Company. He was almost thirty years old, and he spoke almost no English.

"Well, actually, that first week, he was capable of three phrases,"

Paul Horgan recently recalled. "'Yes,' 'thank you,' and 'please.'" Horgan himself later attained considerable fame as a novelist and man of letters, but in 1923 he was working as a scenic designer with Rosing's opera company, collecting the experiences he would presently distill and transform into his first novel, *The Fault of Angels*—in which he included, among other characters, a charmingly bemused Russian émigré opera coach named Colya Savinsky (Colya being the Russian diminutive for Nicolas). Horgan is now professor emeritus at Wesleyan University, where I'd tracked him down and found him filled with fond memories of those years. "When Colya first arrived, he was pale, small, trim, with black eyes and a fascinating intelligence, always in perfect control while always affecting a mild bewilderment," Horgan told me. "He dressed in black at all times, like a clerk. But, as I say, that first week he had only these three phrases, by which he was somehow able to convey to me his wish that I should help him learn English. I gave him a copy of *The Pickwick Papers* and instructed him just to start reading it and under no circumstances to have recourse to a dictionary. And that is what he did: he read it avidly while rehearsing the opera company, and in a couple of weeks he was speaking fine Dickensian English."

I asked Horgan what he meant when he said that Slonimsky read *while* rehearsing the company.

"Just that," Horgan replied. "Colya would sit there at the piano playing out a piano score flawlessly, from memory, with impudent efficiency. He'd even memorized all the cues, so that he'd be interacting with the stage directors and the singers. And as he played he'd be reading *The Pickwick Papers,* which he had perched on the piano easel before him, and he'd be turning the pages in the middle of his playing, entirely absorbed."

"Yes," Slonimsky said some time later when I mentioned Horgan's recollection to him. "I'd memorized the piano score for virtually every opera in the standard repertoire back in my conservatory days, as a hobby. And my work as an accompanist in Paris had, of course, refreshed my memory. So I'd use the time to read. I read Anatole France's *Les Dieux Ont Soif,* I remember, during the rehearsals for *Carmen.* But I was mainly reading English. I was having a terrible time with phonetic pronunciation. O-u-g-h, for example, bothered me frightfully. You know—'through,' 'though,' 'bough,' that sort of thing. Or vowels—I couldn't *hear* the difference, let alone reproduce it. And the t-h diphthong. On the boat over, a book I consulted had suggested that one achieved the t-h sound by sticking one's tongue between one's teeth. What kind of crazy language was this, I remember wondering, that forced you to stick your tongue out every time you used the definite article? And, of course, the idioms were impossible. Friends would ask me how my day had gone, and when I'd say, 'I worked hardly,' they'd all crack up. It wasn't until the company was doing *H.M.S. Pinafore*—remember that passage 'I never use the big, big, D. What, never? . . . Well, hardly ever'—that I suddenly saw the light on *hardly.* Actually, I learned a great deal of my English from Gilbert and Sullivan, although, as you can imagine, this produced some strange results in the coffee shop."

"The fact is we all became so charmed with Nicolai's mispronunciations that we took them up ourselves, and this certainly didn't make things any easier for him," another of Slonimsky's friends of the period, the harpist Lucile Johnson Rosenbloom, told me. "For instance, he would tell people about his Awunt Isabelle, and they'd correct him, and he'd say no, 'awunt' must be right, because that was how Paul and Lucile both pronounced it." Nicolas had suggested that I phone Mrs. Rosenbloom, recalling that he and Horgan and their colleague Rouben Mamoulian (he had been recruited by Rosing as a stage director for the company but soon moved on to greater fame in Hollywood) had formed a fan club around the beautiful harpist in the Rochester Philharmonic Orchestra—"the Venus de Milo with arms," they'd called her. "It was a wonderful time," she told me. "Nicolai had somehow managed to rent an apartment in a little white wooden house, which he left perpetually unlocked, and our group would repair there almost every night, late, following all our various engagements. George Eastman was sparing nothing in those days, and he'd gathered an extraordinary group of people together there in Rochester: the conductors Albert Coates and Eugene Goossens, and, later, the composer Otto Luening. So we'd all collect at Nicolai's and discuss how very stupid everybody in the world was except us—we were being playful, it was never malicious. And the thing was that Nicolai had discovered a novelty store, so that in Nicolai's house if you reached for a candy it was invariably made of soap; if you reached for a glass of water it turned out to be a dribble glass and you got soaked; if you tried to light a cigarette the match would explode, sending colorful sparks in all directions. He had the whole place booby-trapped with his enthusiasms. That was Nicolai's discovery of America, and we were all getting to experience it through him. That, and his discovery of English. For he seemed to be constantly memorizing new words—lists of them at a time, the longer and more abstruse the better—and then working them into his conversation as quickly as possible. 'Parcevendageous'—I can still remember that—I think was his own invention, meaning second- or third-rate. Or 'accubate,' which was to eat while lying down. Or 'pediculous,' from the Latin word for louse, as he'd inform us, meaning lousy. He and Paul and Rouben had formed this Society of Unrecognized Geniuses, but they had to disband it a few years later, because they'd all become too famous."

I asked Mrs. Rosenbloom whether Nicolas dwelt at all on the horrendous events associated with his flight from Russia, which, after all, had occurred just three or four years earlier.

"Not at all," she replied. "Not once, ever. He didn't seem the least bit traumatized. Or, rather, he seemed entirely caught up in the intensity and vitality and energy of this new land." Mrs. Rosenbloom paused for a moment, then sighed. "Oh," she said. "I do thank you for calling. I've got into a wonderful mood just thinking about all this."

I had asked Horgan a similar question about Slonimsky's sense of his dark past, and he had agreed. "He displayed no sense whatever of the tragedy of the history which had preceded his arrival," he replied. "No, our connections were all larkish and prankish. It was a bohemian world of great conviviality. Colya would sit there in his house at his piano and entertain us for hours with his wonderful diversions. 'Le Petit Cochon Qui Se Dégonfle,' I remember, was one piano piece he'd written which was much called for at parties. And then, of course, there were the Advertising Songs."

"Another one of my fascinations in those early days," Slonimsky recalled for me one afternoon, getting up from his table and moving over to the piano, "was the *Saturday Evening Post,* and particularly the unique poetry of its gaudy advertisements. I couldn't get over their language: cynicism set in only much later, I suppose—these early offerings were utterly unabashed. There was one, for example, in which a bearded Germanic doctor was pointing his finger at a beautiful, forlorn female sufferer"—Nicolas now suddenly struck the keyboard, producing a deep, ominous descending underflourish. "And the banner headline above the picture read"—now Nicolas launched into song, unleashing his "unbeautiful tenor voice" (as he sometimes calls it)—AND THEN . . . THE DOCTOR TOLD HER . . ." He momentarily interrupted his song, though not the suspenseful rumbly basso piano accompaniment, "Who knew, who knew what terrible fate lay in store for this poor creature? You read on, mortified, only to discover . . ." He now reverted to his singing self-accompaniment:

> For some time she had not been herself,
> She was ruuuun dowwwn, laaaanguid, tiiiired
> each day before her work began . . .
> One day she called her doctor,
> He advised her to eat bran muffins
> Made . . . according . . . to Pillsbury's recipe
> Pillsbury's marvelous, natural laxative!

At this point, the music suddenly broke free, becoming playfully uncongested:

> He knew the underlying cause of her trouble
> It was a case of faulty e-li-mi-nation . . .

And so forth.

One after another Nicolas now crooned a whole series of advertising songs, his fingers dancing across the keyboard, his head arched toward the ceiling in the manner of a coyote in rapture. "Mother," he urged plaintively at the climax of a song based on a truly bizarre ad for Castoria, "relieve your constipated child!" A few minutes later, he was imploring, "No more shiny nose," in a rendition of an ad for Vauv nose powder ("something to keep your nose from getting shiny, something to relieve you of this oiliness of skin"), which seemed to derive its melodic inspiration from a chorus of Volga boatmen. On a more sprightly note, moments later, he was inviting me to "make this a day for Plurodent." ("It brings to you new beauty, new emotion; it means to you new safety, new delight. . . . Film on your teeth ferments and forms an acid, this vicious film that clings to teeth.")

"Plurodent?" I asked when he'd concluded.

"Yes," he said, thoroughly invigorated. "Of course, it was Pepsodent, but, strangely, the Pepsodent people refused to grant me permission to use their name; I tried to sell my song to them, but instead they threatened to sue me. So a few years later, when I got set to publish the songs, Pepsodent became Plurodent. The nose-powder company had in the meantime gone out of business, so no problem. Strangest of all, the Castoria people gave me unqualified permission to use their name."

Slonimsky quickly dashed off another song, this one for Utica sheets and pillowcases ("So soft, so smooth, so snowy white"). "You see, this idea of advertising jingles was one of my inventions—only, like my grandfather, I was too impractical to think of patenting it. This was 1924, just before the popularization of the radio, and nobody had yet thought of this notion of putting advertising to music, so it was a big innovation. The thing is that although the language of the words of these songs was new to me, the musical language was pure St. Petersburg Conservatory. That Castoria song could be ascribed to Mussorgsky—harmonically, melodically, contrapuntally. It would have received a perfect score from Glazunov.

"But I was changing. Maybe it was related to the fact that during those years I was having to move through so many new *spoken* languages, especially English. In any case, I began developing a longing to expand the boundaries of my *musical* language as well. So that just four years after this"—he repeated the "Children Cry for Castoria" theme—"I was composing this." Slonimsky proceeded to play an eerily modern-sounding piece, made all the more eerie by the way his hands moved across the keyboard, his left hand confining itself to black keys, his right to white ones. "You see," he explained, looking over at me as his hands continued playing, as if on automatic pilot (actually, as if on two *separate* automatic pilots), "the 1920s in music constituted an orgy of dissonance. To have merely joined in that orgy would not have satisfied my vanity. So instead I created this sequence, which I called 'Studies in Black and White,' in mutually exclusive consonant counterpoint—or, to be accurate, in 'consonant counterpoint in mutually exclusive diatonic and pentatonic systems,' as I phrased it at the time, for I was already addicted to polysyllabic self-expression." He slowed his playing down to half time, quarter time. "You see, it's a case of trompe-l'oreille: although it's in fact entirely made up of consonances, it sounds dissonant, because it's made up of the kind of so-called false relations which were forbidden back at the conservatory. Just as I loved puns in English, I loved them in music, too."

Over the years, Nicolas continued to compose—once in a while for full orchestra but more often for piano alone, or else for singer accompanied by piano. In 1928, the year of his "Studies in Black and White," he wrote the song "I Owe a Debt to a Monkey," inspired by the Scopes trial; in 1945, he composed a vocal suite based on epitaphs he'd found on the tombstones in an old New England cemetery, entitled "The

Gravestones of Hancock, New Hampshire." ("Stop, my friends, as you pass by. As you are now, so once was I. As I am now, so you will be. Prepare for death and follow me.") Most of the piano pieces are miniatures, composed from a somewhat cockeyed vantage point. In 1979, Schirmer's published Slonimsky's compilation *51 Minitudes,* a thin volume—just forty-two pages—that happened to be sitting on the piano easel that afternoon. Slonimsky opened the book and offered to display a few of them, beginning with the first, entitled "$\sqrt{B^5}$" or, as Slonimsky now demonstrated delightedly, the square root of Beethoven's Fifth, for what he'd done with this piece was simply to compress all the intervals between the famous notes of the clichéd opening of the Beethoven symphony, as it were, by their square roots. Ba-ba-ba-*bum* thus becomes Ba-ba-ba-*bee,* and so forth. "After a while," he suggested, "you might get to like this version better—it's more salty, more acrid. But what's fascinating is that it's still recognizably Beethoven." Some of the other Minitudes parody a variety of musical styles; for example, there's "Casanova in Casa Nueva, Hollywood, California," which Slonimsky describes as "a deliberately gooey tonal mucilage, imitative of movie music," and which includes such markings as "orgiastico" and concludes with a repeat sign marked "D.C. al orgasmo." Slonimsky played me several more examples, concluding with his "Fragment from an Unwritten Piano Concerto."

It wasn't half bad. I asked him why he hadn't written the full concerto—why, in fact, he hadn't taken his composing more seriously.

"What for?" he countered. "What am I going to do, eat the reviews?"

Didn't he have music welling up inside him, crying out for expression?

"No," he replied. "I don't believe in that sort of thing. Sometimes, admittedly, it can get bothersome—I'm composing away in my head. If I let myself go, it would get to be like a vision, an aural vision—I have to watch it. But I feel no need to write out these symphonies. I know too many geniuses who composed masterpieces and became mental basket cases worrying about how they weren't being recognized. I don't have this problem."

Rosing's American Opera Company in Rochester lasted just a few years; then Eastman withdrew funding for the venture as precipitately as he had originally extended it. But in the meantime Serge Koussevitzky had been appointed principal conductor of the Boston Symphony Orchestra, and, learning of the sudden availability of his surrogate orchestra, he invited Slonimsky to Boston for a repeat engagement. Slonimsky accepted, moving there in 1925. Alongside his other, more official duties, and notwithstanding his minimal competence in spoken English, Slonimsky was soon delivering short introductory lectures on symphony concerts at the Boston Public Library. Paul Horgan, who was present at some of these, recalled for me one occasion when Slonimsky introduced a performance of the Dvořák Cello Concerto by praising the abilities of the evening's featured soloist, "that talented spaniel Pablo Casals."

In Boston, Slonimsky met Dorothy Adlow, a recent Radcliffe graduate. "Seven years younger than me," he says, "and an eternity wiser." She was the daughter of Russian Jewish immigrants who had begun as pushcart peddlers and then prospered. (Her father ran a furniture store and spoke English with the Irish lilt of most of his customers.) She herself had studied art history in college and, shortly after graduation, had become an art critic for the *Christian Science Monitor*. In that capacity, she would prove to be the only consistent breadwinner in the Slonimsky household for most of the ensuing years. By the late twenties, she and Nicolas were inseparable companions.

By the end of 1927, meanwhile, Slonimsky was spending less time with Koussevitzky. He had launched a small ensemble of his own, the Chamber Orchestra of Boston, announcing that he would be devoting his programs principally to baroque and ultramodern compositions, and that he himself would be the conductor. In Rochester, it seems, what little time Slonimsky had not spent studying English he had spent studying conducting—specifically, the conducting of Albert Coates and Eugene Goossens. Coates, in fact, had taken him on as a student. "I was a particularly inept student," Slonimsky recalled one afternoon. "For one thing, I seemed unable to give a decisive downbeat. That can be a problem for a conductor—and a calamity for the orchestra." But over time he improved. He found the downbeat, and by 1928 he seemed capable of conducting the most complex modernist compositions—indeed, the more complex the better. In particular, he became captivated by the growing achievement of American avant-garde composers (he took to them the way he seemed to take to all things American)—this at a time when virtually no one else was paying any attention to them. For example, he became a close friend of Henry Cowell, the master of dissonant counterpoint and startling tone clusters. Cowell allowed Slonimsky to conduct the premiere of his Sinfonietta with the Chamber Orchestra, and then encouraged him to contribute a composition of his own to *New Music,* a quarterly, recently founded by Cowell, that was to become the fount of American modernism. Slonimsky contributed his "Studies in Black and White," which ran in the Fall 1928 issue with some success. Cowell subsequently made Slonimsky an associate editor of the journal.

Slonimsky continued to identify himself with the fledgling American modernist movement and to champion its composers. The composers, in turn, championed him, for what that was worth. At one point, Cowell published an article in the magazine *Aesthete* titled "Four Little-Known Modern Composers: Carlos Chávez, Charles Ives, Nicolas Slonimsky, and Adolphe Weiss." The afternoon we were talking about this period, Slonimsky pulled a copy of the article out of his file and showed it to me. "Can you imagine?" he said. "Charles Ives, a 'little-known' composer. Extraordinary." Slonimsky went on to tell me about a day when Cowell took him along on a trip to New York to pay a call on Charles and Harmony Ives, at their brownstone, on East Seventy-fourth Street, where Ives, who was fifty-three, was still convalescing from a heart attack he'd suffered years earlier. Slonimsky described the chamber orchestra he'd recently founded and asked Ives if he would allow it to perform one of his works. Ives pulled out an old manuscript, which he had composed between 1903 and 1914 but which had never been performed, and asked whether something along its lines might do. This was the score for *Three Places in New England.*

In his autobiography, Slonimsky has recorded his impression of that moment:

> As I looked over the score, I experienced a strange but unmis-
> takable feeling that I was looking at a work of genius. I can't
> tell precisely why this music produced such an impression on
> me. The score possessed elements that seemed to be mutually
> incompatible, and even incongruous: a freely flowing melody
> derived from American folk songs, set in harmonies that were
> dense and highly dissonant, but soon resolving into clearances
> of serene, cerulean beauty in triadic formations that created a
> spiritual catharsis. In contrast, there were rhythmic patterns of
> extreme complexity; some asymmetries in the score evoked in
> my mind by a strange association of ideas the elegant and yet
> irrational equations connecting the base of natural logarithms
> and the ratio of the circumference of a circle to its diameter
> with the so-called imaginary number, a square root of negative
> quantity. The polytonalities and polyrhythms in the Ives score
> seemed incoherent when examined vertically, but simple and
> logical when viewed horizontally.

I often found myself wondering during the weeks I spent chatting with Slonimsky and reading his writings, to what extent he *loved* music. At first, paradoxical as this may seem, I even wondered whether he loved music at all. But, of course, he does. The proper questions are: How does he love it? What does he love in it? For it seems to me he doesn't love music as most people do. Slonimsky seems to me a very sensual man, in his way, and a man of deep emotions beneath his play-

ful surface, yet his appreciation of music is hardly sensual or emotional. He doesn't get carried away by its so-called spiritual quality.
Sometimes he almost ridicules—at any rate, he certainly downplays—
the sensual aspect of musical experience. He is not someone who is
ravished by the *sound* of music, the sensual experience of that sound,
its emotional or spiritual referents. "Waves rising and falling, that sort
of thing," he said to me one day. "The waves on the gulf of Finland just
used to get me seasick. I don't see what value there would be in experiencing music in that way." Rather, his ear is so precise that he hears
right through the sound to the structure, and it's the structure that
quickens and vitalizes and transports him. I once discussed this with
one of Slonimsky's best friends in California, the composer David
Raksin. "It's true," Raksin said. "Nicolas doesn't appear to be ravished
by music, he doesn't ecstasize. He's a cool guy—his flame burns a low
blue." And that flame is intellect. Leibniz once wrote, in one of his
famous letters to Goldbach, "Music is a hidden arithmetical activity of
a mind that does not know it is counting." But Slonimsky *hears the
counting.* For him, the love of music is a mathematical passion—it is
calculation taking flight, a structural transport. For Slonimsky, I came
to realize during the weeks of our conversations, structure *is* emotion.
And in that sense, that afternoon in 1928 on East Seventy-fourth
Street, he was indeed being ravished by the score of *Three Places in
New England.*

   Ravished or not, he would find it a damnably difficult piece to
envision conducting. "There was, for example, the second movement,"
Slonimsky recalled, "in which two bands seem to be entering a village
square from opposite sides, both playing in standard 4/4 time, but one
playing at a third faster rate than the other. This section could get
pretty tricky for the conductor, because if you addressed yourself to the
side of the orchestra that was playing faster, you ran the risk of losing
the slower side, and vice versa. I'd encountered a similar problem with
a canon by Wallingford Riegger, in which he had half the orchestra
playing in 5/8 time and the other half in 2/8. Those boys really liked to

mix things up. But it happened that I had discovered in myself a curious capacity: I seemed to be able, on the spur of the moment, to divide my brain in half, so that with one arm I could keep one tempo while with the other I projected an entirely different one. It was really quite simple." Slonimsky proceeded to demonstrate this weird talent, whose exercise seemed to transform him into a berserk semaphore messenger. His movements were brisk, powerful, exact—hilarious. He slowed down to give me a chance to verify the separate tempi, but my mind boggled in the attempt. "One of the critics," he now declared, without abandoning the performance, "proclaimed that my conducting was evangelical, for my left hand knew not what my right was doing." His eyes were gleaming joyously—full of mischief.

This marvelous capacity and Slonimsky's overall rhythmic hypersophistication served him in good stead on the night of January 10, 1931, when he and his orchestra premiered *Three Places in New England* in New York City's Town Hall. "The program went off without incident," he recalls. "I wasn't even disturbed by the concertmaster's whispering 'So far so good' at the conclusion of each movement. The reviews the next morning were mixed, but Ives himself, who attended the concert—something unusual for him—seemed satisfied. Interestingly, a few weeks later I went down to Havana, Cuba, to conduct a similar concert—Ives, Ruggles, Cowell—and the musicians there had far less difficulty negotiating the rhythmic complications of those pieces." Within months of thus presenting the premiere of one of the most important pieces of twentieth-century American music, Slonimsky was granted his American citizenship.

In the meantime, Ives, who was independently rich from his days as an insurance executive, told Slonimsky that he would like to sponsor him on a return trip to Paris so that he could "rig up" concerts of American music there. This foray, in the spring and early summer of 1931, proved immensely successful. Slonimsky arranged to give two concerts in Paris and was able to engage one of the city's finest orchestras, which he had sufficient time to rehearse properly. The indefatigable

Edgard Varèse, who was then in Paris, churned up a firestorm of publicity and anticipation. Announcements blanketed the kiosks. Slonimsky himself composed the program notes, encapsulating *Trois Coins de la Nouvelle-Angleterre* as *"géographie transcendentale par un Yankee d'un génie étrange et dense"* and Carl Ruggles's *Men and Mountains* as *"une vision brobdingnague par un inspiré de Blake."* Audiences packed both concerts, which also featured works by Cowell, Riegger, and Chávez, and the reviews were dazzling. "We have *sans blague,* just discovered America, thanks to a Christopher Columbus who left Russia for Boston," declared the weekly *Gringoire.* "This Christopher Columbus is called Slonimsky." Other reviews hailed Slonimsky for *"une oreille et bras excellents, une remarquable autorité, une souple intelligence."* Exercising some of that *souple intelligence,* Slonimsky now took time out from his triumph to accompany Dorothy Adlow, who had come along on the trip, on a brief visit to the Mairie, where the two of them were wed, Varèse serving as best man.

So successful had this trip proved that a second one was almost immediately arranged for the following winter, this time to include Budapest and Berlin in addition to Paris. The first of Slonimsky's second pair of Paris concerts, in February 1932, included works by Ives, Cowell, and Dane Rudhyar, and the Paris premiere of Béla Bartók's First Piano Concerto, with Bartók himself at the keyboard. The second concert featured the world premiere of Ruggles's *The Sun-Treader,* Varèse's formidable *Arcana,* and then, for balance, Brahms's Second Piano Concerto, with Arthur Rubinstein as soloist. Once again, Slonimsky was showered with rave reviews, but this time Paris was only a workup for Berlin, where he had been engaged to conduct the Philharmonic itself.

This proved to be one of the transforming moments of Slonimsky's life. "Never had I enjoyed such professional cooperation and competence," he recalls. "We went through four rehearsals with no complaints whatsoever. Indeed, what with all the newfangled percussion instruments I'd brought along, the Berlin Philharmonic players were like children in their enthusiasm. They particularly enjoyed the Lion's

Roar, a bucket through which you pulled a rope. It had a wonderful name in German—the *Löwengebrüll.* During the concerts themselves, the sound that the orchestra achieved was close to perfection."

Slonimsky's glorious triumph in Berlin was to have a sadly constricted horizon, and as we sat talking about it that afternoon, and he pulled out a file to show me the yellowed clippings, he wasn't so much boastful as bewildered, still—dumbfounded that such promise could yield so little. The works—Ives, Cowell, Varèse, Ruggles, and so forth—evoked controversy, but the praise for Slonimsky's conducting was nearly unanimous. Surely the most impressive came from the redoubtable Alfred Einstein, of the *Berliner Tageblatt,* dean of the German critics, who hailed Slonimsky as "a talent of the first rank, of a quite elemental capacity to convince orchestra and audience alike." The words seem to have branded Slonimsky to the core. *"Ein Talent ersten Ranges"*—on several occasions, I heard him mutter them quietly, like a mantra, in persisting sad amazement.

Upon Slonimsky's return to America, his success continued for a few more seasons. He toured. In March 1933, he presided over yet another epochal premiere, this time of Varèse's *Ionisation,* scored for forty-one multifarious percussion instruments—a seemingly chaotic welter of sound deep under the surface of which lay a structure of shimmering precision. Varèse presently dedicated the piece to Slonimsky. Surprisingly, Columbia Records accepted *Ionisation* for a single disk, but it soon became evident that the complexities of the piece were beyond the capacities of the percussionists from the New York Philharmonic who had been commissioned to tackle them. Instead, Slonimsky assembled a remarkable impromptu pickup ensemble, including Cowell pounding tone clusters on the piano, the composer Paul Creston on the anvils, Wallingford Riegger rubbing the guiro, the composer Carlos Salzedo on the Chinese blocks, and a very young William Schuman, who was assigned the crucial task of pulling the Lion's Roar. Varèse himself manned the necessary pair of sirens, which he had managed to borrow from a retired city fireman.

From this final triumph, Slonimsky pitched headlong toward disaster. Several months earlier, he had had a successful outing to Los Angeles, where he conducted the L.A. Philharmonic to considerable acclaim. On the basis of that performance, he'd been engaged to preside over the Philharmonic's entire summer season at the Hollywood Bowl. Then, in July 1933, arriving to take up his assignment, he resolved to program a vigorous selection of contemporary work, starting with *Ionisation* itself. Such a bold undertaking, however, while it might have worked for a single concert in a downtown auditorium, was bound to cause trouble at the staid and saccharine Bowl. Slonimsky stuck to his guns, insisting on the importance of exposing contemporary audiences to contemporary music and looking forward to the controversy. But those audiences proved instantaneously hostile, the orchestra mutinied, and the trustees quickly intervened. As Slonimsky puts it, "following the first concerts of the series, I was given the bum's rush out of Hollywood."

And suddenly his conducting career started to break up. The speed with which this happened is somewhat mysterious. Surely Slonimsky's adamant insistence on the necessity of programming vigorous, challenging, complex new music worked against him in the profoundly conservative context of mainstream American tastes. But now history, which had once made him sane, was also working against him. Ordinarily, he might have been able to return to Berlin, the scene of his greatest triumph, but this was already 1933, and Berlin was now cut off. (Even the year before, the Nazi critic Paul Zschorlich had excoriated the degenerate music that Slonimsky was trying to foist on the pure Aryan public. "The leader of this impudent exhibition was naturally a Jew," he pointed out in his review in *Germania*. "Slonimsky can call himself a hundred times an American, but one has only to watch his shoulder movements to recognize that he is a 100% Polish Jew.")

And then again, perhaps Slonimsky simply didn't have a talent for managing and exploiting his initial successes. This was not the sort of thing St. Petersburg intellectuals were well versed in doing; on the contrary, they were generally averse to any worldly exertions. At any rate, Slonimsky's conducting career was cut short. Nowadays, when, despite all his remarkable accomplishments, Slonimsky speaks of himself as a failure, this is what he really seems to have in mind—what he can't get out of his mind. As his former assistant Ana Daniel parsed it for me one afternoon, "the conducting clearly mattered to him enormously; in fact, in a way, Nicolas got everything he ever wanted except the one thing he ever really wanted, and that disappointment has surely remained a sorrow the rest of his life."

On the other hand, maybe he did get the one thing he ever really wanted and, in fact, got it that very summer. For all the while he was battling with the orchestra and the trustees at the Hollywood Bowl, he was also monitoring developments back east, where Dorothy was seven months pregnant. Returning to Boston in defeat, he was presently consoled by the arrival of a daughter, whom he immediately named Electra—after the Greek word for "amber," or for some such reason. Within months, the debacle at the Hollywood Bowl was receding into irrelevance. He was too busy teaching his baby daughter Latin.

II.

"Like the gaseous remnants of a shattered comet lost in an erratic orbit"—or so Nicolas describes the situation in his autobiographical manuscript—"occasional conducting assignments came my way." And occasional compliments as well. At one point, for instance, Arnold Schönberg compiled a list of good guys and bad guys among then-active conductors, and there were only two good guys—Eugene Goossens and Nicolas Slonimsky. But by the mid-thirties such assignments had virtually ceased. He would now have to cobble together a livelihood in some other manner—a requirement rendered all the more urgent by Electra's birth. He managed to get various odd jobs. For a while, he had a radio program in Boston. He taught Russian sporadically at Harvard. He offered private lessons in piano and composition.

"I charged two dollars a lesson, but I invariably failed to look at my watch—much to the distress, I imagine, of my captive students," Slonimsky recalls. "Some of them, though, I must say, nearly drove *me* over the precipice. I had one sixteen-year-old kid, for example, who protested vehemently at my assigning him the slow movement of a Mozart sonata, because he felt he wasn't getting his money's worth per number of notes played. And then there was a society matron who came to consult with me one day about a symphonic poem she claimed to have conceived. When I asked to see the score, she said no, I didn't understand—that was precisely where she required my help: to arrange what she heard *in her imagination*. She proceeded to describe a flat desert, horses galloping in the distance, a rising storm (violins, drums, whatever), the wind subsiding, a full moon rising (perhaps, she suggested, to be represented by a lilting flute)."

Increasingly, Slonimsky, now past forty, was turning to research and writing in his adopted language. As early as the mid-twenties, when he'd been consulting reference works in order to prepare for introductory talks prior to Boston Symphony concerts, he had begun to evince a certain compilation compulsion. "I was astonished by the tremendous discrepancies I encountered in dates for composition, publication, premieres, births, deaths," he recalls. "There were wholesale contradictions not only between but even within the various established sources. So I became something of a detective, burrowing for primary sources—contemporary reviews, correspondences, and so forth—writing letters to the principals involved whenever that was possible, trying to ferret out the truth and impose some order on the chaos."

Slonimsky started compiling his files—files on top of files—and was soon deploying his discoveries in ever more imaginative matrices. His continuing devotion to and fascination with modern music inspired the first of these efforts, the redoubtable *Music Since 1900,* which was initially published in 1937. In the years since, this book has gone through four editions, with updates in 1949, 1965, 1971 (that edition swelled to 1,595 pages), and this past year Slonimsky released a new 390-page supplement. If the purpose of the work was disarmingly simple—to make a day-by-day chronological listing of every significant happening in the field of music since 1900—the execution was exhaustively thorough. In the preface to the 1971 edition, Slonimsky endeavored to explain his straightforward principle of inclusion: "I have established a simple criterion: when in doubt, do not delete. Better to have a hundred bits of musical flotsam and jetsam in circulation than to omit a single potentially important event. The fear of leaving out an interesting work has even invaded my dreams. One particularly vivid nightmare was that I had overlooked a really sensational item—the 'Red Army Symphony' by Brahms, written in 1938, and dedicated to Marshal Voroshilov." And, indeed, virtually everything makes it in. A British music critic once dismissed an unfortunate composer's sequence of new compositions by wryly observing that they would probably just "disappear into that impeccably kept graveyard of our century—*Music Since 1900*." Endurance records for "pianofortitude" and for harp playing underwater, the schedule for the inaugural run of the Chopin Express between Vienna and Warsaw, Scriabin's horoscope, and the arrest of a Rumanian diva for spying during the First World War are all recorded. Under January 4, 1915, we learn of the American copyrighting of "'I Didn't Raise My Boy to Be a Soldier,' a sentimentally pacifistic tune by Al Piantadosi . . . challenging in quickstep time anyone to place a musket on his shoulder or make him shoot some other mother's darling boy . . . (650,000 copies were sold in the first three months of 1915)." In a note on that entry, we are invited to follow the changing course of American attitudes toward the war by way of the successive copyright dates for various sequels to Piantadosi's song, including: "I Didn't Raise My Dog to Be a Sausage" (April 21, 1915); "I Did Not Rear My Boy to Be a Coward" (October 18, 1915); "I Did Not Raise My Girl to Be a Soldier's Bride" (June 24, 1916); "America, Here's My Boy" (February 16, 1917); and "I'm Glad I Raised My Boy to Be a Soldier" (April 14, 1917). But Slonimsky's chronology is extraordinarily rich in serious revelation as well. Even a random browse through the year 1912, for example, elicits within just a few pages: May 29, the premiere of Debussy's *Prelude à L'après-midi d'un faune* by Diaghilev in Paris; June 26, the premiere of Mahler's Ninth Symphony ("a year, a month, and eight days" after the composer's death), with Bruno Walter at the podium, in Vienna; September 3, the premier of Schönberg's Fünf Orchesterstücke, Opus 16, in London; September 5, the birth of John Cage, in Los Angeles; October 16, "after forty rehearsals," the premiere of Schönberg's *Pierrot Lunaire,* in Berlin; and then, on November 17, "suffering from an excruciating toothache, exactly five months after his thirtieth birthday, Igor Stravinsky completes, in Clarens, Switzerland, *Le Sacre du Printemps.*"

Slonimsky was seldom satisfied with a mere date entry. Instead, for example, in the case of operas he'd include detailed and vividly wrought synopses of the plots; major symphonic works were granted crystalline, profoundly intelligent musical analyses, often complete with orchestration. Somewhere along the line, partly to rouse himself from the numbing stupor of his seemingly endless lexicographical task, Slonimsky hit upon the challenge of encapsulating every entry—no matter how long or exhaustive—within a single sentence. This artifice, he explains, also helped to ensure "the Aristotelian unity of place, time, and action within each item." The resulting sentences sometimes read as dazzling virtuoso performances in their own right (especially when one realizes that their author had only been exposed to English for the first time not much more than a decade earlier). Thus, for example, consider the entry for April 27, 1905 (the sole utterly bogus entry in the entire volume); the name of the composer in question is a fairly transparent anagram:

On his eleventh birthday Sol MYSNIK stages, in the recreation hall of High School No. 11 in St. Petersburg, in which he is a student, the world premiere of his politico-revolutionary opera in eleven scenes, *The X-Ray Vindicator,* scored for three countertenors, basso profundo, piano, balalaika, toy pistol and a static electricity generator, the action dealing with a young scientist confined in the dreaded Peter-and-Paul Fortress for advocating the extermination of the Tsar and the termination of the Russo-Japanese War, who escapes by directing a stream of Roentgen rays at himself from a hidden cathode ray tube as a Secret Police officer enters his cell, putting him to flight in superstitious horror by appearing as a skeleton, and then calmly walking through the open gate to resume his terroristic propaganda, with petty bourgeoisie characterized by insipid arpeggios on the balalaika and the playing of the waltz *On the Dunes of Manchuria* on the phonograph, revolutionary fervor by the songs "The Sun Goes Up, the Sun Goes Down, I Wish the Tsar Would Lose His Crown" and "We Fell as Martyrs to Our Cause Because We Scorned the Tsarist Laws," the X-Rays by chromatically advancing sequences of diminished seventh chords, and Freedom through Terror by blazingly incandescent C major.

With each new edition of *Music Since 1900,* Slonimsky has wrestled with the question of an appropriate, worthy cutoff date. The 1971 edition achieved a transcendent culmination with its entry for July 20, 1969: "The Harmony of the Spheres of the Pythagorean doctrine that interprets the position and movement of celestial bodies in terms of musical concordance is mystically manifested as first men step on the silent surface of the moon." The 1986 supplement ended just slightly more prosaically with July 13, 1985: "'Live Aid,' the first global rock concert"—the telethon for African famine relief undertaken simultaneously in both London and Philadelphia—is "watched by something like 1,500,000,000 people . . . with the Philadelphia portion utilizing about 90,000 nails driven into the 23,744-square-foot plywood stage and 75 miles of cable connecting 16 tons of lighting equipment with 2 Million watts of power, and involving 37 acts and 30 equipment changes, with hundreds of spectacular celebrities gracing the stage with their uninhibited crooning and howling presence, and hundreds of humble roadies donating their essential labor." (In a sense, perhaps, Slonimsky identifies with these last characters: he's now completing a distinguished career as a humble roadie with the ongoing road tour of the history of music.)

Every edition of *Music Since 1900* has included a fascinating—if wildly idiosyncratic "Appendix of Letters and Documents." Included among the letters are many that Slonimsky elicited from some of the foremost composers and music critics of our time—Ives, Varèse, Schönberg, Webern, George Bernard Shaw—answering his questions about the actual chronology of such things as the invention of the twelve-tone system (the one from Schönberg in this regard is especially significant and is often quoted). The documents Slonimsky includes range from encyclicals on sacred music by Popes Pius X and Pius XII (with their "Blacklist of Disapproved Music") through the *Peking Review*'s pathbreaking treatise, "Has Absolute Music No Class Character?"—with stops along the way for, among other things, the "Ideological Platform of the Russian Association of Proletarian Musicians" (1929) and "The Musical Ideology of the National Socialist (Nazi) Party" (1934). But without a doubt the treasure of the 1986 *Supplement*'s "Documents" section is a strange, once highly classified U.S. Department of the Army report, from 1954, which Slonimsky managed to wrest from a grudging bureaucracy through a Freedom of Information Act suit; it explores "Communist Vulnerabilities to the Use of Music in Psychological Warfare." Slonimsky even reproduces the official stamp, "Regraded Unclassified Order Sec Army by Tag Per 7502444," on each page.

Slonimsky frequently appends notes (in a smaller typeface) to his chronological listings in *Music Since 1900,* in which he provides samplings from the contemporary critical response to premiered works. While his fascination with the acceptance or, more usually, nonacceptance of the unfamiliar, of course grew out of his own experiences as the premiere conductor for many avant-garde works, his curiosity about the subject presently became more general, extending back to the critical reception of now classical compositions. He began compiling files on the subject, and in 1953 he distilled those files into one of his most celebrated sourcebooks, the *Lexicon of Musical Invective,* a compendium, as its subtitle explains, of *Critical Assaults on Composers Since Beethoven's Time.* The bulk of that volume consists of a remarkable cavalcade of righteous indignation arranged alphabetically by victim (Bartók, Beethoven, Berg through Varèse, Wagner, Webern), but what is perhaps Slonimsky's finest inspiration comes at the end, with a thirty-page "Invecticon," a cross-referenced alphabetical listing of individual terms of derision. A random trill from the Invecticon, for example, runs: "FRIGHTFUL (Berlioz); FROG LEGS, thrown into violent convulsions (Wagner); FROGLIKE SEXUALITY (Krenek); FRYING PANS (Wagner); FUNGI, hateful (Liszt); FUTILE (Berg, Debussy, Gershwin, and Schönberg)."

One afternoon, while discoursing on the nonacceptance of the unfamiliar, Slonimsky recited for me, by heart, two antimodernist poems he'd included in his *Lexicon.* The first one he'd managed to unearth in an American newspaper of the 1880s. Entitled "Directions for Composing a Wagner Overture" and signed "A Sufferer," it concluded:

> For harmonies, let wild
>   discords pass;
> Let key be blent with key in
>   hideous hash;
> Then (for last happy
>   thought!) bring in your
>   Brass!
> And clang, clash, clatter,
>   clatter, clang and clash.

Slonimsky delivered the last line with zest and syncopation, and immediately launched into the second poem—this one, also anonymous, from a February 1924 issue of the Boston *Herald* and inspired by a recent Stravinsky performance. It began:

Who wrote this fiendish
   "Rite of Spring,"
What right had he to write
   the thing,
Against our helpless ears to
   fling
Its crash, clash, cling,
    clang, bing, bang, bing!

Instead of finishing his rendition of the second poem, he observed, "'Clang, clash, clatter' and 'Crash, clash, cling.' The new not only sounds horrible to each new generation—it sounds horrible *in an identical way.*"

I asked him why he had never brought the *Lexicon* up to date, including more recent examples in revised editions, as he did with most of his other lexicographical projects.

"Because it can't be done," he replied quickly and emphatically. "That's the sad point of it. Critics simply don't vesuviate the way they used to. That sort of vituperative inflammation has gone completely out of fashion. I mean, one critic once described the first movement of Bartók's Fourth String Quartet as conveying 'the singular alarmed noise of poultry being worried to death by a Scotch terrier'; the third movement, he said, reminded him of 'the mass snoring of a Naval dormitory around dawn.' Who ever says that sort of thing anymore? Or my personal favorite, a German review of my own 1932 performance of Wallingford Riegger's *Dichotomy:* 'It sounded as though a pack of rats were being slowly tortured to death, and meanwhile, from time to time, a dying cow groaned.'" Slonimsky paused for a moment, savoring the image—and the sound. "It's even better in German. Not just torturing them to death, but torturing them to death *slowly. Langsam!* There's a positive genius to such rhetoric. Nowadays, a critic may say that music he doesn't like is ugly, but he's unlikely to say that the composer is ugly, which is what one of the critics I cite said of Debussy. And no one goes in anymore for the kind of personal attack you get in that 1841 review of Chopin I included in the book: 'There is an excuse at present for Chopin's delinquencies; he is entrammeled in the enthralling bonds of that archenchantress, George Sand. . . . We wonder how she can be content to wanton away her dreamlike existence with an artistic nonentity like Chopin.'" Slonimsky's eyes opened wide, his face displaying fresh astonishment, as if he had never before heard such words—even though he had memorized them. "The critics in those days had passion. But back then at least people got worked up about music—it occupied a central position in cultural life. New music took a passionate stand—and critics responded in kind." It occurred to me as Slonimsky spoke that this sort of language has not so much fled the world as shifted arenas: it is precisely the sort of language one now finds in film reviews. This in turn suggests that there was once a time when new music commanded the public presence, the urgency, the immediacy that new films do today.

Through the 1940s and into the fifties, Slonimsky whiled away his energies in other ways as well. He followed up some earlier conducting visits to Cuba with a tour of South America in 1941, which resulted, a few years later, in his widely heralded survey of the region's vigorous contemporary composing scene, *Music of Latin America.* He published a series of essays about music on the children's page of the *Christian Science Monitor* and presently brought them together in a book entitled *The Road to Music,* which he dedicated "To Electra, Against Her Will." In 1948, he perpetrated *A Thing or Two About Music,* a scattershot recollection of anecdotes from music history, which was greeted with almost universal critical acclaim, except for one devastating pan, in *Music Library Notes,* which he wrote himself.

"He was round the house pretty much all the time," Electra recalls nowadays. "We lived in a two-bedroom apartment in a respectable working-class district, well situated, close by the Boston museum, the library, Symphony Hall. It was crowded—keep in mind that he was using it as an office and my mother was writing there as well—but it was all they could afford. There was never any money. My mother used to think of him as semiretired, and that made it okay. He'd participate in household chores. For instance, he'd wash the dishes, because he could make a pagoda out of them as they dried, but he'd invariably leave the pans, because they just weren't interesting. He'd breakfast in leisurely fashion, read the *Times,* expostulate about the day's events, putter around, and finally you might be able to get him to focus on work. Even in those days, there was a harem of successive secretaries— generally nubile young maidens who would become embroiled in all the household dramas, part of the collective superego trying to get Genius Boy to do whatever it was he was supposed to be doing."

Dorothy Slonimsky's family tried to persuade Nicolas to get a job as a bandleader in Miami Beach. (After all, he was a musician, wasn't he?) But he demurred. In general, he seemed to be backsliding into the habits of the St. Petersburg intelligentsia—know-it-all good-for-nothing.

In the mid-forties, Slonimsky's inspired puttering achieved its apotheosis in an astonishing work he compiled, whose title is *Thesaurus of Scales and Melodic Patterns.* The *Thesaurus* is a sort of musical index—a catalogue made up of rows of notes rather than words. Specifically, it is, Slonimsky explains, "an ordering of every possible succession of notes arranged by intervals as counted in semitones." In more than two thousand entries, Slonimsky has managed to generate every conceivable sequence of scales. Intellectually, the breakthrough that allowed him to accomplish this feat came when he dispensed with the traditional division of the octave into two unequal parts—a perfect fifth and a perfect fourth—and instead divided the octave exactly in half, to form two tritones ("the dread *diabolus in musica* of the medieval theorists," as he acknowledges, adding, "Bach himself had his knuckles rapped for flirting with such a division in school—but those German teachers were all sadists"). From there, he ordered his melodic patterns by successively filling in the intervals to form new scales. The afternoon Slonimsky went through the volume with me, delving deeper and deeper, across page after page of carefully laid out scales, each scale differing just slightly from the one before, he quickly lost me in his astral explications of the book's subtleties. Seeing that he'd done so, he doubled back. "Never mind about the musical implications." he said. "It's *beautiful*—it's Mondrian."

Other musicians agreed. Arnold Schönberg labeled the *Thesaurus* "an admirable feat of mental gymnastics," averring, however, that "as a composer I must believe in inspiration rather than mechanics"; Howard Hanson described the work as "revolutionary" and "immensely valuable"; Arthur Honegger labeled it *"absolument remarquable"*; and Leonard Bernstein, in time, would praise it as "an astounding feat of invention and knowledge."

However, the various publishers whom Slonimsky initially approached, though they were fascinated by the manuscript's premise and dazzled by its execution, expressed virtually unanimous agreement that its chances of commercial success were dismal. "Over and over," Slonimsky recalls, "I was told, 'It's great, but there's no chance of its selling among the hoi polloi.' That, by the way, is a redundancy: 'hoi' is already 'the.' But finally, in 1947, a small outfit brought it out, with virtually no promotion, and, mysteriously, the book sold, sold some more, and then positively took off. None of us could figure it out. It turned out that what was happening was that *jazz players* had heard about the book and were using it as a sort of rhyming dictionary, a kind of melodic shake-and-bake. One of the sales guys told me, 'Yeah, it's a real hot item up in Harlem.' Coltrane, for example, was assigning it to his whole band." (Some have gone so far as to suggest that Coltrane's innovative "sheets of sound" were actually sheets of Slonimsky.) "All sorts of people were coming into stores who had no idea what a thesaurus was—they didn't know from Slonimsky. They'd ask for the Resorious by Slumsky, or the Notorious by Plumsky—but the book was selling. It's gone through six printings."

Even so, Slonimsky's cult notoriety remained circumscribed, and his financial productivity downright marginal. A few years later, however, he was suddenly, though briefly, able to marshal his mammoth store of useless knowledge for practical profit. One day in 1956, he was invited to be a contestant on the nationally televised quiz show, *The Big Surprise*. He competed in the category "Misinformation," and week after week he successfully batted down popular misconceptions and artful stumpers in all sorts of areas. By the sixth week, he had attained thirty thousand dollars, all of which he was now invited to risk in going after the hundred-thousand-dollar prize. He had never made anything like thirty thousand dollars before, nor had he ever attained such a level of public notoriety. Strangers were stopping him on the street to ask if he was going to go all the way; bookies were taking bets on his chances. Nowadays, he says wistfully, "There is no greater glory than making money in public." But in the end he decided to pocket the thirty thousand dollars. Mike Wallace, the show's host (yes, *the* Mike Wallace), asked whether he'd like to try answering the seven remaining questions, just for the fun of it. He agreed to and, effortlessly, he did. A Boston paper the next morning ran his picture on its front page, with the headline LOSES $70,000, HAS NO REGRETS.

Increasingly, during these years, Slonimsky was being drawn into the world of conventional musical lexicography. Editors, perhaps annoyed by his penchant for tripping them up in their errors but obviously impressed by his investigative zeal whenever he could be aroused to display it, invited him into their deliberations on a more official basis. He began contributing to Oscar Thompson's *International Cyclopedia of Music and Musicians* in 1939 and, upon Thompson's death, rose to its editorship in 1946; he remained at the helm there through 1958, supervising the fourth through the eighth editions. In 1949, he produced a supplement to the third edition (1940) of *Baker's Biographical Dictionary of Musicians* (which had been launched in 1900 by Theodore Baker, a pioneer American musicologist), and in 1958 he was appointed to preside over an entirely revised fifth edition. Slonimsky had reached the age of retirement—he was sixty-four—but in a profound sense his career was just beginning: he persisted at *Baker's* through a sixth edition, in 1978, and a seventh edition, in 1984. It proved an endless labor; as the critic Alan Rich recently commented, Slonimsky is condemned to work "in the manner of the painters of the Firth of Forth bridge, where the job, once completed, is ready for recommencement." He had become the Keeper of the Files, Monitor of the Obituaries ("You can't get into musical heaven without St. Nicolas seeing you off at the gate," an admirer recently commented), Weigher of Worth, and Assigner of the Adjectives. (Aficionados study each new edition, trying to gauge the subtle realignments in Slonimsky's assignment of key adjectives—"brilliant, celebrated, famous," "eminent," "distinguished," "noted," and "remarkable" among them—at the head of his major entries. Most individuals in the *Dictionary* are initially identified only by vocation and nationality—"British pianist," say, or "Danish soprano"— but about 10 percent of them rate adjectives, and these adjectives have become the subject of Talmudic disputation among the *Dictionary*'s fans, who try to determine whether "brilliant," for example, is more or less laudatory than "remarkable." Slonimsky has recently introduced a new term, "seeded," which he appears to reserve for rock idols, but no one has any idea what *it* means. Some surmise it's a play on "seedy," but when Slonimsky is asked he merely smiles delphically and says, "Tennis.")

Baker's is widely considered the finest existing single-volume dictionary of musicians on the market (albeit a *huge* single volume, with 2,575 double-column pages, and weighing over seven pounds). Its coverage of a vast range of figures across the history of music is consistently thorough and authoritative. Abram Chasins, the composer-pianist and radio commentator, recently said, "When Slonimsky writes about musicians, the people themselves emerge, not just what they wrote but who they were. His writing is informed by a charm and warmth and individual personality you don't find in most other contemporary dictionaries, and yet it's objective. His analysis of musical forms is invariably exact, and his critical judgment absolutely pristine.

And this is true of his treatment of all his subjects, whether they arrived on the scene four hundred years ago or just the day before yesterday." Thus, Slonimsky's entry on Handel contains crisp explications of the composer's entire musical output and also supplies a vivid character squeeze, including the facts that "Handel remained celibate, but he was not a recluse. Physically, he tended toward healthy corpulence; he enjoyed the company of friends but had a choleric temperament and could not brook adverse argument." Or, more recently, Luciano Pavarotti: "Idolized by the public as no tenor has been since the days of Caruso, he plays the part of being Pavarotti with succulent delectation. . . . Like most tenors, he likes himself immensely. Unlike most tenors, he does not get involved in scandal." Slonimsky is always on the prowl for the bizarre detail, and he invariably frames the trophies from his indefatigable researches with liberal dollops of his own sly wit (as in the case of Gusto Tenducci, the "celebrated Italian castrato, b. Sienna 1736, d. Genoa 1790" who "was nicknamed 'triorchis' on account of the singular plurality of his reproductive organs that enabled him to marry"). Such details crop up throughout the volume, but they're especially liable to occur when Slonimsky is considering the achievements of the avant-garde. We discover, for example, that in addition to his other achievements the composer George Antheil contrived "a torpedo device in collaboration with the motion picture actress Hedy Lamarr," for which "they actually filed a patent, No. 2,292,387, dated June 10, 1941." Farther on in this entry, Slonimsky notes that "Antheil was the subject of a monograph by Ezra Pound entitled *Antheil and the Treatise on Harmony* . . . which, however, had little bearing on Antheil and even less on harmony." In the John Cage entry, we are informed that *4'33"* requires that its performer play nothing for the length of time stipulated by the title. We are also told, "It was followed by another 'silent' piece, *0'0"*, an idempotent 'to be performed in any way by anyone,' presented for the first time in Tokyo, Oct. 24, 1962. Any sounds, noises, coughs, chuckles, groans, and growls produced by the captive listeners to silence are automatically regarded as an integral part of the piece itself, so that the wisecrack about the impossibility of arriving at a fair judgment of a silent piece since one cannot tell whose music is not being played is invalidated by the uniqueness of Cage's art."

In the last two editions of *Baker's,* Slonimsky has taken to including a substantial, though quirky, selection of contemporary popular performers. Sometimes these entries seem designed as much to puncture the self-seriousness of the lexicographical profession as to mock the vagaries of popular taste, as in a passage near the beginning of his entry on John Lennon: "He was educated by an aunt after his parents separated; played the mouth organ as a child; later learned the guitar and was encouraged to become a musician by the conductor of the Liverpool-Edinburgh bus." More often, however, they simply afford Slonimsky an opportunity to filter his genial contempt for those vagaries of taste through the medium of his own ebullient rhetoric. Thus, of Guy Lombardo: "The result is a velvety, creamy, but not necessarily oleaginous harmoniousness, which possesses an irresistible appeal to the obsolescent members of the superannuated generation of the 1920's." Of Frank Sinatra: "In May 1976, the University of Nevada at Las Vegas conferred on him the honorary degree Literarum Humanitarum Doctor in appreciation of his many highly successful appearances in the hotels and gambling casinos of Las Vegas." And, finally, Slonimsky's description of the death of Elvis Presley, which "precipitated the most extraordinary outpouring of public grief over an entertainment figure since the death of Rudolph Valentino. . . . Entrepreneurs avid for gain put out a mass of memorial literature, souvenirs, and gewgaws, sweatshirts emblazoned with Presley's image in color, Elvis dolls and even a lifesize effigy, as part of a multimillion dollar effort to provide solace to sorrowing humanity."

From the evidence of entries like these, one might easily assume that Slonimsky's belated musicological career has been one extended lark. No assumption, however, could be less well grounded. One afternoon, Slonimsky caught me looking at a rave British review of the latest edition of *Baker's* headlined SEVENTH HEAVEN. "Funny," he said. "It seemed more like Dante's *Inferno* to me." Indeed, on the question of a career in lexicography Slonimsky had had misgivings from the start. He recalled for me what it had been like reviewing the galleys of *Baker's Fourth* as he prepared his revisions for the fifth edition. "There were an incredible number of errors, but it took a tremendous amount of concentration to weed them out," he explained. "At one point, I came upon a little scribble in the margin left by one of the earlier editors. It said, 'I will go mad if I have to continue this for a long time.' I took this as an omen. And it's been known to happen. Consider poor John Callcott, whose case I included in the *Dictionary*." (Of John Wall Callcott, 1766–1821: "His mind gave way from overwork on a projected biographical dictionary of musicians, and he was institutionalized just before he reached the letter *Q*. He recovered; but not sufficiently to continue his work.")

Slonimsky loves to bewail the difficulties of the lexicographical profession; he can carry on for hours, retailing instances of absurd impasse and hopeless travail. He has written on the subject frequently, and the prefaces to the various editions of *Baker's* are rich with anecdotes of near-apoplectic exasperation. That particular afternoon, Slonimsky summoned up the case of Helen Traubel, a singer "who preferred to date her birth several years after the scission of her umbilical cord." (Luckily, Slonimsky explained, she was born in St. Louis, where a tradition of excellent record-keeping goes back to Napoleonic times, so it was not terribly difficult for him to upend her conceit.) From Traubel, it was a natural progression—progressions in such conversations with Slonimsky are seldom so smooth—to the great conductor Leopold Stokowski, who, Slonimsky said, "was born in London in 1882 but preferred to have entered the world in Krakow five years later." He went on, "One day, I got a letter from the folks over at Riemann's, the German dictionary, informing me that I must have got it wrong in my account and that they were henceforth going to cite Krakow, 1887, as the correct version, since they'd just 'gotten it from the horse's mouth.'

I wrote back informing them that they must have gotten it from the other end of the horse, enclosing a copy of the birth certificate, which I'd managed to procure, to prove my case." Slonimsky now free-associated from Stokowski to Stravinsky, with whom he waged a drawn-out controversy regarding *his* birth date, and the date of his departure from Russia as well. "Luckily, there I had a spy inside his household and was hence able to examine the actual passport."

From dubious births, we proceeded to annoying deaths. "One of my main problems is that composers decide to die out of alphabetical order," Slonimsky said.

I remarked that, come to think of it, he must greet each evening's newscast with a certain foreboding, given the obituary havoc it could play with his completed entries.

"Actually not," he said, doubling back. "No, deaths are perfectly okay." He rummaged around among his papers and dug out a sheet headed "Stiffs, October 1985," which consisted of a neatly typed list of musicians who had died that month, along with the places and circumstances of their deaths. "Now, of course, with all these I'll still have to double-check and get proper documentation. But that's okay; that's just bookkeeping. No, what's really terrible is when they *don't* die. The zombies. For example, I once had a perfectly unimportant Austrian ballet composer, one Alois Ludwig Minkus, who was born in Vienna in 1826 and was then attached to the Imperial Theatres in St. Petersburg until 1891, when he was pensioned off and immediately vanished. Obviously, he must have died sometime, but when? Where? It took me years, literally decades, of sleuthing before I was finally able to determine that he achieved his heavenly reward back in Vienna on December 7, 1917. But, I mean, you can't just leave a parenthesis dangling like that. And that's only one case. There are dozens."

I asked him what other sorts of problems he ran into.

"Transsexuals!" he exclaimed. "Composers who've had sex-change operations. What pronoun do you use? That, I assure you, is not the sort of thing my predecessors in this line of work ever had to contend with."

The worst, though, the worst of everything, the horror of horrors and the bane of his existence, Slonimsky now informed me, were the inadvertent factual errors that, once born into print, refused to die and, indeed, spread exponentially from one sourcebook to another, eternally. They haunted his sleep like vengeful wraiths. They haunted his mailbox, too. For, over the years, Slonimsky has received thousands of letters from correspondents throughout the world. Some of them come from formal contacts—informants. He has one in Bulgaria, for instance, who keeps him apprised of compositional doings there and, whenever possible, in Albania, too. He has another in Beijing, as well as people in Siberia and Egypt and Australia. Others are sent in by more casual contributors, whom he acknowledges in one of his prefaces when he thanks the "legion of anonymous (for their signatures are usually illegible) archivists." But over the years he has also attracted the attention of some true fanatics—people who scour each new supplement or edition and inundate him with their corrections and emendations and *his* omissions. "When I got one particularly vitriolic letter from one of these fellows," Slonimsky recalls, "one Stephen Ellis, from Glenview, Illinois, sideswiping my 1971 supplement to *Baker's* as 'grossly incomplete' and 'shockingly out of date,' with *pages* of examples, my first impulse was to dash off a note saying 'Sirrah!' and perhaps challenge him to a duel in the high Russian tradition. But I quickly thought better of it and instead struck up a correspondence, and he has proved an absolutely invaluable resource person. The thing about him and several of my other fellow conspirators—Dennis McIntire, in Indianapolis; Michael Keyton, in Dallas; David Cummings, in Britain; Samuel Sprince, in Boston—is that they're usually nonmusicians and nonacademics, and often they can't even read music. They're obsessed amateurs, and they know more about music than the most erudite musicologists. Some of them, admittedly, have their idiosyncrasies. Sprince, for instance, is a fantastic energumen and a champion complainer. He sends me these thick dispatches typed out single-spaced, both sides, on sequences of disparate-sized little pages, always concluding with a complaint about the Boston weather—and he's *really* into zombies. They're his specialty. He keeps lists of musicians born before 1900, arranged by birth year." Slonimsky rummaged among his papers and fished out a page headed "1894." "Look," he said. "He even has *me* on one of them. And then there's Keyton—he's a mathematician, who somehow became fascinated with the soloist who gave the world premiere of Tchaikovsky's Second Piano Concerto, in New York City, in 1881, an otherwise utterly insignificant pianist named Madeline Schiller. One day, he happened upon a picture of her in a newspaper of the period, he fell hopelessly in love with her, and since then he's managed to unearth over a hundred articles on the woman. I mean, these are the kinds of madmen I run with."

Only slightly less horrible than the outright mistakes—although in a way even more exasperating, because so easily avoidable—are misprints. And in the most recent edition of *Baker's,* the seventh, these have for some reason seemed exceptionally numerous. "My God, there's never been anything like it," Slonimsky said, cringing as he hefted a copy of the first printing of *Baker's* seventh edition onto my lap. "A complete disaster. I'm going to have to wear a hood the rest of my days. Monasteries won't even accept me. The shame, the derisive laughter will pursue me to my grave. Thank God they've already sold out the five thousand copies of the first printing so that we've been able to correct some of the grossest errors in the second printing. But this process of correcting the volume has produced a whole batch of new ones." He cited several examples—seemingly niggling matters that nevertheless left him mortified. He shuddered. We were silent for a moment, letting the terrors disperse, and then I asked him, "What does it matter? Why is it so important to you?"

"If you ask me what is the significance to the world that I have everything down precisely correct, the answer is zero. I have no huge Copernican ambitions, no need to transform the known universe. It's just that in doing my first book, *Music Since 1900,* I kept finding all these discrepancies, all these manifest impossibilities, and it became a game for me. I invented new research techniques—for instance, placing ads in Russian émigré papers in New York City to nail down a death in San Remo. Or, take nineteenth-century Latin American composers: they're particularly troublesome . . ." With Slonimsky, any abstract question quickly dissolves into a miasma of particular instances, but I tried to steer him back. "I just don't give up, that's all. I can't stand it," he said. "It's like when I come upon misspellings in the morning paper, a paper that *no one but me is ever going to read*"—he waved a hand toward a copy of the New York *Times* lying on the sofa—"I can't help it: I *have* to correct the errors before throwing the paper away." Sure enough, the front page was tattooed over with a pox of minuscule inked-in emendations. "I have to destroy them or they literally show up in my nightmares. I have a very rich dream life—no Freudian content, just pieces of paper that need to be picked up. And my mother, criticizing. Strange thing, though, about my dreaming—I never lose my chronological awareness, even while I sleep. My mother showed up in my dream the other night, nattering on about something or other, and I said, 'But, Mother, you must be a hundred and twenty-nine years old.'" Slonimsky smiled. "I don't know. Sometimes I ask myself, 'Why is it so important?' But I guess it's just that I write, I publish, and I have to know whether what I publish is true or not."

But why, I asked him, had he drifted into this lexicographical vocation at all? What did it do for him? How did it answer his needs and fit into his history?

"Ah," he said, "that's another question." He paused. "Perhaps it's genetic. You know, that uncle of mine who used to keep up that vast *cartotheèque* on Pushkin and other Russian writers, and my grandfather who was famous for debunking all manner of Hebraic superstitions in the name of enlightened science. Perhaps—I don't know—it's a continuation of the exhibitionist tendencies of my childhood, the need, still, to show off my precocity and garner all that admiration."

Perhaps. But one evening a few weeks later I was talking with Steve Wasserman, a New York editor who treasures Slonimsky's enormous lexicographical achievement, and Wasserman said, "The strange thing about Slonimsky is that in a certain sense, for him, *Baker's* has been one gigantic, heroic feat of sustained procrastination." When I mentioned Wasserman's comment to Ana Daniel, Slonimsky's former secretary, she almost concurred. "Almost, but not exactly," she said. "It hasn't been so much a simple act of procrastination as a vast procrastinatory dirge—an extended act of mourning."

Nowadays, whenever Slonimsky imagines that someone is trying to pull a fast one on him, he's likely to protest, "Look, you know, I wasn't born yesterday. I was born twenty-two years ago, when I first moved to California, but *not yesterday.*"

He originally came to Los Angeles in flight from Boston, when that city became intolerable to him following the sudden death, by heart attack, of his wife, Dorothy. He seldom talks about her these days, but when he does it's clear that she was an enormous presence in his life, and is an enormous absence. In the years he has been based in Los Angeles, he has traveled throughout America on lecture tours and throughout the world on research junkets, but he has never been back to Boston. "I warned her against marrying me," he said to me one day. "I suppose she saw me as a lost soul to be saved, but it's too terrible for words what she sacrificed for me."

I asked him if he imagined that he had ruined Dorothy's life.

"No," he replied instantly. "There was, after all, Electra."

Los Angeles, for Slonimsky in 1964, offered a sort of fresh beginning, a tabula rasa, and he was particularly charmed by how rasae the tabulae were with almost all the people he met. He taught music appreciation at UCLA until 1967, when, as he puts it, he was "irretrievably retired . . . owing to irreversible obsolescence and recessive infantiloquy." He was popular with the students—"He is a terrific piano player, who puts on quite a show almost every lecture," one evaluation read—and they, for their part, never ceased to astonish him. He has a whole routine he loves to fall into about the answers he used to get to his test questions—Monte Verdi; Shosty Kovick; "Beethoven's three symphonies, the First, the Fifth, and the Ninth"—and the *explanations* for those answers: "Schubert composed the Unfinished Symphony, also known as Finlandia." Why? "Because you talked about Finnish music, and I wasn't sure whether it was finished or unfinished, so I put them both in." He invariably concludes, "Socrates would have been no match for my students."

For Slonimsky, one of the big advantages of Los Angeles, and especially the Westwood area where he lives, is that it contained "a pullulation" of potential secretaries, the California "odalisques" without whom he couldn't function as a dictionary-maker. ("Odalisques!" he reports that one of them exclaimed to him one day. "I know what they are—there's one in Central Park.") Although he savors (and sometimes exaggerates) the intellectual innocence of his secretary-wards, they, for their part, have all been appalled by *his* innocence in the matter of managing his own business affairs. (This is an estimation they share with Electra.) To hear them tell it, publishers are always putting things over on Slonimsky. They point, for example, to his inability to demand a just royalty on *Baker's,* or to demand any royalty, or even to negotiate at all. He meekly accepts whatever is offered. For the sixth edition of *Baker's* in 1978—which sold over twelve thousand copies at seventy-five dollars apiece—Slonimsky received a flat fee of thirty thousand dollars. For the six years of work on the 1984 edition, Schirmer Books (which had in the meantime become an imprint of Macmillan) paid him a flat fee of fifty-seven thousand dollars, of which more than two-thirds went to pay his secretarial and other office expenses. That edition has already sold over eight thousand copies at almost a hundred dollars apiece and sales are continuing handsomely, but Slonimsky will not be seeing another penny. He is not well off; indeed, his principal source of income these days is his occasional lectureships. "But it's partly his own fault," one of the former odalisques told me, in exasperation. "He's absolutely supine in the face of power—or imagined power. Maybe it comes from his background in the Russian intelligentsia, but for him outward success would blow everything. Intellectuals aren't supposed to work or to be seen working; they're supposed to putter, brilliantly, and they're certainly not supposed to haggle over something as insignificant as money. Anyway, it's easier for him to be self-deprecatory than to be visibly successful."

Notwithstanding his borderline economic existence—or rather, precisely in standing with it—Slonimsky has over the years become a vital presence in the contemporary music scene of his adopted hometown. We were talking a bit about that scene one afternoon as I drove Slonimsky over to a salon concert at the Beverly Hills home of the contemporary music patron Betty Freeman—one of a regular series of such private concerts, but a special one, because it signaled the beginning of New Music America Festival, a weeklong national celebration of contemporary music being staged throughout Los Angeles. At first, I didn't know *what* we were talking about.

"For some reason," Slonimsky said, "the ones they spawn out here are especially furfuraceous."

Which ones?

"The composers." Two beats, a smug smile spreading across his face. "From the Latin, *furfur,* dandruff. Hence furfuraceous: flaky." Of course. "In fact, I'm acquainted with several of the flakes out here. I even infiltrated their magazine, *Source*—they published two of my pieces, mistakenly imagining that I was one of their kind. One of these flakes, Philip Corner, once published an interesting composition in another issue of *Source*. It consisted of the simple injunction 'One anti-personnel type CBU bomb will be thrown into the audience.' But it was never performed. Another of my flaky friends is Ken Friedman. When he told me that the finale of his Third Symphony was the Los Angeles earthquake of 1971, I naturally became curious about the orchestration. 'You don't understand,' he told me, with barely disguised contempt. 'The earthquake *was* the finale!'"

But perhaps Slonimsky's greatest triumph on the local scene, he now informed me, came one spring evening in 1981 when a gentleman calling on the phone introduced himself as Frank Zappa. "I couldn't believe it," Slonimsky said as we wove among the palm-lined drives into Beverly Hills. "He spoke to me about Varèse and that book I did about musical scales, all quite knowledgeably, and then asked if I'd mind coming up to his house in the Hollywood Hills for a visit. A few days later, as had been agreed, he sent a limo down to fetch me. We went up to the house, and it turned out he's a tremendously sophisticated musician. His studio includes an immense Bösendorfer piano, which even features nine additional keys in the bass. I mean, as my friend David Raksin says, you don't tune the thing with a tuning fork, you have to use a Richter scale! Anyway, far from what you might expect on the basis of his hoary reputation as the head matron of the Mothers of Invention, Zappa turns out to be an entirely regular family man, with a lovely wife of long standing and four children, one of whom, his teenage daughter Moon Unit, I met that evening and found especially fascinating. For, as you may know, she is a specialist in that strange lingo they speak in the school corridors and shopping malls of the San Fernando Valley. She can deliver whole paragraphs in the Valley language and you can't understand a word of it." Slonimsky spoke with the evident admiration of a fellow linguist. "She patiently explained to me the use of several of these Valley locutions, like 'gag me with a spoon' and 'totally grody to the max,' some of which she later incorporated into her famous record, and a few months later, when I got a new cat, I named him Grody-to-the-Max, in her honor. Anyway, Zappa asked me if I'd like to try out the Bösendorfer, and I played the coronation scene from *Boris Godunov,* which is rich in those deep bass sounds, and then he asked if I'd play some of my own compositions, and I played the last piece from that series of mine called 'Minitudes,' and then he asked if I'd be a featured soloist in his next concert. I laughed and said sure, but when? And he said, 'Tomorrow. We can rehearse the band in the afternoon.' Which we did, and which is how I came to perform as a soloist backed up by Zappa's band at their 1981 concert in the Santa Monica Civic Auditorium. Zappa introduced me to the audience as 'our national treasure, Nicolas Slonimsky,' if you can imagine such a thing, and, to my astonishment, some of the fans shouted out 'All right!' Everything went well, and the applause at the end made me feel positively inebriated."

A few days later, I phoned Frank Zappa to hear his side of the story. He told me that he'd first heard of Slonimsky years ago, as a young teenager growing up in the California high desert community of Lancaster. At the time, he'd had a collection of R & B singles but only two albums, a Stravinsky *Rite of Spring* and his favorite, a Varèse. He'd read everything he could get his hands on about Varèse, and of course he'd repeatedly come upon the name Slonimsky. As the years passed, he'd followed Slonimsky's writings. "But I had no idea he was living here in L.A. Somehow, I figured a guy like that wouldn't want to live in a bleak place like L.A." The moment he learned that Slonimsky was a virtual neighbor, he called him up and invited him over. "He's incredible," Zappa told me. "He played my Bösendorfer, and nobody has ever played that piano as loud as that man—and not jumping up and down like a madman, just from the strength of his arms and his spirit. He's a human dynamo: he's got a fantastic brain, and a body made out of molybdenum. And another thing I really like about him is his clothes. That first evening, when he was standing there, his clothes didn't match, but they were obviously cool, and you just knew that this was one of the Real Guys. It was an honor to be able to play with him."

No sooner had Slonimsky and I arrived at Betty Freeman's than I lost him in the crowd. Actually, what happened was that someone near the entry as we were coming in was commenting that the trouble with most twentieth-century music, especially of the twelve-tone persuasion, was that there weren't any tunes you could whistle, to which Slonimsky immediately replied "Nonsense!" Whereupon he proceeded to whistle—or, at any rate, to hum breathily—the theme from Schönberg's *Klavierstück,* Opus 33a. This performance naturally attracted an audience, and he was off and running—being Slonimsky. That gave me a chance to talk with some of the other guests, and it became obvious that Slonimsky was well known and well loved in these circles.

"He's such a delightable man," someone commented, noticing how we were both gazing over at the same man. "He hasn't lost the ability to be delighted." The speaker, a shortish expansive man who seemed to be no slouch at enthusiasm himself, proved to be Alan Rich, the critic and writer on music for *Newsweek,* who now lives in Los Angeles (just a few blocks from Slonimsky, it turned out) and is the cohost of these salons along with Betty Freeman. He began telling me about the day, some fifteen years ago, when he first met Slonimsky. "It was at Lake Placid, and we were going to be on a panel together, and as I saw him entering the room I became tongue-tied. I was terrified." Why? "I mean, if the Washington Monument were to walk into your living room, you'd regard it with a certain degree of awe, wouldn't you? And Slonimsky is a *monument* in the history of modern music. In my college days, LPs were becoming popularly available, and all you had to do was partake. I never had to go through the trial of being won over to new music—its triumph was already evident, the battle had been won. But with Nicolas, this is the man *who did it,* who wrote for *New Music,* who fought for and lobbied for and championed and suffered for new music. He's one of the heroes."

This estimation was echoed a few minutes later by Charles Amirkhanian, the composer and radio producer from Berkeley. "He was literally fifty years ahead of his time," Amirkhanian said. "I was talking to a friend the other day about the new music scene in New York City in the early fifties. You know how many new music concerts there were per year in New York City as late as, say, 1950–51? Maybe three or four, total. And twenty years before that Slonimsky was refusing to compromise: he was trying to perform new music virtually exclusively. It was heroic work, but he was undertaking it in an absolute cultural vacuum, and I guess he just recoiled: he retreated finally into lexicography. But for anyone under forty-five he's a living link to that era, to Ives and Cowell and, especially, Varèse." Amirkhanian said he had occasionally stayed overnight at Slonimsky's on his visits to Los Angeles. "He seems to enjoy having me around," he said. "He tells me, 'We're coconspirators in the distortion of music history.' I think he's profoundly lonely, at a certain level: all his contemporaries are gone. He has this strange pattern: he sleeps, he gets up, he sleeps some more, gets up again—all night long. At one point, around three in the morning, I woke up and came out of my room, and there he was, pacing in the living room, with a sheaf of papers in one hand and a pen in the other. 'I'm rewriting the Bach entry,' he told me. 'Rewriting it entirely.' And he did the same with Mozart and all the other major entries. I'm convinced that he conceived of this new edition of *Baker's* as his magnum opus, his testament, his ultimate statement."

A few minutes later, I circled back through the crowd to Slonimsky, who was engaged in a jovial colloquy with John Adams, an accomplished young composer from San Francisco. Slonimsky was catching up on Adams's latest work—completion dates, premiere dates. I could see him filing away all the details in his memory for transcription onto his cards. It struck me that Adams, who is in his boyish late thirties, was about the same age as Henry Cowell had been—for that matter, as Slonimsky himself had been—when Slonimsky was first championing new American music as a conductor. And here Slonimsky still was, every bit as aware of the newest, most contemporary manifestation of music history, every bit as open and engaged, as he had been back then. A conversation between the generations, I said to myself, observing the scene. But later on, rethinking that formulation, I realized that Slonimsky and Adams were separated by more than a single generation, by more than two—indeed, by more like three.

A few days later, the generational spread had widened to almost four. Slonimsky was about to lecture to an undergraduate music-appreciation class. He was serving a three-week stint back at UCLA, as a Regents' Lecturer, a position that involved his delivering a formal public lecture, which he'd do later that evening, and, in addition, making himself available to any regularly scheduled classes that might want to draw on his wisdom; this was to be one of those classes. There were about twenty students, ranged in rows in a wide, squat room, facing a piano, and the group looked to be about as much of a tabula rasa as any he'd confronted twenty years earlier: their teacher had presumably tried to impress upon them the world-historical significance of their visitor, but the students appeared to have escaped absolutely unscathed from the onslaught of this knowledge (Ives? Varèse? Cowell? Koussevitzky? *Baker's?*), and they just gazed up at their odd-looking guest with blank, amiable expressions. He was wearing shiny black shoes, black slacks, a black jacket, a striped shirt (open at the collar), a set of black suspenders, which framed his bulging belly quite elegantly, and, pinned to his lapel, a colorful NEW MUSIC AMERICA FESTIVAL button.

He gazed upon his audience for a moment and then shuffled over to the piano, upon the lid of which he set a narrow black satchel, which was similarly bulging. His tongue protruding just slightly from the corner of his mouth, he finger-poked out the melody of the trumpet call ordinarily used for signaling the start of a horse race: he delivered it with great brio but then climaxed on a decidedly wrong note, at which point he winced and looked up in mock confusion. He stumbled across the keyboard for a few more moments with his pointer finger, as if trying to arrive at the proper send-off, but presently he gave up and instead turned to the class. "Rousseau," he began, "as you no doubt recall, says somewhere in *Émile* . . ." He paused for a moment, gazing at the class. "Jean-Jacques Rousseau, the philosopher," he enunciated carefully, "in his book *Émile* . . ." He shrugged and continued, "Anyway, he advises, 'The student must enjoy his lesson.'" At this point, he returned to the piano, sat down on the bench, and began playing a series of bass harmonies with his left hand. "Some of you may be familiar with Chopin's 'Black Key' Étude," he said. "When I was your age, or a bit younger, studying at the conservatory, I found it a terrifically tricky piece to play until one day I noticed that you could perform the right-hand part much more effectively"—he reached into his satchel and brought out a mysterious, brightly colored spherical object—"if you played it with an *orange*." Suddenly, he launched headlong into a spirited rendition of a now entirely recognizable melody, quickly and dexterously rolling the fruit up and down the black treble keys straight through to the climax, whereupon he grasped the orange tightly and hurled it down full force on precisely the right tone-cluster. The orange bounced off the keyboard and rolled over toward one of the students. "You can have it," he said. "Music should be nourishing as well." He was already playing a new progression of chords with his left hand, these quite dramatic and foreboding, and he continued, "Now, there's a particularly pesky violin passage in Wagner's *Tannhäuser* Overture which I've always found, when attempting to negotiate the piano transcription, works much better if you play it with"—his right hand darted back into his satchel—"a *brush!*" An old shoebrush, to be exact, with which he proceeded to slap the high keys with improbable precision and to hilarious effect. "Well," he said, calming down, "you get the idea." He had at any rate got their attention: the students all suddenly seemed genuinely interested in just who this man might be who had thus so abruptly hijacked their seminar.

One kid asked Slonimsky where he came from, and he replied, "I was born a long time ago in a town which has twice changed its name in a vain attempt to exorcise the stigma of its having been my birthplace. I'll let you figure it out." He then improvised a set of similar riddles regarding his exact age, generalizing from these to a consideration of the average ages of all sorts of categories of musicians. "As a lexicographer, you find yourself wondering about such things," he explained. "It helps keep you awake. Anyway, I have determined that, statistically speaking, for some reason organists live the longest. Scholars and pedagogues come next; then conductors, who tend to be pretty durable. Among instrumentalists, don't ask me why, but those handling the bigger instruments, like double-bassists and trombonists, tend to outlive your average violinist, who, in turn, outlasts the average flutist or oboist, who are apt to be of frail physique. Among singers, on average, tenors burn out faster than bass singers. And in all categories mediocrities outlive the great artists by a vast margin."

The kids were making wild guesses about his birthplace, so he decided to give them a nice, fat clue, saying that it was somewhere in Russia. This got him talking about serf orchestras. "Serf orchestras," he said. "That's s-e-r-f. Nothing to do with California—not the Beach Boys. These were the traditional folk orchestras formed by the Russian peasants during the czarist times, when they were living like slaves. Now, these serfs were generally illiterate and they certainly couldn't read music, so each player in the serf orchestra was assigned a different unique note, which he then had to play eternally—or, I mean, whenever he was performing in the orchestra. For example, you could be condemned to be E-flat or G-sharp forever—just that note, whenever it came up in the melody. Once, when I was researching something else in some stacks of old Russian journals, I came upon a note which read, 'Reward: F-sharp and A-flat, escaped from the orchestra. F-sharp is a tall fellow, bald, big blue eyes; A-flat is shorter, rounder, dark hair.' But this may be why Stravinsky was so fond of melodies with just four or five notes—that is what you always ended up with as the serf orchestras became depleted. In fact, if you want to compose a Russian folk song, the recipe is simple. Take any five notes in a scale and repeat them at random." He went over to the piano and, remaining standing, demonstrated the method, building out from his improvisation with limpid clarity. "Suppose," he continued, "you want to compose a spontaneous French impressionist *chanson*—say, some Debussy." He was suddenly crooning away, accompanying himself with a progression of swelling chords, "*Viens ici, je t'attends, je t'aime*... It's simple, you limit yourself to six notes from two mutually exclusive major triads. See?" He played the notes one at a time. "You can compose an entire opera like this." He was singing again, his back arched, baying at an imaginary moon. "*Le soleil de minuit, sur la mer Méditerranée*... Admittedly, a geographically impossible opera. Or, if you try the reverse—two mutually exclusive *minor* triads—what you get is one of those dark, ponderous, lugubrious German arias: *Das Licht . . . die Nacht . . .*"

One of the kids asked him about South American music, and this set him to reminiscing about his travels through Latin America back in the forties. Presently, he was talking about the Brazilian master Heitor Villa-Lobos: "Now, there was a composer who was larger than life. Tall tales seemed to aggregate around his persona. There was one about a trip he took into the jungle—he was always venturing into the jungle to stalk authentic indigenous melodies—and about how he was captured by cannibals. Now, Villa-Lobos was quite portly and very interesting from the cannibal standpoint. But somehow he persuaded them to let him play his cello—in this story, he was traipsing around the jungle with a cello—and he did convince them, they let him, after which they all fell down before him, worshipping him as their new god. And that's *just the beginning* of the story. Well, subsequently I asked Villa-Lobos about that particular tale, and he denied it, but with Villa-Lobos you never could tell. He was a wonderful composer. I really should play you some Villa-Lobos. Let's see." He pulled up the piano bench and sat down. "This is his 'Alma Brasileira.' I hope I can remember it. I haven't played it in over twenty years." He could have fooled us: he tore into the piece with astonishing vigor, negotiating the intricate rhythmic patterns with absolute authority. When he finished the room was still.

He simply rushed to fill the stillness with more stories. From Villa-Lobos to Gershwin (how most pianists get "I Got Rhythm" all wrong: "It's not I got-one-two-rhy-thm, it's supposed to be I-one-got-one-rhy-one-thm, completely even; I asked Gershwin about this one day and he agreed that it's always being misinterpreted") to Schönberg (his triskaidekaphobia) and on to Bach and then Rossini. "*You* are an endangered species," he informed the students, "because I could go on forever."

One of the kids asked him who was the greatest living composer.

"Hmm." He paused, momentarily stymied. "Hmm. I take the Fifth Amendment on that. They're all my friends."

At length, his talk did in fact conclude, after which he was surrounded by the departing students. ("What did you say your name was
again?" "Was it Vladivostok?") But as we walked back toward the car I
returned to Villa-Lobos. "Were you serious?" I asked. "Have you really
not played that piece in twenty years?"

"Well," he admitted sheepishly, "actually, I was cheating there a
little bit. It just happens I was thinking about that piece this morning,
and I rehearsed it in my head in the shower."

"In the shower?"

"Well, you know, the fingering."

Quite a vision. I asked him what it was he was remembering when
he remembered a piece like that. Was it the sound of the music or the
sight of the printed page?

"Neither," he replied. "I remember the structure."

The site of the public lecture that evening was a bit more formal—the
main auditorium of UCLA's Schoenberg Hall. And Slonimsky appeared
a bit more formal himself: he had donned a tie and a gray sweater-vest
under his black jacket, and he had slicked his hair down. A nice crowd
had turned out, and Slonimsky addressed it from a raised stage, all
miked-up and bathed in bright arc lights.

He performed a medley of feats at the piano. Some I'd already witnessed, earlier in the day at the undergraduate class or else in the
weeks before that at his home, but there were a remarkable number of
fresh ones: his inventory seems limitless. For example, while talking
about his ability to split his brain in half so that his right hand could
conduct at one tempo and his left at another—an ability that proved
terrifically useful in his conducting of modernist works—he averred
that he could also do this when playing scales. He went over to the
piano and announced that he would now play a continuous C-major
scale with his left hand in 4/8 time, like this, while simultaneously
playing an E-major scale in his right hand in 5/8 time, like this. He rat-
tled off some quick mathematical calculations and told us that he'd

start here, at these two low notes, and that if he was going to get it right we should expect his two hands to reach these two high notes, these ones here, simultaneously, and that then he'd take the scales down again. And that is precisely what he proceeded to do, effortlessly.

And he told wonderful stories—of lexicographical detection, of the vanity of geniuses, and of the wisdom of babes. But something strange was going on. The words were right, the ideas, but his timing was off— his *presence* was off. He looked haggard, mildly disoriented. He seemed to be merely going through the motions and not to be connecting. For the first time since I'd started following him around, he suddenly struck me as an old man. "Well, what do you expect?" I found myself asking myself. "He's ninety-two years old." And I'd never thought a thing like that in his presence before.

At length, the evening ended, and I went backstage to join him. Magic: suddenly everything had changed back. He was surrounded by his fans, holding court, once again in the pink of good humor. After a while, he came over to me and said. "The lights! They were right in my eyes. It was terrible. I couldn't see anybody out there. I couldn't gauge anyone's reactions." And it occurred to me at that moment that it is precisely—and almost exclusively—Slonimsky's sense of fellow feeling, of being a living part of a live discourse, of offering himself *and getting a response,* all the inspired bluff and bluster, that accounts for his un- canny youthfulness. Pith him of that—put him out there on the stage alone—and the grace bleeds away: he's left with his haunting demons, his myriad senses of failure. He counts on people.

I drove Slonimsky home. "I just heard from Virgil Thomson, in New York," he told me. "Electra was having dinner with him, and he asked after my health, and she replied archly, 'Physically, he's all right.'" He laughed fondly. "Ah, well," he said, repeating his slogan, "I may not be endurable but I am durable." He paused. "I was thinking about it today. Do you realize that if Mozart had lived to be as old as me, he could have been Chopin's buddy and the mentor of the young Wagner?" It was a remarkable assertion: not many people capable of making such a statement are still capable of framing it. It was strange, too, to realize that the entire expanse of music history between Mozart and Wagner consisted of barely one century; and conversely, it was startling to be reminded that this man sitting next to me was almost a century old.

We pulled up to the curb by his house. "At least, I'm still ambulatory," he said. "And, for all its odd folds, Electra's estimation notwithstanding, my brain still does function. Every morning, when I wake up I lie there staring at the ceiling, and I give myself a little test. I ask myself, 'In what city was Miaskovsky's Thirteenth Symphony premiered?' *Because it's a trick question!* You'd think, of course, that it was Moscow. But it wasn't—it was Winterthur, Switzerland. And if I can get that right I know that I haven't gone senile during the night, that everything's okay, and so I get up and go feed Grody."

Postscript (1998)

Almost a decade later, as spry as ever, Nicolas had revised his actuarial calculations. "Had Schubert lived to be as old as me," he'd inform visitors with extravagant nonchalance, "he could have been *my* nanny."

And indeed, Slonimsky, loyally flanked by Grody the entire while, eventually survived well into his one-hundred-and-second year—as productive, too, as ever, almost to the very end (he produced seven books across his nineties, including entirely new editions of both *Baker's* and *Music Since 1900*).

For his ninety-ninth birthday, his former and current odalisques contrived a surprise mass sleep-over—all of them clad in prim, proper nightgowns—complete with a late-night house call by a striptease nurse. (As the festivities waned and Nicolas doddered off to his bedroom, he advised his charges that none of them had better attempt to follow him there. "Even in my advanced years," he warned them sternly, "I could still sire a child." "In your dreams, Nicolas," they replied in fond unison, "in your dreams.")

Of course, Nicolas survived virtually all his contemporaries, and in fact outlasted most of those a generation or two younger than himself whose lives he'd chronicled in *Baker's*. For the most part he retained a steady equanimity over this state of affairs, though he took one death particularly hard, that of his great pal and fellow avant-gardist-at-arms, Frank Zappa, at age fifty-two, in late 1993.

Not long thereafter, around the time of his one-hundred-and-first birthday, Nicolas began suffering a series of mini-strokes—almost, it seemed, a new one with every fresh beat of his heart—and over a period of months it was as if his uncanny lucidity fled him entirely. He would jabber on and on about The War, and when asked which one, he'd reply, self-evidently, "Why, the Finnish War, of course." (Some wondered whether he hadn't retained his antic taste for puns to the very, very end.)

One visitor commented how, "It was as if he'd completely lost any sense of himself. The only thing that survived, entirely unscathed, was his vanity. He was enormously pleased with himself. He had no idea who he was; he just knew he was Hot Stuff." I tried this characterization out on a neurologist friend of mine, who noted how "That just goes to show how the seat of vanity in the brain, as it were, exists entirely distinct from that which the person may be vain *about*. Or anyway, the sense of self that precedes and grounds and propels a lifetime's achievement can manage to survive well beyond the far side of all that achievement."

I mentioned these comments the other day to Dina Klemm Ormenyi, one of Nicolas's final and fondest odalisques, and she demurred slightly. "It's not that he didn't know who he was exactly," she explained. "He might not have known who *you* were, but he knew who he was. And that's the really strange part, because it wasn't really vanity one saw in him there at the end so much as contentment—in Nicolas, of all people! And maybe for the first time in his life. I know it's hard to believe, but Nicolas Slonimsky died entirely serene."

Nicolas Slonimsky closed his own *Baker's* parenthesis on Christmas Day, 1995.

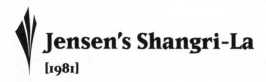

Jensen's Shangri-La
[1981]

From its name—the Louisiana Museum—I was half expecting some bayou vista. The view from the window of the director's office, however, was of a broad green lawn girdled by a profusion of tall, dense trees; a smattering of modern sculpture; a dip about two hundred yards off, where the plateau gave way to bluff, then sea strait—a band of blue—and, off in the distance, about seven miles across the calm water, Sweden.

The Louisiana Museum, that is, in Humlebaek, Denmark.

"There, all right," said Knud Jensen, the museum's founder and director, as he speared a memo from his desk, folded it neatly, threw it away, then reached back into the wastebasket, retrieved the folded page, and left it on top of a pile of similarly reprieved documents. "Okay, let's see. Is that everything? I think so. Well, there's always something, but I think . . . No, wait." Looking up at me, he smiled at his own mild confusion. "People accuse me of being a perfectionist, but I'm not. On the contrary, I know what perfection should be, so I realize each evening how far short I've once again fallen. By now, I'm miles and miles behind!"

Speaking about Jensen with museum people and artists in the United States and Europe, as I was preparing for my visit, I'd heard him described, variously, as an elf, a pixie, Ariel, a leprechaun, "the kindest man in the museum world," and King Puck. Danes are almost always described this way; people tend to have Hans Christian Andersen on the brain when it comes to Danes. Or Victor Borge. But it was true: the short, brisk, white-haired man who came circling round from behind his desk to greet me seemed wholly unconnected to any Viking ancestors. "Ah, yes," he said, chuckling, when I offered the observation. "We Danes do have a hard time squaring our current lives with our supposedly fierce Viking heritage. Our history classes at school are somewhat demoralizing: we start out very big and important, the scourge of the world, and then it's just one defeat and dismemberment after another."

He started to guide me out of the office, stopped, excused himself, went back to his desk, riffled through several piles of papers, passed a hand over a bookshelf, sighed, gave up on whatever the project had been, and returned to the door, muttering something about tomorrow. Jensen, I came to realize during the ensuing week, perpetually projects an aura of benign befuddlement—he seems to be moving in a cloud of good-natured confusion—but he is *not* confused. He may be thinking about a lot of things at once; he may even enjoy the pose of innocuous disorientation; but he's a masterly organizer. From that diffuse cloud dart startlingly succinct aphorisms and hard-edged decisions. He may not be a Viking, but during the past twenty-five years he has amassed one of the loveliest and best-loved treasure hordes of modern art in Europe.

"Well," he said as we left his office and descended the single flight of stairs into what had once been the vestibule of a Victorian-era manor house and now constitutes the entry hall at Louisiana. "Where do you want me to start?" I suggested that the museum's name might be a good place.

"Ah, yes," Jensen agreed. "People do have trouble with that. Actually, we had nothing to do with naming it Louisiana. The name came with the estate. This house was built by the estate's founder, one Alexander Brun, during the 1850s. He was a comfortable landed gentryman, with a strange fixation: over the years, he wed a succession of three wives, each of whom was named Louise. Somewhere in there he founded the estate, and named it after one or all of them."

As Jensen was speaking, we'd walked around to a porch, which opened out onto the lawn I'd observed from his office window. The trees were even more magnificent from ground level: a blue-green cedar, a flowering magnolia, a tall, distinguished pine, a wide, low cotoneaster, a gorgeous ginkgo, and—perhaps most awesome—a tremendous blood beech, breathing like some deep burgundy giant in the springtime breeze. "The grove is very much Mr. Brun's legacy," Jensen explained. "He was the president of some sort of Danish beekeepers' and fruit-tree-growers' association, so he planted all sorts of exotic and remarkable trees during his time here. Owing to one of the perpetuation clauses in the deed to this property, Louisiana is, I think I can safely say, the only museum in the world where presentation of an entrance ticket entitles the bearer to the cutting of his or her choice."

From the vantage of the porch one could see another special feature of Louisiana: an unparalleled sense of the human provenance of art. People milled in the late-afternoon sun, sat on picnic blankets, slept on the lawn, or cuddled in the shade, more like neighbors than visitors. There was a great sense of relaxation, of familiarity—none of the stiff propriety, the soreness at the back of the knee and the base of the spine that I usually associate with museum-going. As we sat for a few moments on the porch steps, Jensen said, "I have noticed that you can classify the world's museums by their metaphorical images of themselves. Some—the Tate, the Museum of Modern Art—seem like arsenals, tremendously imposing and exhaustive in their thoroughness. Others seem like cemeteries, an endless array of tombstones; some museums are almost self-consciously mausoleums, devoted to the eternal flame of an individual artist—a Rodin, for instance, or a Vasarely. I've always thought of the Guggenheim as a temple and the Centre Pompidou, in Paris, as a forum, in the ancient sense, or else a circus fair. At Louisiana, we've tried to create a refuge, a sanctuary, a sort of Shangri-la." I suggested the image of a deer park. "No, no." Jensen objected. "Or at any rate, in the deer parks I know of, animals are penned in—they've become docile and domesticated. We've tried to preserve the wild and slightly dangerous element in art."

Although there are dozens of sculptures scattered through the grounds of Louisiana, only three bronzes are visible on the part of the wide lawn seen from the main porch. In the foreground rests a small, sensuously smooth and lyrical abstract concretion by Jean Arp. In the middle distance, slightly larger than life-size, stands a squat figurative maiden by Henri Laurens. And at the edge of the bluff, magnificently framed against the dapple of sea and sky, looms one of Henry Moore's huge abstract reclining figures. From the porch, thanks to the play of the perspective, the three bronzes seem the same size, occupy the same amount of visual field. The tiny Arp, at any rate, holds its own and establishes a confluence of form and presence with the massive Moore—a dialogue seemingly mediated by the quiet, gentle Laurens. Their placement evokes a myriad of triangulations—the interrelationship, for instance, of pieces that are abstract, figurative, and abstractly figurative. "It's strange—this whole wide lawn, and all it can take is three pieces," Jensen observed. "I've noticed that when you create a human enclosure, a walled-in square or rectangle, you can put in five, seven, ten pieces of sculpture. It's as if the pieces were slightly tamed by the cage. But against a natural backdrop you can seldom have more than three, no matter how large the space. You know the work of Konrad Lorenz, the great ethologist—his writings on animal behavior and territoriality. That is why the sculptures at Louisiana are spaced as they are: Lorenz has shown that all living things stake out their natural territory, require their breathing space. Sculptures, like all great art, are, of course, living things. I once tried to move another piece onto the lawn here, but the others got very angry; they withheld their lustre as if in resentment. Anyway, three is the ideal number. We have three Moores, three Calders, three Ernsts, three Arps, three Kienholzes. In fairy tales, as we all know, one is lonesome, two is sterile, but three—ah, three is fertile, the number of possibility. Thesis, antithesis, synthesis. Flaubert once wrote that it takes three particular details, when describing any fresh new scene, to establish its substantial reality in the reader's mind, to give it a sense of lived-in three-dimensionality. Freud, too, has many things to say about three."

We got up from the porch and took a little walk along the edge of the lawn and then into the encircling grove. The corridors of the museum, as they span out northward from the manor house, are virtually invisible, completely absorbed into the surrounding nature. Occasionally, one catches glimpses of visitors walking through low glass passages from one exhibition hall to the next. Outdoors, there's a fresh surprise every few feet. "The children call those the 'Muppet Show,'" Jensen said as we happened upon a view of three whimsical Max Ernst beasts—a turtle, a bird, and some other sort of thing. "And here's an army of little stone creatures by my Danish friend Henry Heerup." They looked as if they were marching in from the sea—petrified Viking dwarfs.

"I've always had a love of journeys," Jensen said, thrusting his way through a jungle of ferns toward a sudden clearing—the terrace of a cafeteria, upon which were straddling three medium-sized Calder stabiles. "I am fascinated by the sense of around-the-bend—the expectation, the anticipation of a voyage. That's always been a key element in our planning at Louisiana—lots of around-the-bend." The Calders, two black flanking one bright red, revealed an unexpected maritime aspect: they were cast like proud sails against the sea. Some children chased a blue-yellow-and-white mobile that circled gently, high atop the red metal mast of the center stabile. We ambled back toward the lawn and emerged near the Laurens. Small children love the Laurens; they relate, perhaps, to her short, stubby legs, her low waist, the soft tumble of her half-enveloping blanket. They try to shinny up the knee to grab an arm. Or else they sit beside her, nuzzling her sun-warmed calves. She's like a very nice baby-sitter, and picnicking parents leave their kids to her. The Moore, meanwhile, attracts a slightly older crowd. Eight-year-olds understand Moore; they recognize a giant lap, and they climb aboard to perch. As we walked by, I noticed one boy curled inside a hollow, intently reading Tolkien, not the least bit distracted by a frisky band of seven-year-olds burrowing follow-the-leader through the holes and over the promontories at the other end of the platform. Jensen looked on, beaming, well-established smile lines spreading out from his eyes, his white hair blown back by the breeze. "I suppose I should worry a little bit about the wear and tear," he remarked. "But even Moore says it's good there's at least one place where the children can provide a natural polish."

"Knud, at age sixty-five, retains the wonder and exuberance he must have had when he was five or six," says one of his associates at the museum. "Nothing is ever routine. About everything, there is an almost childlike enthusiasm. He wears all the rest of us clean out."

Knud Jensen was born in 1916, in Copenhagen. His mother, Christiane, was thirty-seven at the time, and there were already two daughters, aged ten and twelve. His father, Jens Peter Jensen, was forty-six and had long since given up hoping for a son, to whom he could leave his cheese-exporting business. "It was like being an only child, only more so," Jensen recalls. "People sometimes describe me as impatient, overeager, headstrong. I think this has something to do with how spoiled I was. I had not one but three doting mothers; my sisters—who, by the way, were both out of the house by the time I was ten—used to compete with each other at indulging me."

Jensen regales his companions with memories of Copenhagen during the twenties—his sisters' flapper friends, his own long discussions with the family chauffeur, the summers in the family villa, about fifteen miles north of Copenhagen, and not far from where Louisiana stands. He attended public schools, "along with children of all classes," and almost from the start he reveled in literature. During his adolescence, his favorite authors were Poe and Rabelais; earlier, he'd steeped himself in the faerie world of his countryman Hans Christian Andersen. His father, an autodidact who'd had to suspend his own schooling at age fifteen, when *his* father died, had built up an extraordinary library of valuable and cherished old books. "It was not a collection gathered by the meter but, rather, the library of a life," Jensen recalls, lapsing into bittersweet nostalgia as he leafs through a catalogue he once had prepared—first editions of Andersen, Kierkegaard, Poe, Rabelais, and Goethe, among others. "Many years after my father died, once I'd started the museum, I decided to sell the library. Sitting through that auction was a tremendously masochistic experience, because I loved the books. But it was no doubt better that they nourish other people's collections. And the proceeds helped cover some of our construction costs. The books became bricks—meters and meters of bricks."

Jensen had begun showing a head for business by the time he entered college, and between 1936 and 1938 his father sent him abroad to Germany, France, Belgium, England, and Switzerland, partly to deepen his comprehension of the languages he would be needing once he'd joined the family firm. Languages came easily, but while he was learning them he developed an increasingly consuming passion for literature and, soon, the visual arts. At the University of Lausanne, he composed a senior thesis entitled *Les Influences des Arts Primitifs sur l'Art Moderne.* In the introduction to the essay, he quoted a sentence from Gide: *"L'influence ne crée rien, elle éveille—la puissance d'une influence vient de ce qu'elle n'a fait que de me révéler quelque partie de moi encore inconnue à moi-même."* (Influence creates nothing: it awakens. The power of an influence comes from the fact that it has only revealed to me some part of myself that was still unknown to me.) The choice of quotation was doubly autobiographical, in that it described both Jensen's situation at the time and the aspirations he came to embrace as his vocation. Jensen returned to Denmark early in 1939 and informed his father that he would not be going into the family business after all but, instead, wished to pursue some sort of career in the humanities. "My father was disappointed, a little doubtful, but generally supportive," Jensen recalls. "The funny thing was that after about three months I began to miss the excitment and tangibility of commerce. And I went back to him and asked to return to the firm."

Soon thereafter, Hitler invaded Norway and Denmark. From the outset, the Danes acquitted themselves with remarkable valor and honor, rescuing, for example, most of their Jewish population. (The small harbor town of Humlebaek, facing neutral Sweden at a narrow point along the Øresund strait, was one of the principal launching points for midnight smuggling operations.) Jensen plays down his own contributions to the Resistance; as the only son of an old and ailing father, he says, he had to be careful. Others tell stories of how the Jensens gave Resistance fighters innocuous work in their company's warehouses, allowing the buildings to be used as hideouts. When Jensen *père* died, in 1944, Jensen *fils* was only twenty-seven; nevertheless, he took over the business. Hans Erik Wallin, a former advertising executive who is a longtime friend of Knud's and is now his colleague at Louisiana, recalls meeting him on the street soon afterward: "Knud was quite agitated. Several of the other cheese exporters, the veterans, considered him something of an upstart and were trying to maneuver him out of the cheese-exporters' association. But Knud insisted he wasn't going to allow that to happen—'If you do something, you do it right,' he said—and within a few years he had become, like his father before him, president of the association."

"I very much enjoyed the business," Jensen told me one evening as I sipped coffee with him and his wife, Vivi, around the kitchen table, following a delicious dinner at their home, about a mile from Louisiana. "I loved the morning drives out to the country, the conversations with the farmers, the stimulation of commerce. During the first few years after the war, Denmark, which had emerged relatively undamaged, was very much the farm for all of Europe, so the work was important and the business good. But I was really living a sort of double life." Jensen had all the while maintained his literary interests. He spent most of his free hours in the company of Copenhagen's bohemian community, such as it was—writers and painters and poets who whiled evening into night scanning Rilke and Baudelaire, Eliot, Auden, and Isherwood. "I loved being with writers, even though I was no writer myself," Jensen recalls. "I was the one they sent for beer." The parties would drift from tavern to tavern and eventually back to Jensen's modest, three-room downtown apartment. "At a certain point, I would have to retire to the bedroom, leaving them to their disputations. The next morning, when I got up for work at six-thirty, I'd find them sprawled all about the apartment, draped in curtains they'd taken down for blankets."

"Yes," Mrs. Jensen puts in, smiling, as she pours fresh coffee. "I was one of those underneath the curtains." Jensen had first seen Vivi Arndal during the war, sitting at a restaurant table with two friends, while he was on a date with another woman. Vivi must have been a stunner; she still is. Vaulting over the intervening difficulties—her escorts, his companion—he called out to her, lobbed a few one-liners. Nothing quite took. "Several months later, however," Jensen recalls, "I was on the top deck of a ferry, and next to me was standing a woman all bundled in a hood. I used the old 'Don't I know you from somewhere?' approach, but once I'd got her down to the ferry bar and she'd lowered her hood, I had to gasp, 'Gosh, I do! I do know you!' This was Vivi."

The first months after the liberation, in May 1945, were a heady period. Jensen would procure gasoline on the black market and spirit Vivi off to the country. Vivi, a schoolteacher with a special interest in psychology (she subsequently compiled Rorschach inkblot interpretations from many of the greatest artists of our time, though she guards this collection with absolute discretion), quickly became part of his bohemian circle, and slept in his curtains. In 1946, Jensen traveled to the United States on business for several months, leaving her behind. He established contact with Kraft and Swift and other American corporations, which had by then begun to expand their European operations.

Returning to Denmark, Jensen went straight to a travel agent, bought two tickets to the Faroe Islands (the home, about three hundred miles off Iceland, of Vivi's maternal relatives), and then called on Vivi to propose marriage. Everything blew up in his face. Vivi laughs about it today. "I didn't like his attitude," she says. "He bought the honeymoon tickets before he'd even proposed. He was too sure of himself." The fact is that while Jensen was away Vivi had fallen in love with another member of the circle, a painter. A few months after she rejected Jensen's offer, she married the painter; presently, Jensen also married someone else. Both marriages lasted less than three years, but it took almost a decade for Jensen and Vivi to get it right. Jensen has yet to visit the Faroe Islands, although he talks about them with a passion he ordinarily reserves for the work of Henry Moore.

His business, meanwhile, was undergoing a phenomenal expansion. Within a few years, he had guided it through a fivefold increase in sales and personnel. And the other side of his double life was blossoming simultaneously. In 1945, he and a friend, Ole Wivel, founded a small publishing house, specializing in contemporary literature. Three years later, Jensen helped to finance the launching of *Heretica,* which became one of the most important Danish literary magazines. Then, in 1952, he acquired the controlling interest in Gyldendal, Denmark's oldest and most distinguished publishing house—it was founded in 1770—which had been on the verge of falling into the hands of foreign speculators. "Jensen is the ideal owner to work for," one of Gyldendal's senior editors told me one day, when I stopped in at the Copenhagen headquarters of the firm. "There's no expectation that the company will make money. We are not criticized if we do things that fail, as long as they have quality. For that matter, Jensen hardly ever interferes with the running of the house at all. The thing with the supermarkets last week was quite the exception."

A few days later, I asked Jensen about the supermarkets. "Our salespeople were trying to persuade us to start marketing our books on racks in supermarkets, which is something that is beginning to be popular here," he explained. "All the figures support the idea, but I had to veto it. It was a question of morale. I felt that it would hurt the feelings of the book dealers, and we shouldn't hurt their feelings, because they support us and work very hard."

By the early fifties, Knud Jensen was well established in Copenhagen as a business and civic leader. He would not, however, have merited a place on anybody's list of major European art collectors—or even, for that matter, of significant Danish collectors. To his three-room apartment he brought a taste for uncluttered walls; he owned a single Picasso drawing and one Munch print. He lacked, in his words, "the collector's mania, the need to possess." But with his acquisition of Gyldendal and the completion, later the same year, of a large cheese factory and warehouse, he suddenly found himself with a lot of empty walls. "It was like a dam bursting," he recalls. "I suddenly began acquiring all kinds of things for all those new empty spaces." Not satisfied with his own new walls, he soon forged an association of forty Copenhagen companies to carry out an ambitious program called Art in the Workplace. The companies began pooling resources, buying artworks from young Danish artists, and circulating the pieces in traveling shows. "This program wasn't for the offices of management," Jensen explains. "We figured that managers could fend for themselves. Rather, these shows visited workers' canteens and rest areas. The art ran the gamut from traditional to modern Danish style. Some of it was quite difficult, and sometimes the workers complained. I remember one fellow who stared at a painting a long time and then got up and walked away, muttering in disgust, 'At least, it should have a gold frame or something around it.' We didn't condescend and we didn't bend, and there was some resistance. But the moment a show had moved on and the walls were again empty, the workers would demand, almost in unison, 'Where's *our* art?'"

Through *Heretica*, Gyldendal, and Art in the Workplace, Jensen was beginning to build a reputation as something of a cultural power in Copenhagen. One afternoon, a journalist invited him to appear on a radio interview show to discuss the situation of the Danish Royal Museum of Fine Arts. The museum's longtime director—a man who loved Matisse and loathed Picasso, and, for that matter, anything more adventuresome than Fauvism—had recently resigned, and the future direction of the museum had become a matter for public debate. "I hadn't particularly thought about the Royal Museum in some time,"

Jensen recalls. "I guess I just took it for granted. But prior to the interview I went over to take a look. And I was dumbfounded. It was a true horror, very much the nineteenth-century bourgeoisie's exaggerated view of its own importance, manifested in the transcendent value of the art it prized. It was a real art temple—huge, fat columns, a broad, forbidding marble staircase, rows and rows of plaster busts, dark alcoves. During the interview, I therefore started criticizing the museum, saying that it was a relic and had nothing to do with the art of our time. 'So what do you propose?' the journalist demanded. Well—just improvising—I suggested that they ought to move out into the museum's large park, get a good architect, build a low pavilion, with not-too-high ceilings and good lighting, and move all the modern stuff out there. The main thing was to make it inviting, so that all the people who walked through the park—the young mothers, the maids with their perambulators, the old pensioners—would have an oasis in the park. Well, parks are sacred in Copenhagen. Even though the city has dozens of parks, and some of them are ugly, and some have too-tall trees and too-shady groves—idyllic but also unsafe—they don't let you touch a single tree. People told me I was crazy: 'How can you violate the green areas of our town?' It was nuts. But I got fascinated by the idea. I thought, Damn it, maybe I could do it myself."

At first, Jensen merely played with the notion, in moments of idle speculation, but increasingly it began to play with him. He was becoming possessed. He began thinking about where such a museum could be placed. There were already twenty museums in downtown Copenhagen—historical, geological, military, civic, and so forth. Jensen noticed that people seldom visited those museums during the workweek, and that on weekends they did everything possible to get out of town altogether. Private cars were becoming more popular, and Danes loved to take single-day excursions, to places like "Hamlet's castle," in Helsingør. Jensen began to think of his dream museum as the terminus of such an excursion. He had in the meantime moved out of town and up the coast about twenty miles. A single man once again, following the dissolution of his first marriage, he was now living in a comfortable house on the outskirts of Humlebaek, a quiet town not far from the summer haunts of his childhood. And he began poking about. At one point, for instance, he visited the novelist Isak Dinesen (he was her publisher), who lived nearby on a small, wooded estate, and tried to interest her with visions of a museum of modern art. "Oh, is there a modern art?" she asked, and he dropped the subject.

"One afternoon in 1955," Jensen recalls, "my dog and I were taking a stroll about a mile up the coast, when we came upon an old, deserted estate . . . a poetical, enchanted wilderness." Jensen and his dog had ventured into Louisiana.

"In some ways, it was even more beautiful than it is today," Jensen told me one afternoon as we walked through the grounds. "The tennis lawn had become a jungle. There were broken-down hothouses, splintered stables. The walls around the rose garden—over there, where we now have the cafeteria—were crumbling, and the garden itself had become a thicket. It was a tremendous, wonderful mess, and I knew I had to have it." Easier said than done. Louisiana, which was in probate, had already been spoken for, by the town of Humlebaek itself. "And they had already drawn up elaborate plans for the estate," Jensen says. "They had in mind three principal uses—as a senior citizens' home, a graveyard, and a sewerage plant: a macabre combination that I somehow couldn't envision."

During the next several months, Jensen worked feverishly to transplant the three proposed projects to other sites. The pensioners' home was fairly easy, the sewerage plant a bit trickier, and the graveyard positively fiendish. "I had so many teas and cakes with the pastor of the neighboring church and his committee, trying to persuade them to expand their little graveyard in some other direction, that at last I was almost a candidate for the cemetery myself." But by year's end the encumbrances were cleared away, and he was able to buy Louisiana, for approximately thirty-five thousand dollars. At that point, Jensen was overextended. His money was tied up in the cheese business and the publishing house; the purchase of the estate had been something of a stretch. So he cleaned out the main building, installed a number of Danish paintings, some Greek and pre-Columbian bric-a-brac, a few chairs and benches, and hid the key under the doormat—and for a while the Louisiana existed as a word-of-mouth museum. If you happened to hear about it, you were welcome to go out there and let yourself in. There were occasional concerts—evenings of Carl Nielsen chamber music and the like. But Jensen had no real vision of what he wanted to do with Louisiana, and that was just as well, since he didn't have the funds, anyway.

Then, one day in 1956, some American executives from the Kraft Foods Company came to town with a proposal, which was very much like an ultimatum. For almost a decade, Jensen had been selling about 25 percent of his cheese to Kraft. According to Jensen, the executives now offered to buy him out completely; they tendered a good price and suggested to him that if he failed to accept they would not only withdraw their quarter of his business but also could make it difficult for him to find buyers for any of the rest of his cheese. Jensen considered the offer for about two seconds and then accepted. Within a few weeks, his holdings were reduced to approximately a million dollars in cash; controlling interest in a publishing house; title to a dilapidated nineteenth-century estate; and full ownership of a company that produced powdered milk—the one element of his dairy business for which Kraft had no use. He pooled a part of his holdings in a nonprofit Louisiana Foundation; from that point forward, all interest and all profits would go to the museum. "People sometimes imagine Knud to be a phenomenally wealthy patron," one of his friends observed recently. "They figure he'd have to be in a class with the Rockefellers or Norton Simon to pull off the kind of thing Louisiana has become. Well, he's not. He probably could have been, if he'd taken that money in 1956 and begun speculating with it—he's got a good business head. But he didn't. Instead he poured it into the foundation. And now, although he lives a comfortable life, he in no way commands the kind of fortune that his accomplishments would lead you to expect."

"That milk-powder company!" Jensen exclaimed one day. "It turned out to be a gold mine. I had a feeling it might, which is why I kept it, but I had no idea. For years, Louisiana was kept afloat on a sea—or, rather, dunes—of powdered milk. Our manager there proved an extremely gifted leader. Basically, he was running an exporting business. But recently the farmers began to get tired of dealing through a middleman. 'Why should we be subsidizing an art museum?' they wondered. And they had a valid point. I'm surprised they didn't make it earlier. So, anyway, last year we sold it to them, and now Louisiana runs largely on whatever interest we can extract from the proceeds of that sale."

"I'm not sure whether the Kraft deal had come through yet," Vilhelm Wohlert, a thin, somewhat tense, and yet genial architect of sixty or so told me one afternoon, in his Copenhagen office. "I just remember the phone call, and then Knud arriving in his chauffeur-driven Mercedes. He jumped out of the car, wonderfully enthusiastic, transferred to my little *deux-chevaux,* and proceeded to talk all through the drive out. In the rearview mirror I could see his chauffeur in the Mercedes trailing us the whole way. When we arrived at the estate, Knud showed me around the grounds—it was really a jungle—and I suggested that it might be a good idea to bring Jørgen along on the project.

"*Ja,*" said Jørgen Bo, Wohlert's plump, jolly, and extremely expansive colleague. "And I remember your first call. 'Listen, Jørgen,' you said. 'Don't get excited. This is going to be a small, humble job. We're just going to remodel a few stables.'"

Soon thereafter, Jensen's ambitions began to soar. He spent many hours with the young architects, talking about museums and congeniality. At one point, he invited the two of them to spend a few weeks with him on an architectural excursion through Italy and Switzerland.

Upon their return, he put them up in Louisiana's manor house and had them live there for a month. Every few days, he'd come out and join them for a tramp through the underbrush. "I remember a line from a Danish hymn I used to recite as we forged our way through that wilderness," Jensen said one day. " *'Oh, vidundertro du slår over dybet din gyngende bor'*—'O miracle faith, you throw over the abyss your shaky bridge.' After the Kraft sale, when I had some funds to spend, our shaky bridge began to seem a bit more stable. It was now possible to think in terms of some sort of expansion of the manor house. I generally left it up to the two of them to come up with a plan. I had only three conditions. First, the old house had to be preserved as the entrance. No matter how elaborate the museum might become in later years, I knew I'd always want the visitors to arrive through that modest, nonthreatening nineteenth-century entrance hall, to feel as if they were perhaps just coming to visit a stodgy, comfortable, slightly eccentric country uncle. Second, I wanted one room—where the Giacomettis are now—to open out onto that view, about two hundred meters to the north of the manor, overlooking our lush inland lake. Third, about another hundred meters farther on, in the rose garden—on the bluff overlooking the strait and, in the distance, Sweden—I wanted to have the cafeteria and its terrace. The problem was that we didn't have enough money to go all the way down with buildings. We were going to have to have long glass corridors connecting the various exhibition spaces, and I was afraid that these might get boring. 'No,' I remember them assuring me, 'the corridors will establish the character of the whole place.' There was one other principle I tried to emphasize, and that was that there always be a way out. Have you noticed how in museums that feel like labyrinths part of your mind is always stuck on hypothesizing a means of escape? This can be very distracting, and a terribly fatiguing claustrophobia can set in. At Louisiana, I felt that escape should always be just a few walls away. Also, the views of the woods and the lawn seeping in all the time allowed for that perpetual play of art and nature which has become one of our hallmarks. One specific side benefit that has in the meantime resulted has to do with the more adventuresome avant-garde work we subsequently came to show—things we never imagined we'd be exhibiting when we began. I don't like to overpower the visitors, and some of the recent art can get quite fierce. Thus, it's good that we're always offering an out, some safe place to turn the eyes, like a familiar tree, a stretch of lawn, children playing outside—some safe haven from the wild beasts. The point is that you don't want to leave people alone with the beasts."

Once Wohlert and Bo had drawn up their initial plan, the three men spent a weekend charting the whole project with string stretched across the land. Jensen offered some revisions (ironically, one of his main changes was to add a few extra zigzags along one stretch of glass corridor in order to save a tree, a particularly glorious nine-trunked beech), but he generally deferred to his architects. "I left the last word to them," Jensen explains. "I realized that just as I have my ethics they have theirs. Anyway, there were seldom disagreements."

Disagreements weren't the problem, according to Wohlert and Bo. It was just that the goals of the project kept ballooning as they went along. "For long periods, our principal function seemed to consist of informing Jensen about *the physical* limitations on his inspiration," Bo recalls. "Human limitations—problems of finance, zoning laws, relations with neighbors, and so forth—he could invariably surmount. We occasionally had to deliver the bad news on things like gravity." The final plan reflected Wohlert's then recent exposure to the California style (he had been studying in Berkeley for several years), filtered through a Danish love of natural materials. The walls were white-painted brick, the floors red tile, and the ceilings natural pine. The external woodwork was teak with beams of laminated pine. In general, the dimensions derived from the masonry; that is, the various dimensions of rooms and corridors tended to echo the proportions of the individual bricks in their walls. The buildings were long and low-slung, and they tended to recede into the natural profusion that surrounded them. As the years passed, there were to be several additions, but the architecture's understated transparency—its quiet, clean, self-effacing purity—persisted. And recently, when Jensen began planning a vast new south wing, it was Wohlert and Bo who received his call.

"I remember one Sunday morning about two months before the opening," Jensen remarked one day. "As usual, the workers, who had spent the whole week mixing cement and planing wood, were there again—this time for picnics with their families. I was walking along one of the glass corridors when I got this sudden feeling: Damn it, this thing is going to work."

Louisiana wasn't the only thing that was beginning to work for Jensen. While the estate was being converted, he had resumed his courtship of Vivi Arndal, herself now divorced and bringing up a young daughter, Sanne, and this time when he offered marriage she accepted. She and Sanne soon joined Jensen at the Humlebaek home—which Wohlert and Bo were commissioned to enlarge. She must have had some sense of what she was letting herself in for, but over dinner at the house, where they still live, she denies it. "If it weren't for Vivi, I'd have been dead a long time ago," Jensen confides to me when she is out of the room. "I'd have spent forty-eight hours a day over at Louisiana. But she insists I come home occasionally for dinner. She's adamant on the subject of weekends. She drags me away for summer vacations, and I begin to enjoy them the minute I get out of Louisiana's magnetic field. We're even talking about my taking a year-long sabbatical next year—maybe going to the Faroe Islands." (That will be the day, Mrs. Jensen telegraphs with her eyes as she returns: he says that *every* year.)

Once the buildings at Louisiana were completed, in 1957, the question became how to stock them. During the next few years, Jensen's ambitions were fairly modest and somewhat provincial. He focused on contemporary Danish artists and designers. At the time, Danish arts seemed to be coursing along two tracks—the elegant, sleek, constructivist modernism that Americans associate with classic Danish design, on the one hand, and, on the other, the rambunctious, explosive, self-consciously primitivist expressionism of the artists who came to be known as the COBRA group. (The acronym derives from Copenhagen-Brussels-Amsterdam, the cities with which the group's members are associated.) Neither school was receiving much exposure in conservative, staid Denmark prior to the opening of Louisiana, and Jensen, in the early days, felt that his museum could help. He was, in any case, hesitant about competing with the big boys in the field of international contemporary art; he didn't feel he knew his stuff, and anyway the prices were probably too high.

It was a hesitancy that evaporated in 1959, and Jensen credits Arnold Bode with bringing about his change of attitude. Bode had been a promising young painter in Weimar Germany in the twenties—one of the type whose work was denounced as degenerate by Hitler and his cronies. He had lain low, managing to be a Good Soldier Schweik throughout the Second World War. At the end of the war, he emerged in Kassel as a professor of art. During the next decade, Bode became obsessed by the idea that Germany, once the seedbed of modernism, had simply missed fifteen years of that movement's most significant flowering. By 1954, he was able to secure the summer use of three castles in the environs of Kassel as the staging area for an exhibition he called "Documenta." Its subtitle was "The Classics: An Update." Jensen missed it, but in 1959 he ventured south for its sequel, "Documenta II." "You cannot imagine how naïve I was," Jensen said one evening as he recalled those days over schnapps at his home. "I arrived in Kassel like a country hick, like someone who comes in on the four-o'clock train. Up to that point, I had been completely preoccupied with Danish art. Now, for the first time, I saw Pollock, de Kooning, Bacon, Dubuffet. I caught up with the postwar work of Moore, Calder, Arp . . . The abundance overwhelmed me. I said, 'Gosh, I have lived in vain.'"

Jensen paused and remained silent for several seconds. "Ach," he finally said, sighing and shaking his head. "I was so stupid. You know, all those things—finding the estate, Kraft stepping in, building the museum—it sounds as if it were all good luck and good intuition. But I made some terrible misjudgments in those years. In 1954, in Stockholm, I'd seen a terrific Cézanne-to-Picasso show. Instead of being inspired, I was cowed. I imagined there was no way I could compete internationally, so when Louisiana started I confined myself within parochial horizons. And yet I could have started international collecting right from the start. In 1956, a Max Ernst sold for the equivalent of a good Danish painting, a Léger went for maybe twice that, a Picasso three times. By 1960, though, prices had begun to jump right out of my range; in many cases it was too late. When I think of all the things I could have done and didn't, I could tear out all my hairs and run around screaming." Jensen bounded out of his chair at the sheer thought of it, his hands tugging at fistfuls of white hair, his feet pounding a dance of retrospective frustration—and then, just as suddenly, he stopped, lowered his hands, sighed again, and chuckled quietly. "Ah, well," he concluded, "I suppose all collectors face this sorrow. And, you know, there's a danger of inverted hubris in all this: 'By my incredible intelligence and sensitivity, I should have been able to achieve more.' It's our vanity, finally, that condemns us."

Returning to his chair and smoothing back his ruffled mane, Jensen resumed his tale. "At any rate, standing there in Kassel, I knew I had to make a fresh start, he said. "It couldn't be too sudden—I didn't want to hurt the feelings of my Danish artists—but it was going to have to be complete. That very first day, I rushed up to Bode's office and pleaded with his secretary to let me see him. Finally, she got up, walked over to his door, leaned in, and said, 'Professor Bode, there's a man out here just as crazy as you are. Do you want to see him?' I stormed into his office and cried, 'Let me do something immediately! Otherwise, I explode!' And he was very generous. Over the next few days, we chose a hundred and fifty of the best works in 'Documenta II' for showing at Louisiana later that fall. It was the beginning of a great friendship."

Besides Bode, Jensen cites two other museum men as early mentors. Willem Sandberg was the influential, hugely inventive director of Amsterdam's Stedelijk Museum. "He was a visionary practitioner," Jensen explains. "An eighteenth-century Voltairian who was still very much in the present. An encyclopedic humanist with roots in Freud and the Bauhaus, and at the same time with a deep sense of the emotional and the mystical. The first time I visited the Stedelijk—this, again, was *after* the Louisiana had opened—Sandberg had organized a big comparative exhibition of modern and primitive art. It was my old Lausanne University theme. But Sandberg was launching something like fifty shows a year; there were often two or three openings on the same day. He was the Alfred Barr of Europe—very much a father figure to all of us. It's strange—I am as old now as he was then, but I could never imagine myself his equal." Jensen's other mentor was Pontus Hulten, the young and brashly innovative director of Stockholm's Moderna Museet, who went on to become the founding director of the Centre Pompidou in Paris, and after that (in 1985) the founding director of the Museum of Contemporary Art in Los Angeles. In 1958, Hulten, then a young art historian, had been tapped by the Swedish government to organize a gallery for modern works after a wealthy benefactress willed a vast sum—anything!—to get "those horrible modern things" out of the National Museum. Starting with this small nest egg of exiles, Hulten, through contacts with enthusiastic young artists, quickly developed a thriving art center in the otherwise implausible north. "Sandberg was particularly good with the classics of the modern movement, and Pontus with the cutting edge, the newest trends," Jensen recalls. "They were both extremely helpful in allowing me to borrow their shows. In 1960, we had a show called 'The Moderna Museet Visits Louisiana' which drew from Pontus's permanent collection, and we followed that in 1961 with a similar survey of Sandberg's Stedelijk holdings."

By 1961, Jensen had turned the corner in his development of Louisiana into an international institution. There was a regular traffic in contemporary shows among Amsterdam, Stockholm, and Humlebaek, and Jensen, whom museum people had started out by dismissing as "Cheese Jensen," had now graduated to being known as "one of those three wild men of the north." The transition was not universally applauded by Jensen's neighbors and countrymen. In the summer of 1961, Louisiana played host to Hulten's razzle-dazzle extravaganza "Movement in Art," which included works by Marcel Duchamp, Richard Stankeiwicz, and Alexander Calder. As an adjunct to the show's opening, Jensen invited Jean Tinguely, the notorious and celebrated Swiss kinetic assemblagist, to come up and fashion one of his self-destroying sculptural contraptions on the manor lawn. "Tinguely arrived," Jensen recalled, and he immediately informed me he'd need two thousand francs for fireworks. This made me a bit nervous, since only a year earlier his 'Homage to New York' had almost succeeded in burning down the Museum of Modern Art. I suggested that maybe we should have the fireworks master from Tivoli come and supervise, but Tinguely assured me that no, there would be no problem—the rockets, which would be controlled by an electrical impulse at his command, would be aimed at the ground, not at the sky. He was calling the piece 'Sketch for the End of the World,' so I was wary, but I went along. Finally, the night of the opening, the sprawling junk sculpture was in place. It actually consisted of three separate structures between twelve and fifteen feet high, made out of baling wire, wheel sprockets, bicycle chains, a perambulator, a rocking horse, a sewing machine—*everything*—and near the top was a cage with a pigeon inside. This was 'the peace dove' and it was supposed to be released just before all the excitement. Well, Tinguely was famous as a big *farceur,* so there was a large, festive crowd, somewhere between one and two thousand people, including all sorts of press and dignitaries. Soon after twilight, Tinguely started the whole thing up from his switchboard behind a tree. The wheels began whirring, the engine chugging, metal clanging, the rocking horse rocking, a foghorn tooting, smoke and noise, and then, suddenly, there was a big *Bang!* and the rockets started shooting out. It turns out that they went neither into the ground nor into the sky but, rather, straight at the audience. The laughter went from carefree to somewhat nervous to downright terrified and hysterical. The press photographers became war correspondents. Rockets went spraying into the old house. One sputtered straight at the prime minister's chest. I was running around mobilizing doctors, attending to people's small wounds, assuring everyone that Louisiana would pay for the burned clothes, and so forth. Nobody was seriously hurt, but when I looked back at the steaming debris on the lawn I realized the cage had failed to open. The photographers were swarming around the ruins, snapping pictures. Later that evening, back at the party at my house, the phone kept ringing, with newspeople demanding to know, 'What's all this we hear about murdered birds?'"

By now, Jensen was rocking back and forth, savoring the memory with delight. "Well, naturally," he continued, "the next morning there were banner headlines: MACABRE OPENING OF SHOW: ANIMAL SACRIFICED AT LOUISIANA." People called our equivalent of the SPCA, they called the police, and by midmorning the police were calling on me—I remember how they looked to me through my vague hangover—and demanding 'the *corpus delicti*.' Well, I told them I had no idea where it was, but our maid then informed me that it was in the kitchen. Tinguely, it turns out, had brought it home the night before and given it to her, saying, 'Here, take this. Knud can have it fried or boiled in the morning.' It became a huge scandal. The police brought in a veterinary professor from the university to conduct an autopsy—I remember one sentence from his report: 'This bird was killed while alive.' How else could it have been killed? There was a trial, although by then Tinguely had already left; in absentia he was meted out a fifty-dollar symbolic fine. But you should have seen all the discussion this led to— the editorials pro and con. Things weren't helped any when Nam Jun Paik, the Korean-born avant-garde artist, did a performance the following weekend in which he took a bath in an oil drum, destroyed a piano, threw eggs at the walls, and went around with a scissors cutting off the critics' ties. The next morning, we opened our papers to the banner, YET MORE INSANITY AT THE LOUISIANA! Ah, yes," Jensen said, calming himself. "Those were the days of our heroic youth."

Jensen's mood turned suddenly serious. "It was all so hypocritical," he said. "Thousands of pigeons are killed each year to beautify our parks and no one complains. People who wouldn't mind if human beings were being intentionally tortured were scandalized at the thought of an animal's being accidentally killed. I gradually realized that much more was at stake—that a lot of this was angry resentment against modern art. So around this time I decided to organize a series of seminars entitled 'What Is Modernism?'"

By the mid-sixties, Jensen had begun collecting in earnest: to his excellent holdings in such modern northern European and Scandinavian masters as Pierre Alechinsky, Asger Jorn, Henry Heerup, Karel Appel, Robert Jacobsen, Carl-Henning Pedersen, and Richard Mortensen, he was now adding works by Yves Klein, Victor Vasarely, Arman, César Baldaccini, Lucio Fontana, Naum Gabo, Josef Albers, Max Bill, Jean Dubuffet, Antonio Tàpies, Morris Louis, Sam Francis, Ellsworth Kelly, Kenneth Noland, Jim Dine, Roy Lichtenstein, Frank Stella, and Andy Warhol. He was dogged all the while, however, by the worry that the art he was collecting—some of the finest pieces from the forefront of contemporary artistic practice—was fundamentally misunderstood by a large fraction of its potential audience. "I remember a passage in a book by one of your American writers—I think it was Kurt Vonnegut," Jensen remarked one day. "A character suggests that modern art is a conspiracy between rich people and artists to make ordinary people feel stupid. And I've often been concerned about this kind of misperception. There was a gap, especially in the fifties and sixties, between what artists were doing and what many people were prepared to appreciate. This gap led to frustration, which, in turn, produced anger or insecurity—neither of which was a terribly good mood from which to open oneself to new experience."

During the early sixties, Jensen wrote extensively on what he called "the developing crisis of leisure time." In those heady days, there was a general expectation, especially in Scandinavia, that the forty-hour workweek would soon dwindle further, that automation would free workers from mind-dulling drudgery, that society was on the verge of extending a basic level of material sufficiency and security to all its members. "It seemed as if we were at the dawn of a new age, the era of leisure," Jensen told me. "People were beginning to have a lot of free time, and corporations were moving quickly to colonize that leisure through the various structures of popular culture, such as television, spectator sports, vacation packages—all the standardized ways in which people could be turned into consumers of fun. At that time, I wrote a book called *Slaraffenland Eller Utopia—Lotusland or Utopia*—and those appeared to be the options. It seemed vital that some alternative to the mass standardization of human possibility be provided—that material sufficiency not lead to spiritual anemia. This is where art seemed so important, and especially the work of contemporary artists who were wrestling directly with the challenge of individual, as opposed to standardized, expression."

Jensen paused, smiled, and then continued. "I think people in positions like mine—people who try to mediate between art and society—need a lot of self-irony, modesty, and ambivalence. Also, a certain skepticism as to whether art can make anything happen, and just how much a person can get out of art. I mean, there are a lot of truly happy people who have virtually no exposure to art, and, conversely, some fairly evil specimens who are tremendously sophisticated in artistic matters. Still, having said that, I think art can be a vital tool in one's life. You don't have to conceive of art in Olympian terms to see how it helps people to learn to think for themselves, to sharpen their own perceptual capacities and heighten their sense of self, while at the same time allowing an immediate sense of other people's unique, subjective experience. Art thus has an important role to play in staving off the standardization of society. But it can achieve that promise only if we find some way of overcoming that initial frustration—the anger and insecurity—that tends to alienate many potential viewers from modern works." This became Jensen's consuming passion at Louisiana—to create a milieu in which art and people could meet and mingle. His attitude was neither missionary nor pedagogical. He preferred a sort of relaxed persuasiveness—a mild offer tendered quietly and almost tangentially. Although part of the problem was unquestionably the strangeness of a lot of contemporary art, Jensen increasingly came to feel that a major cause of the frustration arose from the very institution of the museum. "You have to realize that museums are a relatively recent aberration in the history of art," he pointed out. "This segregation of art from the world of everyday life has impoverished both. It used to be that a religious person, for example, would enter a cathedral, just as he did every Sunday, and the light might be streaming through the window in a particular fashion or falling upon a statue of the Virgin in a new way— the hue from the window intensifying the deep blue color of the Virgin's garment—or there might be snow on the shoulder of one of the Prophets outside, and our friend would say, '*Tiens*. Look at that. I never noticed that before.' Art existed in town squares, in the marketplace, in theaters, and in homes—you came upon it in the middle of your day, at the corner of your eye. Now Rembrandt's *Night Watch* is enshrined behind thick glass in a dark, cold room in a large, cold museum. They make you stand there, almost pulling you by the hair: 'Look, damn it, you idiot, this is the greatest work of art in the world, appreciate it!' The trouble with many museums is that they impose this kind of demand for aesthetic worship."

For Jensen, at Louisiana, the challenge became the search for a way to return art—"difficult" modern art, especially—to the everyday life-world of its potential viewers. As the years passed, he added a movie theater, a concert hall, a stage for experimental drama. He offered Louisiana as a site for conferences, symposia, and political rallies. There were poets' days and antinuclear expositions. The idea behind all the sideshows was that people might meet the art on their way to something else. In addition, Jensen and his associates soon started interspersing their calendar of modern shows with significant archeological and anthropological exhibitions. For some reason, people who couldn't care less about Malevich or Surrealism swarmed to look at gold from Peru, funeral masks from Egypt, and stone zodiacs from Mesopotamia.

"It's quite extraordinary—there's an apparently insatiable appetite for the antique and the exotic," Hans Erik Wallin, the former advertising man who now supervises, among other things, Louisiana's archeological spectaculars, remarked to me. (Of the four principal administrators who currently guide Louisiana, not one has any academic credentials in art history or arts administration. To the uncomfortable bewilderment of many traditional museum people, Louisiana seems to swim along just fine under the guidance of a former cheese exporter, a former Ford dealer, a retired advertising executive, and a professional painter— "the boys," as Jensen fondly refers to the museum's leadership.) "Our two biggest shows ever, in terms of attendance, were exhibits of Pompeii in the year 79 A.D. and, just recently, the Chinese bronzes and artifacts from the burial site of the First Emperor of Qin—the one who had himself buried with an army of life-size terra-cotta warriors and horses. A museum man once said, 'For success, you need gold or, if not gold, corpses.' Well, there must be something to what he said, because with those two shows people just couldn't get enough."

The Chinese exhibition proved particularly challenging. Wallin not only had to make several junkets to Beijing but was required to entertain a delegation of Chinese officials at Louisiana. "They were, to say the least, bewildered by many of the things they saw here," he recalled. "At one point, as we rounded a bend, I was struck dumb with horror: there before us loomed our large Andy Warhol portrait of a blue Mao with red lipstick. There was a tense moment of silence—I could feel the prospects for a show slipping right through my fingers—and then the leader of the delegation, arching his eyebrows, muttered something to the effect that the late chairman himself had said: 'Let a hundred flowers blossom.'" Wallin concluded, "These archeological shows are very effective. People come for the jewels and coffins, but they end up passing the modern stuff on their way to the pastries."

"Of every thousand persons who come for the archeological extravaganzas," Jensen later agreed, "nine hundred and ninety-nine may pass right by the modern things, but the curiosity of one may be piqued, and maybe the next week he comes to look again. That is our greatest satisfaction. Of course, I don't want to leave an impression that we coerce people here under false pretenses. As you know from my somewhat naïve thesis in Lausanne many years ago, I have always felt how deeply we are indebted to these faraway cultures and how important they have been in the development of our whole modern sensitivity. Alfred Barr's Museum of Modern Art made exhibitions of African and Pacific art and so did Willem Sandberg's Stedelijk, and, as for Louisiana, we would never assemble a show that was not in some way related to the art of this century. During the past twenty-four years, we have had about a dozen shows of this kind, always trying to emphasize the connection *between,* for example, the pre-Columbians and Moore, the Egyptians and Giacometti, Pacific art and the COBRA artists, and so forth. The only exception may have been the Pompeii exhibition, but even that show implied a kind of self-identification emanating an atmosphere of catastrophe—a civilization extinguished in two days and later forgotten—which makes us understand the Pompeians. And even there the 'calcis'—the casts of dying human beings—have inspired artists like Giacometti, César, Richier, and others, which is why we showed works of these artists at the end of that exhibition."

One of Jensen's favorite exhibitions in this context was also one of the earliest—a presentation, in 1963, of the Mexican government's vast European traveling exhibition. "The exhibition was so big we had to show it in two stages," Jensen recalls. "It arrived at the Humlebaek station in a special train—six or seven cars filled with two thousand pieces, ranging from huge, several-ton Olmec heads and little red clay pre-Columbian pots and figurines to works by such modern masters as

José Orozco and David Siqueiros. The nine hundred pre-Columbian pieces in particular were tremendously fragile. I remember the last day, as we wrapped the show ever so carefully under the anxious gaze of four officials from the Mexican Cultural Ministry—it was like holding your breath for a whole day, totally nerve-racking. Finally, we delivered the last case to the train—not a single item had even been scratched and I turned to the four Mexicans and said, 'Come with me.' We got into my car, drove to Copenhagen, parked outside Tivoli, marched in, and proceeded to a little booth where for a couple of kroner—the equivalent of a quarter—you can throw three hard balls at several piles of ceramic plates. I put down a wad of bills, and for the next hour or so we went berserk—reduced the place to a shambles. There wasn't a saucer left whole. It was tremendously gratifying."

Tivoli is generally considered the top children's amusement park in Denmark. There are times, however, especially during the summer, when Louisiana has much the same atmosphere. Again, it's part of Jensen's attempt to make his museum a milieu for living as well as viewing. "Sometimes it seems that children are the world's greatest oppressed minority," Jensen commented one afternoon as we stood at his office window watching a group of kids scaling the Moore. "Children are usually bored at museums, and I feel pity for them: they're nice and polite to us and say they like it. But I don't think you can expect kids to really enjoy art at a museum until they're in their early teens; it's a taste that comes late, so that finding some way to involve them when they're younger can be a challenge. Some museums respond by setting aside a room for finger painting and clay modeling. But that's merely the kind of thing they get at school. Here at Louisiana we've tried to enlist artists in the invention of high-calibre practical and aesthetic objects and environments that are capable of exciting and involving the children. Unfortunately, because of some trouble we've been having with the neighbors, we've had to temporarily close off our largest children's area, but let me show it to you anyway."

As we left Jensen's office and descended to the vestibule, we could see a long line of people in the courtyard waiting to get into the museum. It was the last weekend of a phenomenally successful Picasso retrospective. (Indeed, by the end of the weekend the Picasso show proved to have been the most highly attended exhibition in Louisiana's history, surpassing both Pompeii and the Chinese bronzes. Charter buses streamed in from as far away as Helsinki and Oslo. During the two months of the show, its entry receipts exceeded the museum's budgeted expectations for the entire year. The bookshop dispensed over three hundred and sixty thousand postcards, the cafeteria almost a ton and a half of shrimp.) We moved quickly through the throng, past the exhibition halls, and along the connecting glass corridors. From inside its buildings, Louisiana feels something like a watercourse, a series of lazy pools connected by cascading streams and narrows, debouching, finally, at the cafeteria's terrace, onto a view of the strait. Just past the Giacometti room and before the cafeteria, we veered out of the main stream. Jensen unlocked a side door, and we were quickly pushing through the underbrush on the far side of the museum. As we emerged into a clearing, we came upon four trespassing teenagers. Jensen shooed them away, and they scampered off into the forest. "I don't blame them," Jensen said, laughing. "If I were their age, I'd be down here, too."

In 1978, Jensen had decided to expand his usual practice of inviting one artist each summer to work with the children of Humlebaek on a group installation. Instead, he made the children's projects the center of the Louisiana's entire summer program. Dozens of artists and theatrical groups were invited to contribute pieces around the theme "Children Are a People." (The phrase is a line from a Swedish song, which concludes, "They live in another country.") Most of the action took place near the lushly overgrown, shallow lake to the north of and just below the Giacometti room. A platform was erected on the far side of the lake, and a Huckleberry Finn-type raft made continual crossings to it, powered by a taut rope anchored to both shores and pulled by the children themselves. On the raft's side were strapped life preservers bearing the legend "Who Needs the Atlantic?" On the terrace above, where the three Max Ernst "Muppet Show" pieces dawdled, with their silly grins, one artist contrived a makeshift funicular: a pair of children would climb aboard a narrow seat, get strapped in, and then fly about two hundred meters swooshingly across the lake and down to the platform at the other side. One artist bought an old schooner, sliced it in half across the middle, and mounted the two ends deck to deck, prow and stern to the sky, along the shore, where they became a striking clubhouse. There was a thrillingly steep, bumpy slide, and all kinds of tree houses and hammocks. One artist contrived a soft, red, womblike room, and another made a shallow straw bowl with an enormous wooden spoon; small children seemed to love to climb into the hollow of the spoon and sit. Suspended above the ground there were narrow platforms on which children could stretch out and flap large goose wings hinged to the structures. In another corner of the woods lay a moss-covered Volkswagen Beetle.

The show's success was tremendous, but so was the opposition it aroused from the neighboring church. Jensen walked me around the now silent lake, parted some branches, and showed me the site of the difficulty. On the other side of a chain-link fence dividing the museum's grounds from those of the church lies a section of the church's graveyard. "They were very upset, because they claimed the noise of our children having all this fun was, in their words, 'disturbing the sleep of the dead,'" Jensen explained. "There was a big polemic. One man even filed a petition with the ministry of church affairs to have his wife unearthed and her casket moved so 'she could get some peace.' I don't know. If I'd been in her position, I tend to think I would have enjoyed the company. But it presented us with a big problem, and we didn't know quite what to do. My friend the artist Pierre Alechinsky heard about the controversy and cabled me, 'Don't give in unless you hear from the dead themselves, preferably in writing.' Well, we didn't hear from the dead, but I decided that for the present, anyway, for the sake of peace among the living, it was probably better to close off the area." As we walked back toward the museum, however, climbing alongside the tumbling slide, Jensen paused, a gleam in his eye, and said, "Don't you think it would be great to invite Niki de Saint-Phalle and Jean Tinguely up here to make a huge serpent with this slide as its open mouth? The serpent's body could coil around underneath the Giacometti room, and the children, digested, could come out eventually over there on the other side. I'm going to have to ask them."

If Jensen's previous record with artists is any indication, Tinguely and Saint-Phalle will very likely be delighted to cooperate. Archeological shows and children's summers may explain some of Louisiana's popularity among its public, but it takes the contagious enthusiasm that Jensen brings to his relationships with artists to account for the remarkable quality of his museum's holdings in modern art. Jensen is not nearly as wealthy as many museum patrons in the United States and in Europe, yet his collection ranks among the most distinctive and distinguished in Europe. "He came to my studio several months ago with the intention of buying one painting," the noted Israeli artist Menashe Kadishman told me recently. "But he was so lively, so interested, so delightfully involved, that being with him was like being near a fire of enthusiasm. He is a man of love. He radiates passion about art. I got so caught up that I found myself lowering prices, giving him other pieces outright. He ended up leaving with four works!"

Pierre Alechinsky, the Belgian-born master, who has donated an extraordinary canvas entitled *Le Doute* to Louisiana, describes Jensen as *"un conservateur de foudre,"* a lightninglike curator. Morris Louis's widow, Marcella Brenner, was instrumental in seeing to it that Jensen was able to secure three—the magic three—large paintings by her late husband. Henry Moore and Alexander Calder, Naum Gabo and Sam Francis—the list seems endless—have all responded to Jensen's charm. He has countless stories of his relationships with artists. Perhaps the story of his friendship with Giacometti can suggest their tenor. "In 1965, the year before his death, Giacometti was having a retrospective at the Tate Gallery, in London," Jensen told me. "I wrote to him out of nowhere and asked him whether he would allow the show to travel to Louisiana—several letters, actually, but no reply. Finally, on the eve of the Tate show's opening, I flew down to London to see him. I found him in the galleries, applying finishing touches to some of the sculptures; in fact, he was daubing some of the bronzes with little flecks of colored paint. I went up to him and introduced myself. 'Ah, yes,' he said. 'You are the Dane. Absolutely out of the question.' He looked at my face and I must have looked crestfallen, because he said, 'Oh dear, let's go to the cafeteria and at least have some tea.' Well, this tea lasted three hours. We began telling very black-humored stories—especially about cannibalism. For some reason, Giacometti was fascinated by cannibalism. He felt that Holy Communion was a cannibalistic rite. I told a story I'd recently read about a fine Berlin burgher who killed his wife and then canned her mortal remains, which he took to eating at his leisure. After a few weeks, he was arrested, tried, convicted, and sent to prison, but they never located the body. In prison, he complained to the guard about the food and asked him, wouldn't he please go to his house and bring back some of the cans he had stored in the cupboard there? We were all laughing and having a very good time. All of a sudden, Alberto tapped me on the shoulder and said, 'Of course you shall have the show. No problem.'

"Later that year, I invited him to come up and see our installation of the show. He didn't travel much and he had a fear of flying. He once took a five-day boat trip to spend five days in New York City and then took five days sailing back. He had intended to place three figures in the Chase Manhattan Plaza, but when he saw the scale of Manhattan he felt he couldn't compete. We've since acquired those three pieces—the standing woman, the walking man, and the large head—and they're in our special Giacometti room, with the lake as a backdrop. I like to think he'd be pleased. Anyway, he came up by train. We, of course, invited him to stay in the converted boathouse down by the shore where we always put up our visiting artists. But he declined. He preferred to stay in a hotel in the harbor district of Copenhagen, where he could stay up late and trade stories with the sailors. When he came out to Louisiana, we were very proud. The show consisted of over one hundred and seventy-five pieces—it was quite remarkable. We'd taken a great deal of care in installing them, and we were eager to get his response. Well, he went up to the first piece and stared at it fixedly for some moments, then shook his head and muttered, *'Ah, c'est terrible, c'est moche.'* He went on to the next one—same thing. Every few pieces, he'd grumble, *'Affreux, c'est bête.'* It was quite shocking to see how depressed and disgusted he was by everything he'd ever done. I remember thinking, Why does he become so masochistic? But it continued from one room to the next—terrible curses, and not a word about the installation or anything. Eventually, we came back round to the beginning, and it was as if he'd gone through a catharsis. Suddenly, he smiled and brightened. He launched out again, going from room to room, praising the installation and the lighting, commenting on the fine choice of groupings and the beauty of the site. It was an unbelievable transformation.

"A few months later, I had occasion to visit him in his tiny workshop in Montparnasse. He lived the life of a bohemian, yet he was tremendously disciplined. It was said that he kept his money in a little box under his bed. In the evening, he took me on a walk and told me stories. Eventually, we ended up at La Coupole, the huge restaurant, which must have been one of his favorites—the waiters called him Monsieur Alberto. At another table were seated Sartre and Beauvoir; I didn't try to engage them in any conversation—I didn't want to bother them, although I am their publisher here in Denmark. Alberto, meanwhile, continued to hold me spellbound with his stories. He told me about one time when Stravinsky called and asked whether it would be all right if he dropped by for a visit. Giacometti had said, 'Of course,' although he'd never really had any relations with the man and couldn't imagine what he wanted. Presently, there was a knock on the door, and it was Stravinsky's chauffeur, saying that the Maestro was outside, waiting for him in his limousine. Giacometti emerged from his studio and was expansively greeted by Stravinsky, all this being captured for posterity on film by two busy cameramen. Apparently, they were making a documentary about Stravinsky, and he thought it would be impressive to be seen with Giacometti.

"Later that evening—it must have been getting on to two or three, and the tired waiters were nodding sleepily but indulgently in the corner—Alberto told me about a time some years earlier when he'd been commissioned to draw a portrait of Matisse as a study for a commemorative medallion. Matisse was old and virtually paralyzed, but very patient and supportive. At one point, he asked to see the drawings. Giacometti, handing them over, sighed and said, 'It's very difficult to draw.' 'Yes,' Alberto said Matisse replied. 'Yes, it's the most difficult of all.' Two of the finest draftsmen of our century talking to each other like that! Imagine!

"Alberto was tremendously generous. Later during that trip, I mentioned that it was a great dream of ours to be able someday to buy a particular group of his figures, but that we didn't have the money. 'How much do you have?' he asked. I told him. 'Oh, that's enough,' he said." Jensen paused for a moment, then added, "And within two months he was dead. That was the last time I saw him. He died early. He was not at all a man who had finished telling the world what he thought of it."

One day, I asked Hans Erik Wallin, Jensen's associate, what he thought Louisiana would be like in twenty years.

"Oh," he assured me, "Knud will still be running it, and no doubt as he's running it today—with more energy than any of the rest of us. He's like Titian, who ran his studio until he was almost ninety. If it hadn't been for the plague, he'd still be with us, and, knowing how Knud relates to artists, he'd probably be right here."

"I don't care about my obituary," Jensen said one afternoon. "I'm just interested in having a good time while I'm here. Everything I've done, I've done for fun, for my own satisfaction. Anyway, you can't enjoy good notices when you're in your urn." After a moment's consideration, he went on, "Besides, I couldn't help myself. Peter Brook, the great stage director, once said something to the effect that 'there is no deep, inevitable need for theater on the part of society. If theater completely disappeared, it would take weeks for most people to notice. No, theater exists because there are a number of individual people who could not survive without making theater.' I think it's the same with museums and museum people."

My visit was coming to a close, and Jensen was in uncharacteristically low spirits. He'd spent the morning in a meeting with the board of the Louisiana Foundation. During the last several years, Louisiana has finally been receiving support from the Danish state and from greater Copenhagen, as well as from some important groups, including the New Carlsberg Foundation, the philanthropic trust that owns the beer company, and the Augustinus Foundation, which distributes grants on behalf of the family of Peter Augustinus, a Danish philanthropist. This meeting of the board had been called to consider plans for 1982, a year that would see the opening, in September, of the huge new south wing as a site for perpetual display of Louisiana's permanent collection—a wing that was entirely financed by the Augustinus Foundation. "Oh," Jensen remarked, with a sigh, "sometimes it takes herculean strength to maintain the optimism of my board. The next year will be crucially important. The opening of the new wing will be a major test; the eyes of the museum world will be upon us. We're just a small museum in a small country in an increasingly competitive art world. In the last ten years at least a dozen new contemporary museums have opened up in the United States, a similar number in Japan and West Germany—and that's not even counting the big boys—all of us competing for the same limited pool of masterworks. It's very difficult, but you've got to take risks; we especially have to make a stretch right now—to risk a major gesture. The board is being very careful, which is good—I am reminded of a Danish proverb, 'Ideas need wings, but they must have feet to walk on.'—but it is also somewhat exhausting. You see, I am also reminded of a story about our Danish Prince Christian Frederik. In 1814, after Denmark had ended up on the wrong side in one of the Napoleonic Wars and had gone bankrupt, Christian Frederik's advisers came to him with a proposal to close the Royal Academy of Fine Arts as an austerity measure. He refused to do so. 'Poor and miserable we certainly are,' he declared. 'Now, let's get silly, too, so that we can just be done altogether with this business of being a state.' And that academy is there to this day." After a moment's reflection, Jensen continued, "Actually, now that I think of it, my board isn't at all like the prince's advisers. I mean, look, here in this time of economic crisis, we are going ahead with a building program that will double our size, and the board has been extremely cooperative. Sometimes I just get anxious."

In the hall a few minutes later, I passed Børge Hansen, the former Ford dealer who has been Louisiana's business manager since the early seventies. ("I told Knud I didn't know a thing about art. 'I'll stick to the figures and leave the art to you,' I said, and that's how it's been. I go around tending to all the practical matters Knud leaves in his wake.") I asked Hansen about the meeting. "Oh, it went fine," he assured me. "Knud's a little frustrated, but he's always frustrated after these meetings. Face it: Knud is always going to be at least two steps ahead of the rest of us."

"I have a veritable portfolio of snapshots of Knud taken from behind as he's racing off somewhere," said Sanne Bertram, Jensen's stepdaughter, the next day as she drove me out to the airport. Miss Bertram is in her early thirties and the two are quite fond of each other. In addition to being an accomplished photographer, she is completing graduate studies in Spanish. "I remember one time in particular," she continued. "Knud and Vivi and I were on our way to see Alexander Calder, at his home in Saché, France. This was to be the culmination of two years of extremely delicate preparations—contacts, correspondence, courtship, tentative queries, and so forth. We'd flown to Paris, and everything was going to hinge on a series of very tight connections—taxi and train. We were desperately late, and the taxi had got caught in a traffic jam. Knud was pleading with the driver to please, please, hurry. The passenger compartment was stinking up with the smell of this large, smoked Danish salmon that Knud was bringing, along with a bottle of homemade schnapps, as a love offering. Finally, we reached the station just as the last train was scheduled to leave. I have this vivid, vivid memory of Knud racing up ahead, careering through the crowd, the salmon flopping under one arm, the schnapps splashing beneath the other, Vivi and I in hot pursuit. It was so tense, so nearly tragic, and yet simultaneously so hilarious. And the wonderful thing is how Knud realized this, too. How, once we'd made it onto the train—it was pulling out just as we boarded—and into our little compartment, he started laughing uproariously, as if to say, 'How silly! It doesn't matter. What do I care?' When, of course, he cared immensely."

Postscript: Waking Up to How We Sleepwalk (1982)

One afternoon early last fall, Knud Jensen opened the gates of the Louisiana Museum to activists in the Danish and Scandinavian antinuclear movement. "I'm getting a certain amount of flak for this from people at other museums," Jensen told me in his office. Down below, the museum's wide lawn teemed with visitors in all kinds of attire, carrying banners and posters, gathering around booths, collecting literature, sampling pastries, and listening to a poetry reading. One group, near the edge of a small grove, huddled about a folksinger; others meandered through the museum's glass corridors, from one special exhibit to another. Everything was part of a calling out for peace—specifically, for nuclear disarmament. Thousands of visitors had converged from as far away as Oslo, Stockholm, and Hamburg for this day of vigilance and celebration.

"I keep being told," Jensen continued, "that it's not a good thing to mix museumship and politics like this. But I don't know. My coworkers here at Louisiana and I have gone to a tremendous effort to create this sanctuary for art, to see to its long-term preservation, so that it will be here for our children and grandchildren; I guess we consider it part of our curatorial responsibility to do whatever we can to make sure that they will be here to enjoy it."

As we walked among the Calders and the Arps, I noticed that some of the visitors carried black plastic bags filled with air, the necks tied with string. Several people had them, and there didn't seem to be any organizing principle as to who did and who didn't. If you asked what the bags signified, their carriers simply said they'd been given them at the entrance, and then moved on.

The air was beginning to cool, although the sun was still high in the sky when we heard the bells of the neighboring church ring six o'clock. We continued to stroll about, talking and listening. It must have been five after six before we began to notice: first one person and then another, and then dozens all over the grounds, stood frozen, stock-still. Children with their mothers, businessmen, teenagers, farmer types—isolated individuals all over the grounds stood deathly still, limp black bags hanging by their sides.

Only not so still after all. Looking away and then looking again, you'd see that they'd have moved, infinitesimally. They were all moving, in suspension, maybe a few feet each minute—but moving nonetheless, toward the bluff. Afternoon of the Living Dead. By six-fifteen, the "zombies" had coalesced into three vague groups; one proceeding out from the cafeteria terrace to the north, another down the gully that bisects the sculpture park, and the last setting out across the wide lawn to the south. All moved slowly toward and then down the face of the bluff. The rest of us looked on; some giggled nervously. Little kids ran up to the zombies and tried to distract them, to no effect. They simply crept on—not even grim exactly, just absent, emptily compelled. The rest of us jockeyed for position; some took photographs, while others seemed to become even more transfixed than the zombies and stood motionless, staring at their glacial advance.

By about six forty-five, the three columns had begun to converge at the foot of the bluff. Now they continued on out across the narrow lawn toward the sand and the sea strait, seeming utterly deliberate, utterly mindless. There were about two hundred of them. Their black bags hung limp. Any laughter from the onlookers had stopped. The silence was immediate; it wasn't that we didn't know or weren't thinking about what would happen next—time itself seemed to have congealed. Our anticipations had become as suspended as their gait. We watched.

The walkers kept advancing, inevitably; still, it was a shock when the first one entered the water. Or, rather, failed to stop at the water's edge. The wavelets slapped across the man's shoes—a few minutes later he was immersed to his knees. All the rest followed him in, mindless but determined; the sea received them. The water must have been cold, but they continued on. As the small waves rose and fell, wet clothes clung to limbs and torsos not yet entirely submerged. This death march became erotic. Cloth outlined sinew: thigh, groin, arm, breast, hair.

One child broke into tears as the water reached his waist. Unable to continue, humiliated, he bounded free of his trance and out of the water into the arms of his grandmother, who'd been watching from the shore—the strangest figure of hope I've ever seen. The others were in the sea up to their necks before they began to turn. The black bags bobbed alongside their heads; now, moving parallel to the shore, the zombies let them go. Downshore a bit, a low canoe dock jutted out from the beach, and the heads now drifted underneath it, beginning finally to arch back inland on the other side. Slowly, one by one, the sleepwalkers emerged from the water and filed—still trance-slow, dripping, shivering violently—through the doors of a large converted boathouse.

While they were still filing in, I entered the boathouse to talk with some of these walkers. Once inside, one by one they snapped to; friends offered them towels and cups of hot rum. It took over half an hour before the last made it through the doors and back to life. Kirsten Dehlholm, the leader of one of the columns, a woman in her mid-thirties with sharp features, punkishly styled, was drying her hair. "So," she asked, "what did you think of our trained snails?" We were presently joined by Per Flink Basse, a tall young man who'd headed the cafeteria group, and Else Fenger, a somewhat older woman who'd led the lawn contingent. The three of them, along with architect Charlotte Cecilie (who wasn't present on this occasion), have been working together since 1977, when they pooled their artistic resources (Dehlholm had previously been a sculptor, Basse a set designer, and Fenger a lithographer) in founding the Billedstofteater. "That translates roughly as 'picture theater,'" explained Basse, "or 'theater of the image.' We are basically a group of performance artists interested in a theater built out of spaces, rooms, occasions, images, rather than literary sources. We often try to involve others in our conceptions—we usually stage them in public spaces around Copenhagen. We almost always work in slow motion, usually exploring themes from everyday life—eating, sleeping, walking—slowing things down to help people notice them. In a way that's what we were doing here—trying to find an image, a way of helping people to *notice* what is going on."

I asked how the performance had come about. "We were contacted several months ago by the people here at Louisiana who were organizing this Peace Festival," recalled Fenger. "We came out to look at the site, since all of our performances arise from the occasion provided by the site. After we got our idea, we sent out about three hundred letters to people who had worked with us before or expressed interest after seeing our work—we've developed quite a network. We said we were planning a performance for the Peace Festival and that the one criterion was that they must not be afraid of water. As you can see, about two hundred people responded."

"We had two meetings at the beginning of the week," Dehlholm took up the story, "and then we performed our snail walk today. Most of us are strangers, but it's incredible the intimacy and fellow feeling this kind of thing brings out. Look at everyone." Throughout the large room people were hugging each other, laughing, stripping out of wet clothes and putting on dry ones. Any anxious feelings of propriety seemed to have given way.

I walked over and asked one young man, who was punching his head through a turtleneck sweater, why he'd joined the performance. "You know," he said, "a few months ago even, I was more or less ignoring this issue. But Haig and Reagan have really frightened us. When they said it is possible to win a limited nuclear war, we suddenly realized what they're talking about—they meant a war *limited to Europe.*"

"It's funny," said a woman who'd been listening to us. "I had all kinds of associations during the walk besides nuclear war. For one thing I found myself thinking of the boat people in Vietnam. And then— it was so strange—I realized that this is one of the narrowest points between Denmark and Sweden, and that it was out of the little village harbors up and down this coast that the Danes smuggled their Jews across to neutral Sweden during the early days of the Nazi occupation."

"I don't consider myself particularly religious," another listener offered. "But I kept thinking of baptism—and death and resurrection."

"For me," another woman said, "the whole thing became incredibly compelling—almost primal. It stopped being political and became biological. I felt the pull of the sea: I felt primordially alive, and then this feeling of feeling so alive came back on itself and became powerfully political. Because that, after all, is what we must fight now to save. Nuclear war is a threat, precisely, of primordial proportions."

A few minutes later I was standing out on the wood-plank porch of the boathouse, facing the water, talking with Jensen once again. "It's very difficult, you know," he said, "to find new images which can wake people up to the horrible reality of this nuclear war danger; this is vital work which artists are especially qualified to take on, since their very livelihood is image making. The whole world seems to be sleepwalking toward a holocaust. Maybe the image of such sleepwalking paradoxically can help to wake people up."

"Do you realize how long we were out there?" said Dehlholm as she joined us on the porch. "Almost two hours! It's incredible: it felt like maybe ten minutes. It was strange," she continued. "At first I felt incredibly alone, cut off, isolated. It was a scary kind of feeling. But then there came this very strong feeling of being with others, of togetherness, of communion. When two hundred people concentrate that strongly, it gives off an aura. Ordinarily you have a thousand ideas kicking around, and at first we were having our various associations, but as time went on, it became like an emptiness for us. Everything became suspended. It was like a meditational exercise.

"No," she said, and paused for a moment, searching for the right word. "No, it became like a prayer."

Twilight was descending. The strait was flat and silver, and on the water two hundred black balloons drifted out toward the gathering night. Dozens of ships, their lights gradually flickering on, coursed north and south through the narrow strait. It occurred to me that this very place—a crucial access for Soviet shipping out of the Baltic and into the North Sea—could well be one of the first targets for irradiation were a nuclear war ever to begin, and that the folk laughing and partying in the hangar behind me could well be some of the war's first victims.

"Two paths lie before us," Jonathan Schell recently concluded in his remarkable essay, *The Fate of the Earth*. "One leads to death, the other to life. If we choose the first path . . . we in effect become the allies of death, and in everything we do our attachment to life will weaken: our vision, blinded to the abyss that has opened at our feet, will dim and grow confused; our will, discouraged by the thought of trying to build on such a precarious foundation anything that is meant to last, will slacken; and we will sink into stupefaction, as though we were gradually weaning ourselves from life in preparation for the end. On the other hand, if we reject our doom, and bend our efforts toward survival . . . then the anesthetic fog will lift: our vision, no longer straining not to see the obvious, will sharpen; our will, finding secure ground to build on, will be restored; and we will take full and clear possession of life again. One day—and it is hard to believe that it will not be soon—we will make our choice."

To say that artists and writers today have a particular responsibility with regard to this choice is to acknowledge that this particular crisis—the specter of obliteration—bleeds into all areas of human life, and most profoundly into those very areas that have always constituted the life source of culture and civilization. Being, time, vision, presence, co-presence, tradition, posterity—the fundamentals out of which art has always sprung—today all of these are in jeopardy. It's simple: artists are inexorably implicated in the current crisis of vision.

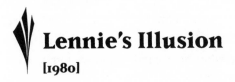

Lennie's Illusion
[1980]

One name they'd thought of was "Better Than Suicide." That idea had surfaced around 4:00 A.M., once the three young writers were well into their second fifth of Jim Beam. They'd just committed themselves to pooling their money and launching a literary bookstore on the West Side of Los Angeles; so, rather than spend more time rehashing their trepidations, which were considerable, they'd set to concocting names. "Lost Illusions" was another possibility. Or "Books Books Books!" One of the guys, who'd been reading Jung, had been taken with one of the voluble master's truisms: "There are two kinds of people you can't change, intellectuals and liars." *"Intellectuals and Liars!"* A half hour and another fifth later, Jung's nomination won the vote.

That was three years ago. Soon thereafter the store opened near the corner of Wilshire Boulevard and Eleventh Street in Santa Monica and quickly became a literary refuge. It didn't exactly prosper—literary refuges seldom do. But it mattered, and mattered profoundly, to a steadily growing clientele, myself included. Money problems dogged the store from its inception. Within six months, one partner had abandoned ship, and, within another year, Leonard Durso was left alone, the last of the three, to steer the precarious venture into a suddenly looming recession.

It ended up being a pretty grim voyage, and, a couple of months back, Durso had to scuttle the store on the jagged reefs of California's bankruptcy laws.

Shortly after that, we were sitting in the ghost ruins of the store,

Lennie and me. A month-long going-out-of-business sale had gutted the stock. The remaining miscellany had been boxed and remanded to the dispensation of the court. Lennie had never gone bankrupt before, and it felt strange. We sat there, downing Beam. Our talk returned to names, and I asked Lennie what he'd name the store today, were he to—

"'Idiot Idealism,'" he said, not even letting me complete the question. "Or no. 'The Albatross.' 'Lennie's Albatross.'"

"This was going to be a store run for and by writers," Lennie said. "That was the idea—the sort of place where people could come and browse and loiter and talk. We had a coffee machine initially, the whole first year. We only stopped because we were getting too many outpatients coming by and spilling coffee all over the books. I mean, they'd come by and get a cup to go. This one guy once, he takes his cup and asks for a lid! For a while we had a donation can, but it was pathetic: At the end of the day there'd be an empty coffeepot and one quarter. One time somebody even stole the donation—that was really heartbreaking."

Lennie's manner had always been wry, laced with sorrow. Even now, when the pain was most palpable—the dark eyes somehow more liquid, the once trim beard a bit more shagged out—the open, vulnerable humor was still there. He downed another shot of bourbon.

Durso is thirty-three. He grew up on Long Island, went to school at Bowling Green in Ohio, as did his two partners. For a while he acted, then increasingly he took to writing—plays, poems, novels. He worked in bookstores, jousted with the Selective Service System for several years, and for many years thereafter worked for the Boy Scouts, of all things. Running a bookstore in California was some kind of cockeyed dream. Maybe he just picked the wrong years to try.

Still, for the three years of its existence, Intellectuals and Liars was, after its fashion, a considerable success. It had one of the best poetry walls in the city and certainly some of the most convivial poetry talk. Most weekend evenings the long, narrow, ramshackle space would find itself entired by spirited readings and after-reading spirits. It was the sort of place writers could visit most any time and find some kindred souls, likewise procrastinating, parsing everything from Dostoyevski to Coover to the current baseball standings. Everyone sensed that the operation was marginal at best, but one tried not to think about that, because it provided such a rich context in a city so lacking in contexts.

There are a lot of reasons Intellectuals and Liars went under. Lennie would be the first to tell you that he did some things wrong. He probably overemphasized poetry. ("That poetry wall was sustained by the fiction—trouble is, I threw more money into the poetry.") He probably overindulged the esoteric. ("As we began, we made sure to stock up on all sorts of books you'd never find elsewhere. But many of those volumes are still here—I can't even unload them in a 40 percent sale. And they just soaked up funds I should have been using on the classics. I mean, when you run out of Tolstoy, that's tragedy. When you run out of Dan Curly, who the hell cares?") And from the start the store was underfinanced. ("Maybe we shouldn't have started in the first place when we failed to reach our initial capital goal. Maybe the whole thing was a mistake.") But two causes loom over all the others—the relentless conglomeration of the book trade and the onset of the current recession.

"You know," Lennie said, "I'd like to think that publishers at one time really cared about what they published and really cared about the survival of small bookstores. Because small bookstores had to be the backbone of their sales, serving the community, sustaining the backlist—not only selling the current best-selling volume of some author but also his earlier tries. But that's changed. And it's not the editors' fault. It's not the salespeople's fault. Most salespeople are terrific people who really care about books; some once owned stores, were book people—only a few could just as well be selling shoes."

Well, whose fault is it then?

"Management. Almost all the once-independent companies have been swallowed up by conglomerates where policy is set principally by accountants and the principal policy is expediency. I mean, look at it: CBS owns Holt Rinehart, Times Mirror owns NAL, some railroad almost just took over Houghton Mifflin. And it goes the other way, too. Harcourt Brace owns Sea World! Only publisher who ever suffered a loss because their whale got sick. Some poor schmuck novelist got a sorry note—they couldn't publish his first novel because Snafu the Whale got diarrhea.

"So there's this division between the sales department and the credit department. Now, you'd think it would be to everybody's benefit that the store lives. But the credit people could care less. Just as it's easier to focus on big blockbusters—Harold Robbins, *The Joy of Diet Sex,* and so forth—so it's easier to deal through big chains.

"Why should publishers care about a little dippy store that maybe grosses $70,000 a year? B. Dalton nationwide probably does that in half an hour. And the publisher dealing with B. Dalton doesn't have to go to each store. He goes to Minneapolis, where one buyer buys for the whole country. That makes for a nice homogenous national culture, which is comfortable and is the best way to deal—*for them.* That's the way they give us cereal, so why should we get books any other way? But it's murder on small bookstores."

How so?

"Most companies for instance have a thirty-day policy. You have to pay for your order within thirty days or you're put on hold, they won't send you any more books. That's crazy. That means you have to turn over your entire inventory every thirty days. You can't do that if you're a small bookstore, especially if you stock backlist. Now, I know a lot of stores—the book comes in, and if it doesn't sell in a month, they just ship it back. We used to keep such a book for at least six months. I gave it a chance. I thought that's what they wanted me to do, let people hear about it, give the book a life. As a writer, I tried to treat the book the way I'd have liked my book to be treated.

"But many of the credit departments have no conception that some of us out here might be trying to run a different kind of operation from B. Dalton's, and that credit policies that make sense for a mass-market mainline store don't make any sense for an intimate effort like this. Some of the credit managers, like the guys at Penguin and Norton, they were at least human beings. But others—Random House!—don't get me started on Random House!"

During the last eighteen months of the store, when somebody would come in and ask for a title, Lennie would ask them who the publisher was, and if it was Random House, he'd tell them to forget it.

"Yeah, they were always putting me on hold. I'd fallen behind in my payments and they weren't going to ship me any books till I caught up. But how was I supposed to catch up if they didn't ship me any more books? If you don't get a steady supply of new things, it gets harder to sell what you have—people don't look as hard."

I asked Lennie what it was like to deal with the credit department at Random House.

"You mean like the time near the end when Random House would not send me copies of one of their books for which I was having a reading— they wouldn't ship me the box unless I paid for all the copies up front— you mean that conversation?"

Yeah, okay, that one.

"It was very tense. I told them to shove it. I told them they were very suppressive people, they didn't give a damn about small bookstores, that this wasn't some kind of joke, this was my life."

What did they say?

"This guy was a robot talking. Ticker tape spewed out of his mouth: Yes, yes, no, I understand, yes, no, we can't do that, policy, balance due, no. You can't even get those people angry."

Even faced with such obstacles, the bookstore had managed to contrive a tentative progress into its second year. Last summer things were moderately healthy, business was slightly ahead of where it had been the year before. But starting with September, sales began to fall precipitously. I asked Lennie what the recession had meant to him.

"It meant I couldn't pay my bills anymore. And why not? Because the dollar isn't worth anything anymore. It meant that people who would normally have bought three books now only bought one. People who used to come in once a week now came in once a month, because they couldn't afford to come in more often. Or they didn't come in at all anymore because they felt guilty. They'd have liked to support the store but they couldn't because the bag of groceries cost twenty-five dollars and it only gave them two dinners, some paper products, and some soap.

"The last few months, sales were off 40 percent. Let's talk about March and April when I would sit in the store from ten in the morning until seven at night—six days a week—and some nights, counting out at the end, I'd only have thirty-two dollars total in sales. One week we did under five hundred dollars. You know what that does to you?"

What does it do to you?

"It kills you. Little by little I was dying here. I mean, I'm only selling books I care about. I'm not selling crap. You have this store you care about and you're bringing in thirty dollars a day, five hundred dollars a week, two thousand dollars a month, which barely pays your fixed expenses, doesn't even pay the publishers anything, they're calling you and hounding you, when are you going to pay? You feel like shit."

Was there a final straw?

"Well, add to all that the fact that my expenses were simultaneously rising. I guess the last straw was when the building changed hands and the new landlord announced he was almost doubling the rent. I couldn't afford the new rent, but I couldn't afford to move, either. I guess I just realized that was it, it was over, I'd failed. I tried to negotiate with various credit departments, but one after another they turned me over to collection agencies, and at that point it becomes hopeless. So, with a great deal of sorrow, and even more a feeling of guilt, I had to declare bankruptcy."

During a period of weeks, whenever I'd spoken with Lennie about his impending bankruptcy, I'd been struck by these pervasive feelings of guilt. The failure I could understand, but the guilt eluded me. I asked him about it.

"It's just the American way, I guess, and the Italian way. I mean, it's not as if I've been hoarding all this money . . ."

How much had he taken from the store those three years?

"Funny you should ask, Lennie said, breaking into a wide grin. Reaching into his pocket, he pulled out his wallet, extracting and unfolding a crumpled index card onto which he'd scribbled a file of figures. "I keep this here just in case I ever start flirting with the idea of another store. Let's see. This is the money I took from this store—not including all the money I was putting into it at the same time, not counting the $14,000 that I poured into this thing initially and which I'll never see again. Okay: 1977—that was a good year, or actually half a year—$2,808; 1978—another good year, my first partner had split, for the whole twelve months, $2,605; then 1979, the peak year, both partners have split, I'm all on my own—$1,938; and finally, 1980, up through April, when I decided to put this thing out of its misery, $545. A nice even bell curve. Three years: $7,897."

So why the guilt?

"I averaged $2,600 a year those three years and I feel guilty because the publishers won't get it. They're only going to get a percentage. I was trained as a child that you don't borrow something from somebody and not pay them back."

But what if the economic system is designed so as to make you fail?

"Sure, sure," Lennie interrupted. "But nobody told me to open this store, nobody told me to specialize in this stuff. I have to accept that responsibility.

"And I feel like maybe I should have done more. A million things go through your head—you didn't do enough. Granted I put in all those hours, lost all that money, the dentist and the doctor visits I never allowed myself, the personal life that was affected, the friendships ruined, the tension, the pressure. But that was my decision, so I feel like somehow I didn't do enough.

"I don't know," Lennie said. "I guess we're trained to think that if we want something bad enough, it succeeds. If you love somebody enough, you'll be able to live with them forever. Of course, at another level, we know that's a lot of crap—love can't keep a marriage together or a store going. Turns out there's more to life than caring. I don't know: maybe it's a crime to want to do only what you want, what matters to you. Anyway, I feel guilty."

What had been striking to me for some time in all of this was how, except for a few isolated run-ins with robotoid credit managers, Lennie's guilt just would not translate into anger. Guilt is sometimes stoppered rage, and there was no dearth of occasion for rage in Lennie's tale. For starters, rage at a corporate system that could calmly deign the bankruptcy of X-thousand small businesses and the forced layoffs of X-hundred thousand factory workers as a legitimate means of "cooling off the economy." Instead of getting angry, Lennie seemed to pour it all back in on himself.

"How do you answer that?" Lennie countered, after a moment's quiet reflection. "All I know is that what I was doing here I cared about a tremendous amount and a lot of people cared about it and I feel guilty because I couldn't make it work. *I* didn't make it work. It doesn't matter whether anyone else could have made it work. I don't care about anyone else."

Lennie subsided again for a few moments. We refilled our cups, he went back to nursing his. As he resumed, free-associating, it began to seem a little clearer that the guilt wasn't entirely self-induced.

"Nothing's worse than talking to somebody over the phone and you tell them you sent a check and they call you a liar. And you did—you *did* send the check. You just want to die. It gets so you don't want to answer the phone anymore. You don't want to open the mail. 'Cause it's the same old shit—more bills, more threats, more demands. Nothing can make you want to do that.

"You put yourself through all this abuse," he continued, "and all you're trying to do is sell poetry and quality fiction. A nice drama section. You're just trying to sell some nice stuff, and these assholes jump all over you like you're some criminal, as if you just murdered some family, you wiped out the seven Dimicos, they're all gone, there are no Dimicos left because you killed them all in your shameful wickedness. And all you were trying to do was sell Kingsley Amis."

But it works, I pointed out. "You do feel guilty."

"Yeah, well, I do. In the long run it doesn't matter whether I succeeded at this—this is a piddle in the universe—but no one told me to do it. No one said, 'Leonard, go open a literary bookstore in West L.A. because they need one.' I did it of my own free will.

"It was a matter of drawing the line: 'This is how I as a person am defining me, here are my definitions.' And you lay them down. And you stand by them. That's all I did here. And I couldn't stand by them."

And that, finally, is what the guilt is all about.

"It doesn't matter whether it was my fault. It doesn't matter if the economy is collapsing. The point is, the lines were laid and I couldn't keep 'em there. This store, which was my line, my statement, is over. It's finished. The guilt is that it's no longer here—that I, with all my background, my smarts, my charm, my talk, my bluff, couldn't keep it going. Basically I just bluffed for three years. It's like I stayed in the bar for three years getting beat up. Stupid. Just to prove some point. And I don't even know what the point was anymore. And now I've been thrown out. And I'm not going back in."

Lennie smiled, always one to find sustenance in an apt metaphor.

So, I asked him—so, what are you going to do now, guilty person?

"I'm going to lay low for a long time," he laughed. "I'm going to disappear. I'm not going to be seen. I'm leaving my ex-partner's number as the forwarding address. I'm going to move back to New York, get a job, make real money, feel what it's like to go to movies on a regular basis, to live a normal life and not feel like a fugitive or an indentured servant. Not space out in the middle of a conversation because the Kramerbooks bill just passed through my mind. I'm going to try to get back to what I'm supposed to be doing, get back to my writing."

Notwithstanding the mire of the past year, Lennie is first and foremost a writer. In fact, he's an exceptional novelist. One of his manuscripts, *Rizzo and Mike,* which has been kicking around New York publishers for some time now—just a little too intimate to have any chance at blockbusting—may be the finest thing I've read on what it's like to try and sustain a relationship today—the need for commitment, the fear of commitment (Mike's short for Michelle). I mention this because Lennie opens the novel with an epigram that could just as well serve as epitaph for his bookstore. It's from the "Matchbook Poem" by Paul Blackburn, and it reads:

> BUT WHY do you always go to the wall?
> Why does he go to the wall?
>
> You go to the wall
> because that's where
> the door is
>
> maybe.

Postscript (1988)

Lennie did move back to New York City, where he soon got a job managing a discount shoe store. "If I was going to have to sell books as if they were shoes," he'd sometimes quip wistfully, "I'd rather be selling shoes." After that he managed a television set rental outlet. He wrote a novel that at one point he was going to call *Retail*. Some years later, he got a job running the student store and teaching English and Speech at a prep school out on Long Island, which is where he is today. He has assured me that, no, he's not going to stock this book in his student store and that, furthermore, if any of his students so much as hears about it, he's going to kill me.

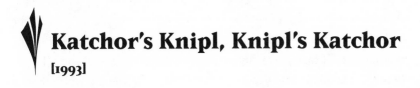

Katchor's Knipl, Knipl's Katchor
[1993]

How old is Julius Knipl, anyway? These days, as he scratches out his decidedly marginal subsistence as a real-estate photographer (his life's third vocation, following stints as a pony-cart concessionaire and, before that, a long time ago, a dance-school instructor), his mind seems perennially adrift in the forties, or maybe even the thirties, his heart's true home. He's kind of ageless. Let's be generous and say he's well into his late middle years. Short, stout, his squarish face distinguished by a pencil-thin mustache, his thinning hair almost invariably covered by the same vaguely rumpled, dark-banded hat, Knipl wanders the city's streets in his baggy, crumpled suit, his camera slung over his back, moving steadily, if somewhat languorously, from one piddling assignment to the next, his mind cut loose in time. He positions himself and his camera on the sidewalk across the street from his morning's quarry (some fleabag hotel, say, or a low-slung office building), and as he waits out the sun's slow transit—waits, that is, until the shadows line themselves up just right—he gives himself over to reminiscence. He summons up the *smell* of soda bottles floating in the dark ice water of those refrigerator cases in the back corners of long-ago cigar and candy stores; or he decants the names of the many drinks you used to be able to order at almost any soda fountain around town—a cherry lake, a Normona, a Latin cream, a Nadjy, a vanilla Tyrol, a grape bosphorous, a Herbert water (featuring in each case the precisely calibrated combination of carbonated water, syrup, and some highly unlikely third ingredient, such as, in the case of Herbert water, half-sour milk).

He snaps his picture and moves on, noticing things all the while: the way, for instance, that at certain hours of the morning passing customers get reflected in the glaze of the fresh cheese Danishes piled in the vitrine beneath a certain deli's cash register. He contemplates the annual harvest of last year's phone books, or the origins of the tall lifeguard stands inhabited by store security guards on the sidewalks up and down Fourteenth Street (the irony, of course, being that when these guards get their man he drowns). Such things can set Knipl to pondering for the better part of a week. Shuffling on toward his next assignment (he is self-employed and does most of his business by way of pay phones and an answering machine), he can pass a newspaper stand and intuit an entire swath of social history, such as the sad fate of those companies which once manufactured the variously shaped iron slugs that standkeepers used to use to weigh down their piles of newspapers. Those particular manufacturers, he realizes, must have lost out some time ago to the distributors of today's cheap, freebie rectangular aluminum weights with their cigarette-company logos. Inwardly, he grieves for the iron-slug manufacturers, just as he worries about the eight-foot-long balloon venders. (It's a tragedy, he mutters to himself, the way they unfailingly choose the wrong location—the financial district, the garment district, the sidewalk in front of the criminal court; a man forced into such a business no longer has the presence of mind to stop and consider the possible uses of an eight-foot-long balloon and so naturally has no idea where to sell them.) He wonders, too, about some of those business establishments occupying the upper stories of many of the city's older buildings—twenty floors up, and still they've bothered to have their names carefully painted on the windows facing the street, even though the names must be completely illegible to passersby down below. (Could it be that people used to have more acute eyesight in the olden days, he wonders. Or maybe there once existed a single, particularly unscrupulous sign painter who systematically worked his way up each new building, floor by floor, pointing at each level to his success at convincing the denizens of the floor immediately below?)

He marvels at the eternal flame under a sauerkraut vat in one of his favorite hot dog stands or, later on, in the park, at the perfect fit of form to function in a trash collector's litter-spearing tool. He never judges, he hardly ever acts; mainly, he just observes. He knows the location of the convertible-sofa-workers'-union cemetery, and which bus passes by its modest entrance—though not as often as it did in the olden days, owing to declining ridership.

After completing another assignment, he dives into a dairy cafeteria, and the cheap ready-made sign above the lavatory basin sets him to musing on the original Section 84 of the Public Health Code, composed by a committee of sanitation engineers back in 1921, a delicately wrought chain of argumentation setting out the legal basis for human decency—"It is in these private moments that one must reaffirm the tacit agreement that exists between all men and women"—whose graceful exposition has been hopelessly garbled and obscured over the years, streamlined and abridged beyond recognition: "Wash hands after using toilet."

Evening comes on, the light begins to fade, and Knipl heads down into the subway, bound for home. He remembers and yet he can't be sure (his universe frequently shimmers like this between precision and indeterminacy): Was he just dreaming, or didn't uniformed men once walk the inside tracks of the city's subway system? They must have been hired to inspect the rails, but they always seemed to have their heads buried in soft leatherbound manuals. (Subway regulations, he seems to recall wondering at the time, or else the Holy Bible. Or did such things happen at all?) He begins to ask himself if some of his other fond memories—the chocolate-filled vending machines bolted to the subway pylons, the subterranean luncheonettes, the advertising ponies—might not themselves have been of a similarly imaginary nature. In the same way that a doctor associates certain physical signs with the end of human life, Knipl knows what to expect at the last stop of any subway line: a trophy manufacturer, a movie theatre converted into a business school, the offices of a wedding orchestra, a bus drivers' uniform-and-supply store, an illegal franchise of a defunct fast-food chain, a plastic-slipcover showroom . . . Knipl notices the way a new patch of sidewalk gradually gets scuffed over to the point where it blends in with its neighboring panels—except, that is, at night, when it alone fails to sparkle. Tonight, as every night, when he curls into the narrow bed in his narrow three-room apartment, Knipl recites to himself, in a barely audible voice, a few lines from the multiple-dwelling law. He falls into a fitful sleep. His loneliness is so palpable, the density of his experience so prodigious, that it's hard to believe he's merely a cartoon character.

But that's what he is.

And he's barely five years old.

Which, of course, raises a question about the age of his creator—Ben Katchor—and here things really get murky. Over the phone, as we arrange an appointment, Katchor sounds, if anything, even older than Knipl. "A voice emanating from a Lower East Side Automat" is how one of Katchor's editors once described that voice for me. It is a deeply resigned voice, a sort of dispirited whine—a sigh in every phrase, a shrug in every sigh. Katchor can't imagine why anyone would want to meet him on account of the *Knipl* strip—he doesn't even believe that there's anyone out there actually following the strip, although Russ Smith, the founder and editor of the New York *Press*, a free weekly downtown tabloid, which has prominently showcased *Knipl* since the paper's inception in April of 1988, assures me that the strip is one of the paper's most prized regular features. "I don't know," Katchor sighs repeatedly during our phone conversation. "I don't know, beats me." At length, though, he finally agrees to a meeting at his office, downtown.

On the subway ride there, I lose myself in a recent *Knipl* anthology, *Cheap Novelties: The Pleasures of Urban Decay*, and as I emerge from the IRT at Fulton Street and head east along the squeezed, narrowing nub of John Street, I feel transformed—or, rather, the world does. The neighborhood seems positively awash in Knipliana—or is it just that suddenly I'm seeing everything through a Knipl lens? There's Farouk

Men's Clothing; the Roxy Food Shop; the Mahony employment agency, advertising its services from a second-floor walkup; an OTB outlet; one shop boasting its proficiency in Vulca-soling ("A nu way to resole!"), while its rival, diagonally across the street, identifies itself simply as "Shoetrician." At the address that Katchor has given me—"a low-rent office building that no self-respecting optimistic business-man would ever want to be discovered in" is how he described the place to me during our phone call—I take the elevator up eight flights, find my way to his door, and knock, and the stooped, lanky figure emerging from behind the opening door turns out to be . . . well, a kid. Hardly more than a teen-ager, from the looks of him: smooth cheeks, flowing dark hair, liquid brown eyes, a prominently bobbing Adam's apple—a beanpole swathed in a black sweater, black jeans, black socks, and white basketball sneakers. But looks can be deceiving. If (deaf) you'd only seen him—or, conversely, if (blind) you'd only heard him—you would probably never have been able to guess that he's ac-tually forty-one years old.

Katchor opened the door wider and ushered me in. "So," he said, without missing a beat from our phone conversation, "as you can see, not much." His digs were dark, the shelves and tables covered with an as yet indeterminate clutter. While my eyes were adjusting to the gloom, he volunteered a bit of the building's history. It had first gone up around 1900, he said—"An old building, but very forward-looking for its time." For a while, the neighborhood had been a jewelry dis-trict, catering to Wall Street, and the building had been filled with such enterprises as pearl-stringing operations. He pointed to some ex-posed bolts in the gray painted floor, left over from some kind of light manufacture. As time went by, the building was occupied by small-time insurance outfits, clipping bureaus, and the like, but by the mid-seventies, when he moved in, almost all of them had moved out. "I've been here one full cycle," he said. "The building was nearly empty when I arrived, it filled up with artist types during the late seventies and early eighties, and now it seems to have emptied out again. I'm still here, though—or part of the time, anyway." A few years ago, he moved out of the city for the first time in his life, to Providence, Rhode Island, but he retains this place and makes a point of coming down for a few days every couple of weeks, to attend to strip business and collect fresh ideas.

My eyes were growing accustomed to the dimness now, and the clutter was beginning to differentiate into an astonishing protean hoard. Bookshelves sagged under the weight of ragged old volumes—an *Encyclopedia of Aberrations, The Elements of Highway Engineering, The Lexicon of the Yiddish Theater,* books on magic and Victorian England and toys and obscure cults. Katchor followed my gaze. "Most of that stuff comes from the outside bins at the Strand," he said, almost apologetically. "I make it a rule never to pay more than fifty cents for a book." The shelves also held a broken accordion, a slew of dusty papier-mâché pumpkins, a couple of door-to-door-salesman trophies (little gilded men striding purposefully, their gilded briefcases swaying). Pinned up on the walls were a faded poster for the 1933 Chicago International Exposition, several New Haven bus transfers, a faded engraving of a Puerto Rican lighthouse, some cards for Capern's Finch Mix, and an array of matchbox labels. "I'm a member of the British Matchbox Label and Booklet Society," Katchor told me, waving toward a pyramid of brittle old boxes in one corner. "The serious collectors usually limit themselves to the labels alone, but, for some reason, I like the whole box—especially the ones from India." He probed among the diminutive packages—All-American, Bird's Eye, Club House ("which actually—see?—happens to have been made in Russia"), The Arc Light, Hotel Astor—and eventually turned up a few of the Indian boxes. "Incredible," he said. "The care those people showered upon such completely incidental objects—*four-color lithography!* Amazing."

Sliding open an ancient wooden filing cabinet, Katchor revealed another collection, this one of cheap, cheap novelties, cheesy toys from the days when the label "Made in Japan" had an entirely different connotation. "I like the cheapest things, the orphans, the ones hanging in the *back* of the kinds of stores that most people would never dream of stepping into in the first place. Slum toys, they're sometimes called. Like this one here." He held out a palm-size plastic doll labelled "Suk'g Baby." Carefully, almost reverently, he put it back. He pulled out a pack of toy cigarettes and then a Voice Tester, a little cardboard pad with a wooden button: push the button and you get to discover the little needle embedded inside—a regular laugh sensation. Strange things.

The building shuddered—a groan, a rattling in the rafters. "Oh, that's nothing," Katchor assured me. "Just the counterweights of the elevator. Gets so you don't even notice it."

I asked him where he had got the inspiration for Julius Knipl.

"Well, one day, several years back, I got a call from Art Spiegelman, who told me to call Russ Smith, I think that's how it was," he said. "For many years, I've contributed to *RAW*, the magazine of avant-garde comics that Spiegelman and his wife, Françoise Mouly, put out. Anyway, Smith used to run a paper in Baltimore, and now he was launching this new paper here, and Art thought that I'd be a good person to do a strip, and so I made the call and Smith made an offer. So I began to think about what I might do in that kind of format. I mean, I've been drawing cartoons ever since I was a child—in fact, I even edited a cartoon journal of my own, this thing here." He pulled out two issues of *Picture Story*—the only two issues, as it happens, one dated 1978, the other 1986. They feature his own work—long, seemingly mundane narratives that turn increasingly surreal—and also strange and remarkable contributions by such like-visioned spirits as Jerry Moriarty, Martin Millard, Peter Blegvad, Mark Beyer, and an anonymous Dutch artist (circa 1840). "Nobody wants this sort of thing," Katchor conceded dispiritedly. "There's no market. Bookstores won't stock them, and when you attempt to get comics places to carry them it's like pouring vinegar into Coke and trying to sell that. Pathetic. So, anyway, here was a chance to do something on a more regular basis, and I wanted to come up with something more—what should I say?—*commercial*. I realized that with a strip you need a principal character who can carry the action of the story from week to week, but I was having a hard time figuring what my character should be. I was mulling that over—now, remember, this was five years ago, and in those days real estate was still hot, and photography was hot, and so, well, I figured *real estate photography!* That ought to be hot." He paused, winced, shook his head disconsolately. "I know, I know—desperate. Just shows you."

I asked him where he got the name "Knipl."

"It's Yiddish," he said. "And it's one of those Yiddish words you can't really translate. It's sort of a nest egg, you know, the little treasure you store away for a rainy day—they say, 'That's your knipl.' And the strip's all about the little treasures of the city—not exactly this city, but almost. This city in some slightly different time—maybe just before I was born. And, in fact, what Knipl does is what I, as a child, thought all grown-ups did—you know, head out into the city, walk around all day, have these little adventures. So it's the past but at the same time not the past, it's very much the present—though maybe it's true that that way of *looking* has been dying out. Everywhere you go these days, there's still so much of the old stuff preserved, as if in a state of perpetual decay, right there, just beneath all the superficial modernizations—the buildings with their sleek new lobbies, and one flight up you're back in the nineteenth century. And this strip gives me a chance to catalogue all that, to work toward something like an encyclopedia of the city. My utopian city, with all its little horrible things. Or maybe not utopian—idealized, rather. The strip is the closest I can come to approximating my perfect city."

And Knipl, I asked—how old is he?

"Oh, I don't know," Katchor replied, seemingly confounded by the question. "Kind of my age, I guess. Forty maybe, forty-five." ("Yeah," Art Spiegelman subsequently agreed, when I passed along this estimate of Katchor's. Spiegelman said he, too, had often wondered about Knipl's age. "But the way forty looks when you're fifteen years old." Perhaps. Or maybe *that's* the secret of Knipl's age: he's invariably twenty-five years older than anyone who happens to be reading about him.) "Forty, forty-five," Katchor repeated. "He's like one of those guys you pass in the world—in the elevator, say—who always seem to be wearing their father's baggy clothes. Though, incidentally, my strips are a big success in Italy. They used to get serialized there in *Dolce Vita*, a now-defunct Milan comics journal. *Knipl* runs in alternative papers in Miami, Washington, Seattle, Fairfield County, and half a dozen other places—the smaller the venue, it seems, the greater the visibility. And, oh, yeah, in San Diego. I have no idea what they make of it in San Diego. But in Italy, maybe, I guess, they loved my strips because of their *look*. The baggy pants, the oversized jackets—just like all those upscale Italian designers."

I asked Katchor about his father. Was he an inspiration for Knipl?

"Not really," he replied. "Not exactly. See, Knipl never really gets involved, he just observes. My father was much more political. He was a Communist Yiddishist from Warsaw whom fate pushed into becoming a landlord. Actually, he'd apprenticed as a tailor, but then he emigrated, first to Palestine and then to Brazil, and he must have got into farming somewhere along the line, because when he eventually arrived here he first ran a combination chicken farm and Communist hotel up in Saratoga. He had a wife and son. His son enlisted in the Army at the very outset of the war, even though as an only child on a farm he didn't have to. He served as a mechanic on a bomber, got shot down over Africa, killed. I'm the replacement son.

"After his son's death, my father traded his farm and hotel for an apartment building in Bed-Stuy and became a small-time landlord, so it was through him that I got to see the inside of that pathetic business. He got a new wife, my mother. She'd been a nurse, but after they were married she was—well, my mother. He never really talked about his first wife—there was a plaster bust of her in a straw basket in the basement, and that's basically all I ever knew of her. But my father was very political, all wrapped up in utopian schemes: about, for instance, how he was going to transform his apartment building into a commune of some kind, which he eventually did—a complete disaster. That, or how he was going to go to the Soviet Union and teach them advanced methods of chicken farming. Which he never did. But he was very involved. He was the one who took *me* to the SDS headquarters. He was so political that he used up all the space for politics in the family—so that the sixties kind of passed me by. I was buried in comics."

Katchor continued, "I mean, occasionally my father serves as an inspiration for some of the things that run through *Knipl*. For instance, the stuff a while back about the Drowned Men's Association." Every once in a while, *Knipl* meanders off, over several installments, into odd, wispy, curlicue subplots. Katchor was referring to a sequence last fall that intimated the existence of an upstate rural asylum for failed small-time businessmen: "At five o'clock each evening, a bus waits on the corner of Roman Boulevard and Rossel Avenue to save those men who have gone under for the third time," one caption says, over a drawing of an idling bus with the logo "Good Riddance" plastered on its side. The place was a retreat for such acquaintances of Knipl's as the journeyman salesman for Golden Calf Brand Pot Cheese, whose desire to make money, after sixteen years, "suddenly went dry, like the rubber gasket on an old refrigerator door." One day he was just gone—his family had no idea where—but "his coworkers seemed to understand." One of them is portrayed shovelling paraphernalia from the top of the salesman's abandoned desk into an open box ("The instinct to survive is perishable," the officemate mutters, "it also has an expiration date") and then depositing the box out back with the trash ("Carbon copies of every order he took," the deadpan caption notes, "a densely packed Rolodex, scraps of paper filled with promising leads and a map of his territory were placed on public display for twenty-four hours"). The pot-cheese man, the salesman for Tsimtsum Industries (purveyors of artificial-leather phylacteries, polyester prayer shawls, and assorted novelty mezuzot), and a defeated kitchen-set vender named Johnny Sumac: they all make their way to the bus and are transported to an idyllic communal resort, where the operators "even run a diesel engine on tracks across the basement of the dormitory building, every twenty

minutes, all night long"—or so a contribution-soliciting man in sand-
wich boards explains to Knipl, back in town, at the local cafeteria,
while proffering a collection pan labelled "D.M.A." Knipl deposits a
quarter, though wondering, "Why save a man from drowning, only to
let him die of homesickness?" The final panel shows a man in a sleeve-
less undershirt sleeping on a narrow bed, a full moon streaming
through a leafy window, and the sound "RUMBABA" welling up from
below. (Katchor is great with sounds.) "Number seven uptown local,"
the saved drowned man dreams.

"And, obviously, that whole sequence harks back to my father,"
Katchor said. "But, if anything, it's been my own experiences that have
provided the bulk of the inspiration for the *Knipl* strip. Just out of
school, for example, there were three of us who started this little type-
setting and graphics business. None of us wanted to get up early, and
this was something where you could do the work itself late at night.
You could work out of very cheap premises, and it was a way of making modest money fresh from day one. Not a lot, but—well, barely
enough to live on, actually. But it really exposed us to a world. We did
everything—pasteup and layout for real low-end magazines, fortune-
telling flyers, gypsy palm cards, self-published rants. We typeset books
on iridology—you know, the science of diagnosing disease through the
patterns and lines in the irises of people's eyes. We produced stickers
for cheap watches—'Fourteen carat,' that kind of thing—and takeout-
deli menus, fish labels for the Fulton Fish Market, come-on pamphlets
for dubious wholesale enterprises. Walking along the street, we'd constantly be coming upon our stuff, discarded, in the gutters. It was grue-
some. But going out to drum up that kind of business, the people who
came in through the door—this is how I learned all about small business." In the biographical notes accompanying his early contributions
to the first several issues of *RAW*, back in the early eighties, Katchor
himself was identified simply as "a small businessman."

"And I filter all that through *Knipl*," Katchor said, "I mean, not
literally—I make things up. For instance, the whole bit about the

newspaper-weight manufacturers. I invented an entire industry solely from my imagination, but then one day a few weeks later I got a letter from this old guy, retired upstate, telling me how he himself had been in that very business—the letter was written on very old-fashioned stationery with a little engraving of the factory itself up in the corner—and he thanked me profusely for, as he put it, 'memorializing it as it really was.'"

I asked Katchor a bit more about his childhood—where he grew up, how he got into comics.

"My first several years, our family lived in Bed-Stuy, but when I was in the second grade we moved to Crown Heights, to an apartment between Washington and Franklin, where Carol Street dead-ends into the shuttle line. I have a terrible sense of dates, but I remember that just before my first year of high school every white person I knew up and moved to Coney Island, almost from one day to the next."

Why hadn't his family moved?

"I don't know. Somebody had to be the last white family, I guess. Everybody else saw it coming. Maybe my father thought it would stop at fifty-fifty. But we stayed on there for several more years, and I went to Erasmus High, in Flatbush, and eventually the family moved to the other side of Prospect Park, to Kensington. My father died there, a few years later, in 1971."

After a moment, he went on, "As I say, though, the main thing I remember from all those years was the immersion in comics. I was hardly alone. All my friends were art historians of the comics, connoisseurs of individual styles, veritable Berensons of exquisitely refined sensibility. We not only knew all the artists, we knew all the *inkers*—we could tell when they changed inkers! We'd analyze every frame, debate each gesture. My own favorite strip was Steve Ditko's *Spider-Man*—this was a decidedly minority taste. Most of the other kids went for the muscle-bound superheroes, and Spider-Man was more scrawny and sinewy. In fact, it wasn't his adventures that excited me so much as the drawing—the stories were good enough, but they were just an excuse for the drawing, whose energy thrilled me. I used to spend hours studying Ditko's conceptualized anatomy, the way he manipulated his characters through space, observing them from every angle, in every position. Somehow, I intuitively realized that this was only a few steps removed from the most serious and elevated forms of representational drawing. I mean, I never went to galleries or anything—this was my art education. And I had my own ongoing strip—a plainclothes-adventure-detective-spy saga. I did attend some classes at the Brooklyn Museum Art School—had a teacher there with sense enough not to discourage me, figured I'd outgrow it.

"And, in a sense, I did. I set aside my cartooning when I went to Brooklyn College. I majored in painting—there, and then for a stint at Visual Arts, and then back to Brooklyn College—and studied the history of art. But I still found myself most attracted to work that told a story, that explored character, that elaborated a philosophical idea. I loved Poussin, for instance. And, as time passed, I found myself thinking about comics again. Only, now I wanted to see if I could render them with all the density of a novel. The point is that, because they exist there on a page, the reader ought to be able to stop, to go back, to step back and get a sense of the whole, to focus in on a single detail. It's not like film, where you're inexorably propelled forward. In comics you can get lost in a single panel for half an hour—and, ideally, the panel ought to be able to bear the weight of that kind of attention."

I asked Katchor about film. Fans of the *Knipl* strip often characterize its visual style as that of film noir—particularly the free-floating, seemingly untethered point of view, with its frequently uncanny foreshortenings. In one panel, the vantage may be the ceiling fan's, while in the next it becomes the curb's. Tight closeups give way to wide scans. Had he been much influenced by film?

"On the contrary," Katchor assured me. "It's the film-noir directors, or so I've been told, who were influenced by the same comic strips that influenced me. Maybe that's where they got the idea for their strange vantages. But those odd angles are never indulged in for their own sake—not in *Knipl,* anyway. They're intended in part to keep things fresh, in part to highlight some sort of relationship that might not otherwise suggest itself, and mainly to *reveal* things, to reveal deeper levels in the narrative."

The style of Katchor's narration is likewise extraordinarily sophisticated and deeply layered. In fact, there are generally no fewer than three separate narrative strands coursing concurrently through a *Knipl* strip. The captions, the voice balloons, and the images all move at their own distinctive pace, often at cross-purposes—competing streams of consciousness. I've heard Knipl described as "a two-bit Leopold Bloom," and the phrase seems to refer not just to his mode of being, the exalted attentiveness lavished on the most mundane of concerns, but also to the manner in which that being, his very consciousness, gradually gets divulged. I asked Katchor to what extent modernist literature had been an influence on his style.

"I don't know," he replied. "Not that much. I mean, I read *Ulysses, A Portrait of the Artist as a Young Man.* I particularly admire Nabokov. I like William James a lot, the poetical way he is able to describe states of mind. I am fascinated by Henry Mayhew, the Victorian sociologist who undertook an incredible dissection of the way the lowliest Londoners managed to live their lives. I get letters every once in a while from a guy in Kansas assuring me that I must have been enormously influenced by the French post-structuralists, people like Georges Perec, but, frankly, I haven't really read them that much, and there, again, the point is, rather, that we share a common source—they, too, were reared on comic strips.

"No, the biggest influence is the strip itself, the challenge posed by each new empty panel. I am deeply engaged by the conflict, the tension, between words and pictures—the way in which the image doesn't have to just illustrate the words but can range quite far afield. At first, you do it just out of boredom—who wants to be slavishly illustrating words all the time? But then it gets to be a value in itself. I spend a lot of time thinking about thinking, about the different tracks that thought and perception regularly take, how they diverge and then realign, how the divergences themselves at times disguise deeper alignments—all that. In that sense, I'm not a surrealist, as some people sometimes claim—I'm a *naturalist*. This is what thinking is like, it seems to me, what remembering is like—or, in Knipl's case, what remembering remembering is like."

Or dreaming that you're remembering remembering.

Knipl is by no means the only outlet for Katchor's creative sensibility. Over the last year, he was simultaneously producing an entirely different and, if anything, even stranger weekly strip, *The Jew of New York,* which climaxed a fifty-two-week run in the April 9, 1993, issue of the English-language weekly, the *Forward,* heir to the old Yiddish *Forverts.*

"You've heard of *that?*" Katchor stammered, incredulous, when I brought up the subject. "I didn't think *anybody* had heard of that. I mean, I know the editor read it, but I can't imagine anybody else did. That strip didn't really go anywhere until about the thirtieth installment. It just kind of wandered around—the wandering strip. But I guess it was serving its function. It filled a space."

Filling a space was indeed precisely how it began—the space left empty, that is, when the *Forward*'s serialization of Art Spiegelman's *Maus II* ended, in early 1992. The *Forward*'s cultural editor, Jonathan Rosen—at Spiegelman's urging—asked Katchor whether he'd like to take over the slot. Rosen's successor, Philip Gourevitch, has assured me that in fact *The Jew of New York* was passionately followed. "Each week, when a new installment arrived, we'd all gather around and try to figure out what it all meant," he told me. "The drawing was magnificent; the plotting—well, it was complicated. But there were people who subscribed to the *Forward* for that strip alone. Others didn't have a clue to what was going on in it, and some of *those* subscribed for its sake alone."

The Jew of New York took place in 1830 and appeared to be historically rooted—in part, anyway. The action revolved (and receded and recoiled and recanted and reverted) around the imminent production of a new play at the Bowery's New World Theatre—a play that was a thinly veiled satire on the at-that-time-recent fiasco involving the proto-Zionist "Mordecai Manuel Noah (1786–1851)," who in 1825 had somehow "acquired Grand Island, in the Niagara River, near Buffalo"—this according to Katchor's opening caption—and then "proclaimed himself governor and judge of Israel and called for the ingathering of all Jews, including the Karaites, Samaritans, American Indians and other lost tribes of Israel." The caption goes on, "He called his 'City of Refuge' Ararat. Nothing came of this grandiose scheme. The Jews remained scattered, Noah went on to become a literary and political lion of New York City, and there our story begins."

The Jew of New York was not Noah himself, but, rather, the name of the play about him. Noah himself barely appeared in the strip at all (another instance of Katchor's near-maniacal penchant for indirection). But dozens of other, vividly imagined characters did appear, in ever more confounding interrelationships. Among them were Samson Gergel, the New World Theatre's scenic decorator and token Jew; Maynard Daizy, the theatre's pompous leading man, who was presently going to attempt to embody the starring role; Isaac Azarael, a middleman in the Oriental button trade; Nathan Kishon, a disbarred *shochet,* or ritual slaughterer, who, disappointed in Noah's utopia, instead spent five years in the wilderness, emerged with a trove of beaver pelts, and returned to Manhattan, where each evening he abandoned his hotel room to sleep in a plot of grass across the street, as naked as an Indian; "a man in a vulcanized India rubber suit" who meandered along and into the North River, reading from a damp old pamphlet containing evidence that Indian tribes were indeed of Hebrew descent; an Indian named Elim-min-nopee (a quintessentially Katchorian construction: l-m-n-o-p), who in fact did recite the Psalms, in perfect Hebrew, every Friday as part of a novelty act; Hershel Goulbat, a violently competitive impresario and Elim-min-nopee's manager, who one evening mistook the sleeping Kishon for a potential rival; Francis Oriole, a fervent entrepreneur with a scheme for carbonating all of Lake Erie in an attempt to cash in on the recent craze for seltzer water; Enoch Letushim, a Palestinian messenger in town peddling soil from the Holy Land; Yosl Feinbroyt, a latter-day disciple of the famed Kabbalist Abraham Abulafia; Mr. Marah, a schemer seemingly intent on stripping Kishon of his beaver pelts; and, toward the end of the strip's run, Professor Solidus, a weirdly veiled playwright and renowned anti-Semitic pamphleteer, whose fear of hotels compelled him to reside on the third floor of the New World Theatre, where his latest comedy, *The Jew of New York,* was about to open. The strip offered a dizzying concentrate of plot, culminating when Samson Gergel's most inspired staging device—a vat of herring simmering in vinegar and water in the theatre's cellar, whose smells were to be piped up to the audience each time Maynard Daizy made one of his ostentatious entrances—caught fire, bringing down the entire place.

The fact is that, far from being unknown, Katchor's *The Jew of New York* proved decidedly controversial, though in an oddly Kniplian fashion. At any rate, it aroused the righteous indignation of Morris U. Schappes, an American Jewish historian who is the editor of *Jewish Currents,* the nearly half-century-old democratic, socialist, pro-Israel, non-Zionist journal of the Association for the Promotion of Jewish Secularism. In June of last year, early in the strip's trajectory, Schappes used the pages of his magazine to rail against this new apparition on the scene, assuring his readers that, though he had two entire books on the actual, true-life Mordecai Manuel Noah on his shelf at home, he could find no reference either to a play entitled *The Jew of New York* or to a New World Theatre in New York. Also, he noted, with an argument-clinching chop, Noah's birthdate was 1785, not 1786. What, he demanded to know, was Katchor using as his source?

In a subsequent issue of the journal, Schappes recorded how "On June 15 I received a letter from Mr. Katchor complaining I had misunderstood him and asking me to 'Do the right thing and print a correction.' Then he [Katchor] added: 'My strip is the fevered dream of an amateur historian in which the "real" lives of New York Jews, c. 1830, are fleshed out and given the breath of poetic truth. There was a "New World Theatre" on the Bowery in New York City. I saw it in my dream. I swear." This reply left Schappes almost speechless. "What," he asked his readers, "was I to make of this effusion?"

I mentioned Schappes's consternation to Katchor—here, at least, was one other person who had followed the strip.

"Ah, yes," Katchor conceded, shaking his head mournfully. "My polemic. Our pitiful little controversy. But it's really true what I wrote him: I came upon Noah in a footnote—that's all I knew about him. I didn't know anything about him, which is why I did the strip. *Knipl* is everything I know; *The Jew of New York* was everything I don't know. And those were indeed the dreams of an amateur historian: he did a little research, he went to sleep, and those were his fevered imaginings."

Katchor looked at the clock on the wall. (He doesn't wear a watch.) "Oh," he said. "It's getting late. I have to be catching my train back to Providence. My wife will be waiting."

"He told you about his wife?" Art Spiegelman sputtered, astonished, when I recounted to him my visit with Katchor a few days later. "I knew him *well*—worked with him on a regular basis—for over seven years, and the entire time I never knew he was married."

Russ Smith made a similar comment. "One evening at a party, he came up to me, shyly, as usual—he's the most modest, self-effacing artist I've ever known—and he introduced a woman, saying, 'This is my wife.' I was flabbergasted. Not only that: turns out he has a teenage kid as well."

The point is not exactly that Katchor is shy; I mean, he is shy, he's very shy. But, rather, it's that usually he doesn't seem to want to burden you with the weight of such inconsequential bits of knowledge.

As he was assembling his papers and sketches and sliding them into a satchel, however, he even mentioned his daughter to me—his stepdaughter, actually. "She's finishing high school, and she really has no use for comics," he said. "It's like me and my father, I guess. Your parents, whatever they're into, it ruins it for you. She finds comic strips terribly boring—I don't push them on her. She sees the strip business for what it is. Terribly hard work, a miserable way to make a living. Pathetic. Hopeless."

I asked him why his family had moved up to Providence. (My friend who has called Knipl "a two-bit Leopold Bloom" surmises that Providence must be Katchor's Trieste.)

"We needed a change," he said. "Both my wife and I grew up and spent our whole lives here in New York City, but it was getting too hard—too expensive, too cramped. I mean, in a better world we'd have gone to Paris or London or something. Providence was easier to arrange. We heard about it because the *Knipl* strip runs in a small paper up there, and some people told us it was a good place. It's all right—there are remnants of a city there. And anyway, the room I work in, that's really not Rhode Island." He paused. "And it's good to get a little distance. Here there's so much stuff it's like I have to shut it out. There I'm dying for it. Like the sound of a car going over a manhole cover, the rattle it makes. There, I don't know what it is—they must bolt the manholes down or something, it's a sound you never hear. And it's a sound you can grow to crave."

He zipped his satchel shut, made a quick last survey of the premises. I suggested that he might be forgetting his notebook. "No," he said. "I don't keep a notebook. If I had a notebook, I'd be terrified of losing it. No, I come down here, get my ideas for *Knipl*, and record them on little scraps of paper." He patted his various pockets. "Actually, this has been a relatively good trip; I'm going home with a few possible ideas." He reached into his back pocket and pulled out a crumpled scrap of paper. "Let's see. Oh, yeah. The brass property lines they embed in concrete sidewalks—what are they for? Fear of lawsuits, maybe." He pulled a scrap out of his shirt pocket. "The milking of the turnstiles—how they go around hooking canvas buckets under the subway turnstiles, extracting the tokens." He turned the scrap over, put it back in his pocket, pulled out another. "The orientation of men's body hair: I mean, the actual *direction* in which it lies on the body, the patterns . . ." He returned that scrap to its pocket and then was silent for a moment. "The best ones are things I never saw the interest in before. Like today I was walking down the street and noticed a very faded, tattered, almost illegible old sign, a sign from—who knows?—maybe forty, fifty years ago, warning about rat poison." He smiled, wonderingly, "I mean, think about it: the rats are long gone, the people who posted the warning are gone, the people they were warning are gone. The sign's still there. It's a knipl."

Postscript (1995)

Some people feel that with his ongoing *Julius Knipl, Real Estate Photographer* strip, Ben Katchor has over the past several years been doing for the comics what Marcel Proust once did for the novel. There are others who feel that, to be more precise, he's been doing for low-life New York what Proust once did for high-society Paris. Clearly, the *Village Voice*'s new editor, Karen Durbin, belongs to neither of these camps. In fact, no sooner had she taken control of the *Voice* last fall, than she tried to jettison the strip altogether. Upon being informed by Katchor, in the excruciatingly meek and yet eerily resolute way that is his perennial manner, that, well, actually, the *Voice* was contractually obligated to continue running the strip at least through this past March (which would have completed *Knipl*'s first year of tenancy on the *Voice*'s pages, Katchor's having only just transferred the six-year-old strip over to the *Voice* from its original home in the New York *Press* a few months prior to Durbin's arrival), Durbin grudgingly acceded—though she transferred the strip's placement to considerably less prestigious digs within the weekly's pages and in all sorts of ways let it be known that, as far as she was concerned, March couldn't come soon enough.

This sad state of affairs in turn was giving David Isay conniption fits. Isay, one of the most accomplished and imaginative independent producers affiliated with National Public Radio, had achieved something last year that many people considered well nigh impossible. As part of a Susan Stamberg profile of Katchor, Isay had collaborated with the cartoonist to produce a sequence of two-minute aural renditions of five of Katchor's most evocative *Knipl* strips, an achievement all the more astonishing in that Katchor's Kniplian universe was never so much aural, or even visual, as it is tactile—or, more precisely, *olfactory*, the distilled essence of melancholy recollection. But with the assistance of such masterful actors and superannuated vaudevillians as Jerry Stiller, Brother Theodore, Joey Faye, and Professor Irwin Corey and the klezmer contributions of Henry Sopozniak, Isay had managed to pull off the challenge and in fact had had so much fun doing so that he resolved to keep on doing it. Scott Simon agreed to provide a regular weekly venue for the future *Knipl* radio-strips on his Saturday morning show, the Corporation for Public Broadcasting (Isay's usual patron) signaled its initial support, and Isay set to remobilizing his team. But now, suddenly, the entire venture seemed newly jeopardized.

Although the *Knipl* strip could continue to appear in marginal papers around the country (even including Iowa City!), the imminent loss of a regular outlet in the very city which was so obviously the strip's palpable home was beginning to make an even-more-than-typically dispirited Katchor consider shutting down the whole enterprise altogether. Isay and Katchor met repeatedly to consider various alternatives, when it suddenly occurred to them, why couldn't the strip simply continue to appear on a weekly basis, completely unmediated, in various locations around the city itself? Say, like in the windows of the Gray's Papaya drink stands at 8th Street and Sixth Avenue and up at Broadway and 72nd? That particular venue appealed to the pair because: a) the storefronts themselves, excruciatingly meek and yet eerily resolute, seemed entirely in keeping with the ethos of the strip itself, the sort of place Knipl might easily dive into in the midst of his daily rounds and where he might overhear the sorts of glancing anonymous conversations or think the sorts of glancing anonymous thoughts that form the bulwark of the strip's weekly reality; and, b) Isay happened to have gone to high school with Gray's daughter.

Katchor set to work fashioning a nifty plastic display case, complete with its own eight-watt interior bulb, within which to house the strip, and Isay contacted the Grays. The daughter and her stepmother took to the idea immediately, but Mr. Gray, when they finally got to him, was considerably more circumspect. "He didn't *begin* to understand the strip, or the poetic appropriateness of housing it in his establishment—this was like an impossible leap of the imagination for him," Katchor reports. "It all became very embarrassing." He hesitated, days passed—"Geez, it got to be like auditioning for Leo Castelli!"—daughter and stepmother continued to work on the dubious proprietor, but in the end he demurred, and Katchor and Isay were thrust back out onto the streets, Knipl-like, with their pathetic little scheme.

Trudging down Second Avenue south of St. Mark's Place, near Isay's studio and across the street from the Orpheum Theater, they happened to gaze into the narrow storefront window of the B&H Dairy, the last scraggly remnant of a once teeming avenueful of such kosher eating establishments. The window was plastered over with placards declaiming the day's fare ("2 eggs any style on our own challah bread," "Create your own juice—carrots, tomatoes, watercress, celery, broccoli . . ."). Isay and Katchor looked at each other and wordlessly concurred: Perfect.

Inside, as they wedged themselves onto the stools along the dairy's narrow counter, Katchor realized it was even more perfect than that: this was the very place where, thirteen years before, he'd first met his wife, scrunched side by side at this very counter. The place had in the meantime changed owners, but Beatrice Poznanski, the fetchingly harried young Polish émigré out of Wroclaw, who's been carrying the dairy tradition forward the past three years (the rest of the staff is unchanged), took to the idea without a moment's hesitation and allowed Messieurs Katchor and Isay to install their case in the front window.

That was a few weeks ago, and Katchor's been keeping the vitrine well stocked ever since. "It's been interesting to watch," he says, "because the strip's getting noticed by a whole new class of people. Before, the people in the strip didn't necessarily ever encounter the strip, whereas now . . . People walking by, in the corner of their eye they might notice this new thing—what is it, an unusual menu display or what? Especially late at night when, with its soft neon glow, it's sort of like a beacon—people feel themselves drawn to it; they stand there hunched, looking—maybe there's an added thrill to be reading it in such a historic and appropriate surround, I don't know. It's all very tenuous."

At lunch the other day, Wednesday, Ms. Poznanski, this Sylvia Beach of the East Village, was looking on during the weekly changing-of-the-strip when somebody asked her why she'd ever gone along with such a scheme in the first place. "Oh, I don't know," she replied, smiling. "They seemed like nice gentlemen. And my son is really into comics." What did he make of this one? "Alright," she said. "Nothing special."

Outside, a few minutes later, Katchor was obviously still smarting from the comment. "And who is this son, anyway," he harrumphed, "some professor of world literature, or what?"

Others, however, were proving more enthusiastic. Mr. Gray's arch-competitor, Papaya King—or, actually, the *son* of Papaya King *(Papaya Prince?)*—glommed the idea instantaneously, and Katchor's been able to install a new vitrine up at their stand at 86th and Third Avenue. He and Isay are currently scoping the Upper West Side for yet another venue.

Meanwhile, Katchor received word that he's just been awarded a Guggenheim for his continuing labors. Isay, on the other hand, learned that a suddenly Gingrich-spooked CPB wasn't going to be funding the *Knipl* radio series after all. But he and Katchor have decided to go ahead with the project anyway, starting in May, on a more attenuated basis—perhaps only once a month at first—while they try to puzzle out some novel and appropriate way of getting the miserable thing funded.

Post–Postscript (1998)

In the end, Katchor and Isay did manage to revive the radio version of the strip, eventually compiling another fifteen or so new episodes. A new collection of the print version of the *Knipl* strips was published by Little, Brown in 1996 (with a lyrically appreciative introduction by Michael Chabon, and to a rave review by Edward Sorel in the *New York Times Book Review*); and the ongoing strip itself found a somewhat more tenable new home in the pages of the *Weekly Forward*. Katchor, meanwhile, returned as well to his *Jew of New York* strip, refashioning it into a soon-to-be-published cartoon (or, at any rate, anything-but-merely-comic) novella.

I telephoned Katchor the other day (he and his wife and daughter had in the meantime moved back to New York City) to see how things were going, and I found him in the pink—or maybe, rather, Ben being Ben, in the gray. He complained about having just returned from Hawaii, of all places. It seems that Art Spiegelman, in his new capacity as the comix editor of *Details* magazine and facing the prospect of an all-sports issue, had hit upon the idea of dispatching Katchor to cover an upcoming surfing tournament. Dubiously Katchor went; dolefully he soldiered on; but, as he now reported, "The waves never broke properly, the tournament kept getting postponed day after day, and in the end I spent most of my time in dark bars talking to the tournament's insurance adjuster."

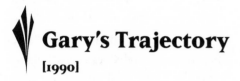

Gary's Trajectory
[1990]

I.

A few months ago, a friend I was talking with began to tell me about a friend of his named Gary Isaacs, who was working at the downtown headquarters of one of the city's top investment houses as an executive in the division monitoring the savings-and-loan crisis. Though Isaacs was just thirty-two years old, my friend recounted, he had previously worked on the Street in several other capacities as well, and before that he'd had a notably successful career in an entirely different field; what's more, it seemed he was about to quit this one, too, and to head off in yet another direction. When I asked my friend what the previous career had been, and, for that matter, what the new one was going to be, he replied that it would be far more entertaining for me to hear the whole story from the man himself, and before I knew it he was on the phone arranging an appointment, which is how, a few days later, I came to find myself in the sleek elevator of one of downtown's better-known headquarters buildings zooming up toward I didn't have the faintest idea what.

Getting off at the pre-agreed floor, I entered a granite-lined vestibule decorated with a large chrome-plated sign identifying the particular activity of this division of the firm: "Capital Funding." I went over to the receptionist and asked for Mr. Isaacs. A few moments later, a young man in a gray suit and glasses emerged through one of those buzz-locked glass doors and introduced himself as Gary Isaacs. Trim but athletically solid, he was clean shaven, with a high forehead and short-cropped, curly dark-blond hair. He seemed a bit shy as he guided me back through a warren of cubicles—a suit in every one—to his office, a good-sized room with a glass wall facing out upon all the cubicles. A computer console sat atop his desk, and stacks of papers and books were piled all about. A well-used whiteboard for writing on occupied part of one wall, and, beyond the desk, a large window afforded a wide view of the buildings opposite (floor upon floor of similar windows, similar offices, similar cubicles). As I took a seat facing his desk, he almost self-effacingly handed me a card, which identified him as "Vice President, Primary Market Group, Financial Strategies Group." There are no doubt dozens of such vice-presidents in this company, but I nevertheless found it somewhat disconcerting to be sitting opposite one so young.

"I guess I should begin by telling you a little about my background," Isaacs said, without any prompting. "I got my college degrees from the Massachusetts Institute of Technology, where I majored in mechanical engineering." Later, in occasional asides, he provided me with a few facts about his earlier life—he was born in Brooklyn, in 1958, and moved, with his family, to Colonia, New Jersey, at age five; his father has run a series of Midas franchises—but he seemed to feel that his life proper had started at MIT.

"I did my principal undergraduate thesis work in the Fluid Mechanics Lab, investigating the fluid dynamics of collapsible structures," Isaacs went on. "Several of us were working on variations of the same problem, trying to model the flow of fluids within the human body—in particular, the flow of blood through the veins in people's legs. One application we were working toward had to do with deep-vein thrombosis, a situation where the blood is flowing too sluggishly through the veins deep inside a person's leg. The question was how to treat this during surgery: whether through a pressure cuff or by massage, and with what sorts of pressure—sudden? gradual? pulsed?—to avoid having the veins collapse almost completely under the pressure, as mysteriously, they were sometimes given to doing. That sort of thing. And, actually, it proved to be an interesting, complicated problem.

"Ordinarily, when you study fluid dynamics you start out by studying flow in open channels, say, or in a system of glass tubes and containment vessels. You learn about turbulence, eddy currents, secondary flows, how different sorts of fluids circulate around different sorts of objects in a channel." He went to his whiteboard and began scrawling a set of equations, and in no time he had lost me. "But in all those cases the geometry is fixed, the shape of the channel is static, it's only the fluid that's moving. Whereas the thing about blood vessels is that the structure itself is malleable, so that the variables start compounding very quickly. As you begin to apply pressure to the outside of the tube, the geometry naturally changes, and then, naturally, so does the flow. And here's where things really get interesting: the changing flow ends up affecting the pressure gradients on the inside walls of the tube such that it starts to collapse *from the inside*. A sort of feedback effect gets started." He quickly charted a series of cross-sections on the whiteboard, showing how a circular tube initially flattened in the middle, leaving two tiny channels still open on either side, and how, eventually, they likewise flattened out almost completely.

"Our group was going at this problem in all sorts of different ways," Isaacs said. "Some people were constructing pure mathematical models on the computer, and others were building actual physical models, with varying levels of sophistication. I myself constructed a relatively primitive device. And then each day one of us had to volunteer his or her own leg for various experiments. As I say, it was an interesting lab."

Isaacs completed his undergraduate thesis by the end of his junior year at MIT. In the months thereafter, he flirted with the idea of becoming an automotive engineer at Ford, and with some other ideas as well, which he said he would tell me about later, but in the end he decided to stay on at MIT for a year and a half to earn a master's degree.

At that point—in February of 1979—Isaacs transferred to the Vehicle

Dynamics Lab, where a team of researchers was working on problems relating to rail vehicles travelling across elevated concrete guideways—monorails, urban transit systems—as seen from all sorts of vantages: aerodynamics, suspension design, materials, guidance and propulsion. His specific project concerned a somewhat disconcerting feature of all standard concrete spans: their tendency to bow in the middle as heavy train cars roll across them—to bend (in the case of an eighty-foot span) by as much as six inches and then spring back with a shudder that under certain conditions (the train moving at certain speeds, the individual cars being of a certain weight) can cause the second car to accentuate the vibration, the third to accentuate it even more, and so on, until, as Isaacs put it, "the folks sitting in the last car would really be having something to think about." Isaacs's task was to analyze the mathematics of the problem—to model it, and predict the behavior of spans of all sizes, and hence be able to come up with some way of compensating for it—and it turned out that the mathematics involved was immensely complicated.

"For a long time, I was really stumped," Isaacs said. "For starters, I spent months in the library, burrowing through all the literature on concrete. Concrete is a subject on which there are more journals, books, digests, and monographs than you could possibly imagine. There must be easily twenty or thirty regular periodicals devoted exclusively to concrete—*Cement and Concrete Research, Concrete International,* and so forth. It's very interesting stuff, concrete is—you know, great compression, lousy in tension, all that sort of thing."

I must have looked baffled. "That means you can push it but you can't pull on it," he explained. "It's like water. Anyway, my breakthrough came . . ." Back he went to the whiteboard. Quickly erasing all the blood-vessel imagery, he scrawled out a new sequence of cross-sections and equations, one cascading into the next, all impenetrable to me. By the time he had covered the entire whiteboard, finally arriving at the solution, he was clearly pleased, but I was still lost.

"So what happened to the trains?" I asked lamely. "What happened to those people in the last car?"

"Actually, we didn't end up recommending doing anything to either the cars or the spans," Isaacs replied. "They just had to jimmy the suspension coils."

Some data came flying across Isaacs's computer monitor, and he excused himself for a moment, went back to his desk, tapped a few keys, peered into the numbers quizzically, reached for a nearby volume, leafed through a few pages, tapped a few more keys, nodded in satisfaction, and returned his attention to me.

"So, anyway, once I'd completed my master's I decided I wanted to work somewhere at the cutting edge of technology. In August of 1980, I took a job in California, with TRW's Defense and Space Systems Group. I mean, just the address of the place was enough to snare me: One Space Park, Redondo Beach. What more could I ask for?

"One of my first jobs there was in the Integration and Test Division—that is, testing already built spacecraft, prior to their delivery for launch. It was an interesting place to work, because you were presented with a lot of constraints. Everything had been designed, tooled, built, and put together long before you even saw the thing. There were elaborate computer models of how the thing was supposed to work, but now there it was, sitting in the High Bay, and it was your job to see if it really did work that way—and, if it didn't, to figure out some way to make it work.

"The testing division had all kinds of subsections, with different groups testing everything from the satellite's telemetry to its capacity for withstanding the sheer vibrations of launch. I first worked with the team that tested the attitude-control system of various satellites—that is, the system that helps the craft determine where it is and in which direction it's pointing, in relation to where it wants to be and how it wants to be pointing, and then makes it possible for it to get from the one to the other by way of firing miniature steering thrusters tucked away on board. The satellite I worked on for almost my entire first year there happened to be the original TDRS, the Tracking and Data Relay Satellite—at that time the world's biggest and most sophisticated communications satellite. It was scheduled to be the first commercial payload delivered into orbit by the space shuttle a few years down the line."

Isaacs pulled out a glossy pamphlet that TRW had apparently put together in those days to celebrate its then imminent TDRS triumph. The cover featured a photograph of the satellite, seen from above, in the Redondo Beach facility's testing hangar—a tall, sleek object folded in upon itself, the way it would later be tucked into the space shuttle's cargo bay. Standing on end, it resembled a modernist hexagonal flowerpot with two gaudy cactuslike protrusions emerging from its top, the whole thing surrounded by a bevy of intent Lilliputian creatures garbed in white smocks. Inside, the brochure featured an artist's rendition of what the satellite would look like once it had been unfurled in space and parked in its geosynchronous orbit, twenty-two thousand miles above the equator: a huge array of gleaming solar panels, diaphanous antennas, delicately gimballed metal dishes, sprockets and cannisters and pods.

The satellite was going to serve several functions, Isaacs told me. Most important, when it was joined by a second, identical satellite parked in a similar stationary orbit on the other side of the globe, the two would constitute a nearly continuous integrated system for tracking the space shuttle and other sorts of satellites orbiting below, and for relaying telemetry for those satellites to and from a single ground station, at White Sands, New Mexico, thereby rendering superfluous the dozens of other ground tracking stations scattered all about the world— often in strategically inconvenient spots—whose existence had previously been required in order to provide much less detailed coverage.

"So you can imagine the importance of precise positioning, precise attitude control, with a satellite like that," Isaacs continued. "And testing for that was our responsibility. We set up an elaborate version of what's called a fixed-base test, which is to say that naturally the satellite wasn't actually going to be flying around there in the hangar, floating in space; rather, it would be affixed to a stable base, and we were just going to surround it with dozens of computers, hooked into it by way of scores of cables, through which we were going to fool its on-board computers into believing, for example, that the sun was positioned at such-and-such an angle, the horizon was over here, and so forth—an environment simulation, the procedure was called. We'd see whether the satellite could figure out where it was and what it was doing—its roll, pitch, and yaw angles—and we'd test its capacity for receiving instructions on how to adjust its position, and its ability to act on those instructions. Of course, its on-board computers weren't actually hooked up to its steering thrusters, there in the middle of the High Bay—or, rather, fuel wasn't actually being fed to the thrusters; the thruster valves just opened and closed ineffectually. So we had other computers, whose job it was to interpret the instructions the on-board computer was sending to the thrusters to make sure they were correct— and then to feed back information to the satellite regarding how such a firing would have affected its attitude.

"It was an incredibly intricate setup, and things were continually going wrong. We'd stand around for days scratching our heads, trying to figure out why an indicator on one of our monitors wasn't on. It could have been that somebody had kicked one of the cables, or maybe one of the pins in a connector had got bent, or the board in back of one of the computers might have come loose, or maybe a chip in the spacecraft had been manufactured incorrectly, or correctly but to incorrect specifications, or else maybe the software had been written wrong—the satellite's own software or else the test's—or maybe the indicator wasn't *supposed* to be on in the first place and somebody had just mistakenly said it was.

"And everything was further complicated by the fact that all the commands going up and the telemetry coming back were codified. You couldn't just type in an instruction to the satellite like 'Now move from

A to B.' There's a certain language the satellite understands—or, rather, different component systems understand different languages. Some receive their instructions in binary format, some in octal, base eight, and some even in hexadecimal, base sixteen. You've got these different codes interacting within the software, and, to compound things, all the numerical information is scaled, because there's only so much bit space, so you've got numbers being sent up in hundredths and thousandths or ten-thousandths or hundred-thousandths, each number sent up with its scaling factor . . . And meanwhile you're trying to find the maybe one digit in the midst of this whole stream that's maybe one digit off. It can become like the world's biggest headache.

"So I was doing that sort of thing, and then, in addition, I was doing some of the more mundane housekeeping tasks—for example, preparing a section of the ground-station operator's manual for the so-called change-of-velocity maneuver that the spacecraft would be expected to perform several times a year once it was deployed. Here the problem was that, though the spacecraft would be parked in a stationary geosynchronous orbit at a particular place, it was going to have a tendency to drift to one or the other of two stable nodes, as they were called, within its orbit, where, for various reasons, it would, so to speak, want to be."

Isaacs got up and started to walk over to the whiteboard.

"Never mind," I said. "I believe you."

"Anyway," he continued, sitting down at his desk again, "we were going to correct for that by performing a 'station-keeping,' or change-of-velocity, maneuver: firing the spacecraft's miniature rockets in such a way as to nudge it back to its original position—in fact, a little past its original position, so that when it began drifting again it might take a little longer before we had to repeat the whole thing. That was the idea, and the other guys in the project knew the theoretical stuff: 'Yeah, sure, you can fire two delta-v thrusters x number of times over the life of the spacecraft, and we'll budget for fuel accordingly.' But it was my job to actually figure it all out and to write up the sequence of commands the

ground-control people would be beaming up to the satellite, over a period of hours, in all those different codes, each time they had to do the
thing. It ran many, many pages, but I did it, and at the time I didn't give
it a second thought."

Isaacs went on to tell me that by 1982 he had moved on to perform
"end to end" system tests on other satellites—tests that were "sort of
like the world's most elaborate video games." These tests integrated all
the components of a given satellite—components that had previously
been tested separately but never as an integrated system. That was all
classified work, he said, and he couldn't really talk about any of it.
While he was deeply involved in that work, the April 4, 1983, launch
date for the space shuttle carrying the TDRS arrived, and he monitored
developments on that front with a certain interest, if only out of the
corner of his eye. "Everything seemed to be going fine," Isaacs recalled.
"They got the shuttle up fine, and later that day they got the TDRS,
with its attached inertial upper-stage booster, out of the shuttle's cargo
bay, no problem, everything seemed to be checking out fine, and then
they powered up the booster engine, which, with its two stages and fifteen thousand pounds of thrust, was supposed to lift the satellite up to
its twenty-two-thousand-mile-altitude orbit, and that, too, seemed to
go along smoothly. The first-stage burn went perfectly—only, then,
with the second-stage burn two-thirds completed, they suddenly experienced some sort of anomaly, and the satellite just disappeared from
everybody's console. Nobody had any idea where it was, or even if it
was still intact or what it was doing, whether it was tumbling, and, if
so, at what rate—nothing.

"I was at work, minding my own business, when all at once people
were literally running up and down the halls, just about knocking one
another over, because this was a big emergency. Sure, the problem had
been with the booster, which was somebody else's component, and not
ours. The problem was not ours, but we were the only ones who could
fix it, and there was over a hundred million dollars on the line with
that satellite, not to speak of the years and years of human effort that

had been put into the thing. They were sending up commands desperately, completely blind—they had no idea where the thing was.

"And there was an incredible element of time pressure, too, because once the TDRS had attained the proper orbit the explosive bolts connecting the satellite to the booster were supposed to be activated—a process that itself required the booster's own battery power—and then the booster would drift away and the satellite's own solar panels would be able to deploy, thereafter satisfying all the craft's energy requirements. Wherever the satellite was, the power in those batteries was quickly draining away—they knew that—and they knew that, at the very least, they had to get the booster to disengage itself from the satellite before the power ran out, because otherwise nothing would be possible.

"So they were sending up this steady stream of commands. The satellite, which, it turned out, was tumbling at something like thirty revolutions per minute, its burned-out booster still attached, was picking up interrupted, staggered portions of the stream, and sending back a steady stream of telemetry of its own—one that the ground station, in turn, once it had finally locked on to the satellite, was likewise receiving only in interrupted, staggered spurts. Remember, those guys weren't sitting there with binoculars evaluating the whole thing; all they had was their screens and monitors, across which an erratic stream of numbers was pouring, and from that they were having both to interpret what the hell was going on and to figure out how in hell to stabilize the situation—and they were having to do all that in real time, and, in fact, immediately. Finally, with only seconds to spare in the life of the booster's batteries, they did manage to get the booster to disengage from the satellite, the satellite to stop spinning, and its solar panels to deploy. Now their only problem was that the satellite was thousands and thousands of miles from where it was supposed to be, and it had just jettisoned the engine that might reasonably have seemed its only way of getting there."

Isaacs wasn't directly involved in the ensuing rescue mission.

"They'd assembled the very top people by that point," he told me. "People a hell of a lot more experienced than I was—people who in many cases had been in the space business longer than I'd been alive. And it was a very intense period. I mean, sure, I was interested, but it wasn't the sort of thing where you could just mosey on over there, peer over their shoulders, kick your legs up onto the consoles, and shoot the breeze. These were very, *very* critical weeks—millions of dollars and years and years of people's lives were on the line."

Isaacs just kept to his own work. A few days later, they came to him. It turned out that since they no longer had access to the booster's huge engines they were going to attempt to nudge the satellite thousands of miles into position just by firing the craft's miniature steering thrusters—that they were going to be executing an elaborate series of exaggerated variations on Isaac's own change-of-velocity maneuvers. They asked Isaacs for all his backup files on the subject, and he handed them over. He briefed them on everything he knew, and then he returned to his own projects. "It was ridiculous," Isaacs said. "They were going to try to replace the effect of fifteen thousand pounds of thrust with these measly, miniature-toothpaste-tube-size rockets, packing less than a pound of thrust each—minithrusters that weren't designed to fire for more than a fraction of a second at a time. They were going to be attempting to adjust the satellite's orbit by almost ten thousand miles powered by the equivalent of a precisely timed sequence of tiny sneezes. I mean, it was all impossible on its face. Only, they did it. It took them nearly two months, but finally they got the damn thing parked exactly where it was supposed to be. It was truly amazing."

Isaacs remained at TRW for four years, working for a while on a concept-design team (producing proposals for new satellites), and for a while after that on a series of advanced-technology studies (producing proposals presupposing technologies that might not even be available for twenty-five years—"processes so advanced," Isaacs explained, "that it would be like showing a TV to George Washington, or to a caveman"). And though the work was exciting, he began to lose interest in it. He was feeling increasingly constricted. "I'd go to work, and it was just a job," he told me. "I did it because I could do it. But, you know, you work on one spacecraft project, you work on another—it's the same process, you have to put up with the same stuff. I mean, yeah, now it's great to talk about, but it was just a job. And then, beyond that, I was tired of being told I couldn't do this, that, or the other because I was too young, or because So-and-So had been there longer and deserved a crack at it first. You got the feeling that you would be allowed to rise to a position where you might really push through innovative projects, only after you'd got so old that the innovative juices would have long since been bled out of you. So by 1984 I was getting restless."

While Isaacs was on a vacation trip back to New Jersey to visit his family, a friend of his father's, a money manager, suggested that Isaacs might want to look into Wall Street, which at the time was busy climbing toward its own stratospheric levels. "I came into town one day," he told me. "I walked into some of the places down on the Street, and, I mean, compared with working in the basement over at TRW, with all the mechanical hardware and the cables and the reaction wheels and the gyros strewn all about—we had gyros down there in the basement, involved in long-term real-time trials, that had been spinning for five years, and it was somebody's job just to monitor the things, to come in each morning and check that they were all still spinning. To go from that into one of these firms with the paintings on the walls, the plush carpets, the gold laminate, the low lights, and the wood panelling and the elevators and the brass and they take your coat when you come in. I'd never seen anything like that, and I said to myself, 'I don't know what they do here, but I want to come back here to work.'"

Isaacs spoke with some Wall Street people ("right firms, probably the wrong people," he said), and they told him that while it was true that the Street was eagerly recruiting technically trained outsiders, it might be better if he first got some seasoning at a business school. So he returned to Los Angeles, applied to UCLA's Graduate School of Management, and was accepted for the fall term.

Generally, he told me, he enjoyed business school, though he experienced a decided clash of cultures. He explained, "I mean, to go from advanced calculus, the sort of thing you used in engineering, where questions had sharp, precise answers, down to the tiniest decimal—from that to accounting classes, where you'd say, 'Yeah, but these figures don't reflect actual cash flow,' and they'd answer, 'No problem, this is how we'll account for it'—clearly, I was in a different world. A lot of it was just make-believe—there wasn't really any money there at all—and for a while that was a tough concept to handle."

Nevertheless, the sort of dogged precision that had been drilled into Isaacs during his days as an engineer stood him in good stead during the internship he landed for the summer between his two years at UCLA. He had come back to New York during the Easter break and walked unannounced into the offices of several firms. "This was a period when they were recruiting mathematicians, statisticians, scientists, engineers—technical wizards of all sorts," he recalled. "'Rocket scientists' was the generic term they'd coined for the whole lot of them, as a sort of a joke. But there I was, an *actual* rocket scientist, sitting out in the lobby. It did give me a certain cachet."

Isaacs was hired by First Boston, being told initially that the firm could use a few extra hands programming over in Fixed Income Research. "But I actually ended up working on a project that was ideal for me," he said. "They had me analyzing the convexity of mortgage-backed securities. That was suddenly a very hot topic on the Street, lots of clients were interested in it. I was at the center of it. I got to speak to a lot of significant people both inside and outside the firm, and the work received a lot of attention. Most other summer interns were spending their time simply rotating from one department to another, but I was getting to make vital, very current contributions."

I asked what a mortgage-backed security was, and why it convexed.

"Fannie Maes, Ginnie Maes—that sort of thing," Isaacs said, getting up and ambling over to the whiteboard. "Okay, this is a simplified version. The thing is that most homeowners make their regular mortgage payments to their banks and figure that the bank will continue to hold the mortgage on their house until they pay it off. Whereas in fact most banks sold off most of those loans a long time ago. They had all this paper, all these mortgages—in truth, they'd lent out all their money—whereas what they wanted was fresh money so that they could originate more mortgages and engage in other sorts of profit-generating investments. So they sold entire portfolios of their mortgages to various agencies like Fannie Mae and Ginnie Mae—for a small fee the banks continued to service the mortgages, to pass the monthly installments along, so that the homeowners never knew the difference. And those agencies in turn gathered together huge pools of similarly denominated mortgages, all of them paying out at a similar percentage and maturing around the same date, securitized them, and then subdivided the pools into more manageable offerings. So that, for instance, an institutional investor could come along and buy a ten-million-dollar piece of a vast pool of mortgages paying out at 10.5 percent through the year 2014. That would be your standard, generic mortgage-backed security—one from which the investor could expect to receive his monthly portion of the payments up until the mortgages underlying it had all paid out. But the point is, he might at some time want to sell off that particular security, or else to buy other securities paying out at other interest rates with other maturities. And the question was, on any given day what should any of them be worth?

"Well, that depended, of course, on the interest rates, the yields, prevailing in the market on the day in question. If the prevailing yield was 10.5 percent, and he wanted to buy an instrument paying out at 10.5 percent, he could expect to pay par; that is, one hundred cents on the dollar. But if the prevailing rates were down, at 10 percent, he'd have to pay a premium to buy a security paying out at such a relatively high rate as 10.5 percent—he might have to pay over a hundred and two cents on the dollar. Conversely, if prevailing rates were up at 11 percent, he could demand a discount, since he was going to be purchasing a security still paying out at only 10.5 percent—he might expect to get it for under ninety-eight cents on the dollar. In other words, the value of mortgage-backed securities is highly sensitive to fluctuations in prevailing yields and interest rates.

"That much was elementary. Everybody knew that. But people generally assumed that, regarding the relationship between prevailing yields and the value of these various instruments, if you charted it on a graph you'd get a straight line. Whereas the line is actually curved— it's convex. There's a reason for that"—and no doubt there is (it has something to do with "the compounding effect when discounting cash flows"), but, frankly, Isaacs, who was now becoming a veritable whirling dervish over at the whiteboard, once again lost me for a while. "Not that it matters when yields are fluctuating by just a few basis points either way," he went on. "The two lines almost dovetail. But, as you'll recall, in the late seventies and early eighties we were seeing huge fluctuations in prevailing yields—interest rates into the high teens, and even the low twenties. And there it really began to matter.

"Now, generally, mortgage-backed securities have a positive convexity. That is, all things being equal, when prevailing yields go down by a single percentage point, the price of the security should go up by more than it goes down when prevailing yields go up by the same single percentage point. And that's all to the good: high upside, low downside, very attractive—people were willing to pay a lot for that sort of profile. But it turned out that there was a catch, because with those big fluctuations in prevailing interest rates you began to see a lot of homeowners refinancing the mortgages that underlay those huge pools. People who'd initially taken out mortgages at 15 percent were prepaying their mortgages, paying them off, refinancing them with loans they were able to get at 10 percent. Tens of thousands were doing so. And suddenly all those investors who were holding those juicy mortgage-backed securities, thinking they'd locked in a 15-percent

yield for the next twenty-odd years—and who'd paid a handsome premium for the privilege—were instead getting paid off right now, today,
and having to reinvest the sudden lump sum at the currently much
lower rates. Ouch: that hurt twice.

"So it turned out that, because of that prepayment factor, mortgage-
backed securities didn't always have nearly as much positive convexity as had been thought; in fact, in some cases they showed negative
convexity. And that's what wasn't completely understood the summer
I was modelling all this for First Boston. In the wake of those wild fluctuations earlier in the decade, several institutions had taken a real bath
on all this—to the tune of hundreds of millions of dollars—because they
didn't fully anticipate the convexity effect on many mortgage-backed
securities. All of them had people desperately working on convexity,
and that summer I was First Boston's man on the case—analyzing the
problem, modelling the behavior, developing software to evaluate
convexity effects, and so forth. Toward the end of the summer, they
brought in research people from all over the company for a seminar
where I presented my findings—I was very popular—and on my last day
I gave another talk, on the current state of the art in spacecraft design,
which was also well attended and quite successful."

After a quick browse at his console, a brief search-and-peck, Isaacs
recounted for me how he returned to UCLA and completed his second
year, and then came back to New York, to First Boston. He was told
that because of his prior success he was welcome to follow virtually
any path he liked. He chose to become a trader of mortgage-backed
securities.

"During the previous summer," he said, "I would come up with the
results based on my pure research, and I'd go over to the traders and
say, 'This is what I think is going to happen,' and they'd look at me as
if I were crazy, and say, 'That's not at all what's going to happen, this
is what's going to happen.' I'd ask why, and they'd say, 'Because it just
is, that's the way the securities trade.' And the point is, when it came to
pricing those securities the traders in effect *were* the market. While I

was convinced of the value of research, I wanted to make it applicable, and to see it working in the real world. It was just like the situation back at TRW, with the guys who'd spent years designing the various components of the TDRS but wouldn't have recognized the completed satellite if they'd come smack dab upon it sitting there in the High Bay, or if it had come hurtling out of the sky and hit them on their heads—which, as you know, it almost did. I just always liked applications—the fun of making things work in the real world—or, anyway, I thought I did."

Isaacs spent the next several months in the general sales-and-trading training program. Then, one day, when he was only three-quarters of the way through his training course, his supervisor came over and said, "They need you on the desk right now." He went down to the trading floor and was told to forget about any further training—he wasn't going back, he was there to stay. He took his place on the huge trading floor, among scores of traders, each hooked up to a telephone with literally dozens of buttons. "It was a whole lot different from research, that's for sure," Isaacs recalled. "It was incredibly noisy. There wasn't the time for any sort of considered analysis: everything was instantaneous, and it was all continuous. You were hooked into the hoot-and-holler, as it was called—everybody had a speaker that was hooked up to all the branch offices around the country, everybody was talking at once, everybody picking out snatches of what he himself needed to hear. At first, it was quite intimidating, but gradually I got used to it."

The things that Isaacs now began trading were brand-new derivatives of traditional mortgage-backed pass-through securities. The investment houses are continually inventing new ways to subdivide their offerings—adding ever more complex and elaborate bells and whistles, as the phrase goes, or else ostensibly streamlining already complex entities into more simple components. In this instance, someone had come up with a scheme to divide mortgage-backed securities into two parts—one made up exclusively of all future payments of interest, and the other made up exclusively of all future payment of principal—and to sell those two parts separately. For a variety of reasons, these instruments turned out to be even more sensitive than most other mortgage-backed securities to the propensity of the underlying mortgage holders to prepay their mortgages; that is to say, to fluctuations in prevailing interest rates. Depending on which way interest rates were going, investors in these new instruments could make a handsome killing or, instead, lose a handsome fortune. "Some of those things were negatively convexed—spectacularly so," Isaacs said. "They had their valid, if esoteric, uses—as sensible hedges for institutions trading in specific venues of other sorts—but they made truly dangerous vehicles for speculation. You saw that every day working as a trader. The trouble was that the pressure on traders was to sell them, period. Move them out. All sorts of institutions—savings and loans, for example—were obviously buying these things on a purely speculative basis. My boss at the time would yell over, 'Get on the hoot-and-holler and tell people these things are really cheap today and that they ought to buy them up'—and that wasn't strictly true. There were times when it seemed like urging a four-year-old to go out and play in the middle of a superhighway. The things is, it wasn't our job out there on the trading floor to be explaining those nuances to people. For one thing, we didn't have the time. And, anyway, all information about these instruments was publicly available: there were just a lot of people and institutions who even after the nuances were explained were just so damn sure of themselves, that they still insisted on playing the vehicles purely for speculation. And a lot of people got burned."

Isaacs paused, and then continued, "It turned out I didn't enjoy trading that much after all. Every once in a while, the sheer immensity of the figures passing over my desk would momentarily become real to me, and that was always unnerving. Beyond that, out there on the trading floor you never got a moment to think, to reflect. Being involved in applications was one thing, but the whole other side of my brain was beginning to atrophy."

Around that time, Isaacs's current firm offered him a job almost

better tailored to his talents and aptitude than any he could have designed for himself. He would be taking ideas developed in research and
making them understandable to traders and salesmen, translating
mathematical models into concepts that could be conveyed to clients—
or else taking problems that the firm's people and clients were encountering in the real world and bringing them up to the research
department, where they could be subjected to quantitative analysis. He
left First Boston for this new job, and as the months passed he became
a sort of all-round troubleshooter for the firm, trying to solve the problems nobody else could. Gradually, he drifted into the job he was currently holding—trying to keep tabs on the savings-and-loan crisis for
the entire firm.

"As I say, I like working on things that aren't working, and the thrift
industry in this country is not working in a big way," Isaacs said. "Essentially, I've had to become a lawyer—or, at least, an expert in this
area of the law." He pulled out a thick volume bound in official federal
tan: The Financial Institutions Reform, Recovery, and Enforcement Act
of 1989. His copy was bulging with color-coded tags and bookmarks.
"This book has—let's see—four hundred and sixty-seven pages, and, as
you can see, there are no pictures, and this is just the *conference report.*
The actual law is three times as long. My job is not only to know this
book inside out but also to follow all the impending changes in accounting standards, legislation, oversight practices, regulations. I'm on
the phone with lawyers and regulators every day, trying to get our
people information on the developing situation before they read it in
tomorrow's papers. I'm the firm's designated expert.

"In part, we're trying to anticipate things that could move markets
and provide us with profit potential—or, at least, keep us from losing
money. And, in part, my clients are the savings-and-loan institutions
themselves—or, rather, professionals in the firm whose long-term
clients include S&Ls, some in worse shape than others. I'm regularly
fielding calls from our own guys: 'Listen, Gary, we've got an S&L out in
So-and-So, and their situation is such-and-such. What can we do for

them? What would be the most effective way for them to meet the new guidelines? How are those guidelines changing? Any exceptions they should know about? What are the regulators saying that hasn't yet hit the papers? How are they saying it? Was their tone positive? Even though they're saying that, do you think they might change their minds in three months? How about in three weeks?' That sort of thing, all day long." He nodded over toward the console. "And the problem is, with a lot of this stuff it's impossible to know. We can't even get solid figures on the basic dimensions of the crisis."

It sounded like the TDRS mission all over again, I observed.

"It's a lot like that," Isaacs said. "Believe me, I've had the thought myself. But one also notices the differences. The environment out in space is filled with all kinds of hazards, but you can model it: there are certain laws that pertain and that are unchanging—you can count on them absolutely—and the spacecraft meanwhile has very sophisticated guidance systems, and, more important, it has deep reserves and re- dundancies built into the system. A lot of the time here, by contrast, we have a much lower level of mathematical sophistication. Sure, the en- vironment is more tangible, in the sense that you can put your hands on it: you can go out and look at the various office buildings, malls, and housing subdivisions the government suddenly owns; you can re- view the bank's records; everything's not floating around, stranded, twenty thousand miles in space. But in another sense the environment features a lot more uncertainty—events you can't possibly predict. It's like trying to mobilize a satellite rescue but not being able to rely on the basic laws of physics—or seeing those laws change every few weeks, in what seems to be a completely random manner. I mean, eco- nomics has its cycles, but we've never been quite so far out on a cycle before, and nothing seems to pertain.

"You've got the federal government changing accounting regula- tions from one day to the next, so that dozens of once healthy S&Ls suddenly turn sick. You've got the fallout from all those speculative ventures—I'm meeting a lot of the same sorts of thrifts over here I last saw over there on the trading floor, gobbling up all those hybrid mortgage derivatives. You've got fraud. It's incredible. The numbers are so huge it just dwarfs any other financial crisis we've ever been exposed to. And, believe me, it's got *terrible* convexity." He paused, and then said, "But, anyway, that's how I pass my time these days."

With that, Isaacs came to a full stop. As he'd been talking, he'd indeed seemed to be suggesting a sense of growing distance from his current vocation. "Well," I said, after a long pause. "I guess the obvious question is: What are you going to do next?"

Isaacs's expression darkened. He got up from behind his desk and went over to the door, which had been slightly ajar. He went out into the corridor, peered around, reentered, shutting the door firmly behind him. He closed the curtains over his glass wall, cutting the office off from the view of occupants of the various cubicles outside, and then returned to his desk.

"The thing is, it has all been a giant mistake," he said abruptly. "I've been miserable the entire time. I mean, sure, it was fine, it was interesting, but MIT, rocket science, the Street—my heart was never really in any of it, even if at times my head was. I was just doing it because I could do it. It wasn't what I really wanted to be doing. There was only one thing I ever *really* wanted to be doing, and now the time has come. I've got to quit fooling myself—I've got to just go out and do it."

And that is?

"This," Isaacs said. He reached into the bottom drawer of his desk, burrowed beneath an overlay of miscellaneous papers, extracted a glossy catalogue, and tossed the catalogue onto the desktop, facing me.

It was the catalogue of the Ringling Brothers and Barnum & Bailey Clown College, in Venice, Florida.

"All I ever wanted to be, from the earliest moment I can remember, was a clown," Isaacs now declared. "I used to pester my parents to take me to the circus every time it came to town. We'd go, and I'd make sure to 'get lost' behind the tents, just wandering around, soaking it all in:

the elephants and the trapeze artists and the peanut venders and the clowns, the clowns—especially the clowns! One of the peak experiences of my childhood was the time my father took me down to see the Circus Hall of Fame, in Sarasota, Florida. I taught myself to juggle by the time I was ten. I taught myself to throw small pieces of food high into the air, or else get somebody else to drop them from third- or fourth-story windows, and catch them in my mouth: M&Ms, peanuts, french fries, grapes. Grapes are especially good—nice aerodynamics, and they don't break your teeth if you miss. With devilled eggs, you don't have a lot of room for error.

"My mom got me a unicycle when I was twelve. I learned to ride it, and I'd play basketball on top of it, juggle. I taught myself to ride it blindfolded—the sort of thing that, if you'd asked me about it at MIT, whether it was even possible to do it, I'd have figured it was like flying a helicopter upside down: theoretically impossible, but doable." Isaacs started toward the whiteboard, reconsidered, and sat back down.

"Actually," he continued, "I applied to Clown College once before—in 1978, after completing my undergraduate program at MIT. It was a highly competitive admissions process—more so, even, than for MIT. Several thousand people applied for a few dozen slots. And I got accepted. But my folks just about threw a fit—they hadn't invested all their hard-earned money in getting me an MIT degree so I could run off and become a clown—with the result that I let it ride. Maybe it's better that I did—better that I proved to myself that I could do all this other stuff. But okay, now I've proved it.

"At TRW, too, I was continually haunted by intimations of my alternative life. It turned out that right down the street from our Redondo Beach facility were the tracks where they parked the big, long, silver circus trains whenever they came to town. I'd duck out of work early to go over and gaze. I love trains, because they're part of the circus. Why do you think I did my master's thesis on trains?

"And then, coming here to Wall Street, I still wasn't able to shake the hankering. In the morning, getting dressed, I'd see myself climbing into my professional corporate suit for another day of doing my professional corporate shtick, and sometimes I'd step back for a few moments, and it just seemed to me so funny that these people were listening to me and taking what I had to say seriously, because all along it was just me, Gary, tooling around on my unicycle. Evenings, I'd head out of here, with all the other suits, and sometimes the incongruity would just overwhelm me.

"But, I mean, I'm tired of all this. I'm tired of coming to work and passing my time coming up with ever more complicated ways of marketing securities, dressing them up with ever more elaborate bells and whistles. I want to dress *myself* up with *real* bells and whistles."

Isaacs went on to tell me how earlier this year, when the circus was in town, he'd taken off from work early and headed for Madison Square Garden to audition, along with dozens of other would-be clowns, and he'd been the only one wearing a suit. (The Ringling Brothers and Barnum & Bailey Circus holds a day of auditions at each of the major stops on its annual tour, and promising candidates are invited to apply for admission to Clown College, which offers an eight-week course of study each fall. Tuition is free, but a six-hundred-dollar fee is required for makeup and costumes. The Ringling Brothers organization operates the college as a sort of clown nursery.) Actually, at that audition Isaacs kept himself pretty much over to the side. The place was crawling with newspaper photographers and with cameramen from the local TV stations, and Isaac didn't want to risk being captured in print or on video, his secret hankering blatantly displayed for everyone to see. Not yet, anyway. He still wasn't sure. But in the days that followed he did summon the nerve once again to fill out the application form (a daunting six-page inventory, with questions ranging from which foreigners you like most, and which least, to when you last cried, and why), and he spent the next several months waiting anxiously.

"And then the other day," he continued, "as I was coming back in from lunch, my secretary gave me a message that Stephen Smith, the director of Clown College, was trying to get in touch with me. 'What are you doing?' she said, handing me the message. 'Running off to join the circus?' She laughed uproariously at her own joke. People here don't have a clue. So I called Smith back, and he said, 'I've been reviewing your application, and I have just two questions for you: First, do you have any idea what you're getting yourself into here? And, if so, are you completely out of your mind?' I answered yes on both counts, and he said, 'Well, in that case I have the honor to inform you that you've been accepted into Ringling Brothers and Barnum & Bailey Clown College's class of 1990.' So there you go."

Isaacs reached into the space between his desk and the wall and pulled out an artist's portfolio. "Another one of the things they don't know about me here is that in my spare time I've been pursuing a parallel career in photography," he said. "I mean, sure, on a much less exalted level—but it's one of the things I've been doing to keep my sanity." He unzipped his portfolio and invited me to examine several examples, a nice variety of images. "One of the things I intend to do is to keep a photographic record of the entire enterprise—a season at Clown College as seen from a clown's point of view," he continued. My gaze had come to rest on a self-portrait he had apparently taken a few months earlier (it was signed and dated 1990), himself standing, facing the mirror in his bathroom. His pose was dour, serious, professional, corporate, the camera held at his chest. Atop his head, however, he'd perched one of those large circular aluminum reflector lamps. He'd frontlit the scene from below, so that his body was casting a goofy shadow onto the blank wall behind. The shadow looked like one of those cheap Martians from the B movies of the fifties, or else some deep-sea diver thirty fathoms down. Clearly—you could see it in the eyes—it was time for this investment banker to be coming up for air.

A few minutes later, I was bidding Isaacs good-bye, thanking him for his story and wishing him well. Once in the elevator, however, I shuddered. I mean, here was a man who probably knew about as much as anyone about the true extent of the savings-and-loan crisis facing our country, and he was saying, "You know what, forget this—I'd rather be a clown!" It was a little scary. But, in any case, I was hooked, and I knew I'd be having to keep up with this fellow one way or another as he launched into his new career.

II.

In mid-August, Isaacs took leave of his job, and of Manhattan, and drove to Florida. Venice is about half an hour south of Sarasota, which, in turn, is about an hour south of Tampa Bay, or roughly midway down Florida's Gulf Coast. Ringling Brothers has had its winter quarters in Venice since 1959; Clown College opened there in 1968 and has been a fixture of the place ever since. Clown College puts its student body up in a motel along the Gulf waterfront about a mile away from the campus, and I managed to reach Isaacs there by phone the evening after the school's opening-day orientation session.

He was exultant. "They had us picked up by a bus here at around eight forty-five this morning," he reported. "About forty of us piled in, and they carted us over to the college, which takes place in a big white hangarlike building, the main structure in the middle of the circus's winter quarters. It's sort of like a big concrete tent, with yellow-and-red pennants streaming all around, and the big colorful circus logo splashed across the building's side—'THE GREATEST SHOW ON EARTH!' We got out of the bus, and they had us gather in front of the main entrance, by the turnstiles. The doors were still closed. This is the building where every year they give the public premiere for each new edition of the circus, before they take it out on the road—it's like a permanent big top. We were all just standing there, waiting for something to happen, and the bus driver banged on the door, and suddenly this roar of music kicked up inside, the doors slid open, and pandemonium had broken loose. We stood there dumbfounded, thunderstruck, weak-kneed: it took a moment for our eyes to adjust to the relative darkness inside, but gradually we could make out bleachers all around, a high triumphal arch of braided helium balloons bobbing high over the main ring, a bubble machine turned up full blast and dispensing a giddy stream of bubbles, and, in the center of the ring, about forty people going full-tilt bonkers at the sight of us. Turned out they were the faculty—there is a one-to-one student-faculty ratio—and they were cheering and jumping around, and somehow their cheers were being piped through the PA system, mingling with the music, so that the whole thing sounded like a huge, full-fledged ovation. For a second, it also looked as if the bleachers were packed, but as our eyes got further adjusted to things we realized that most of the audience was actually made up of full-scale painted cardboard cutouts that they'd propped into most of the seats: really silly-looking figures—kids, parents, pets, swamis. It all provoked an incredible explosion of emotion. I wish they'd had us wired up to measure our reactions: we'd have blown the needles right off their monitors. It's all been worth it. If nothing else comes of this whole thing, it was all worth it for just that one moment.

"Anyway, then they escorted us over to our seats in the bleachers facing the main ring, up there with the cardboard throng. Eventually, the music stopped and the faculty calmed down, and we, who'd taken to whoop-whoop-whooping like those audiences on *Arsenio Hall,* finally calmed down as well. The director of the college came up to the podium to welcome us. He was dressed a bit more formally than the others, which is to say in a white dress shirt, a white silk bow tie, white sneakers, and spanking-white farmer-style overalls. 'I'm Steve Smith,' he announced, 'and I'm going to be your guide through clown hell.' He's a youngish-looking guy, but he told us that he graduated from Clown College almost twenty years ago, with the class of 1971, and toured with the circus for several years after that. Most of the faculty turned out to be graduates of earlier Clown College classes. Several of them are currently active with the circus and have been pulled back from the two touring units for the duration of the college. Somebody was telling me how in 1967, when Ringling Brothers changed owners, there were only fourteen active performers in Clown Alley, and their average age was fifty-eight. Irvin Feld, the new owner, is supposed to have said, 'I know they can fall down, but can they get back up again?,' and to have founded the college the following year in an effort to remedy the situation. Today, there are over fifty clowns in the two units, almost all of them Clown College graduates, with an average age of twenty-three. As you can see, I'm getting started a bit late.

"So Smith began with a quote from Albert Einstein, about how the most beautiful possible experience is that of the mysterious, how the sense of wonder is the fundamental emotion at the cradle of both true art and true science, and how if you've lost it you might as well be dead. He went on to say that during the next ten weeks they were going to be teaching us a variety of techniques. And when you look at the schedule it's almost daunting what they've got in store for us: mandatory workshops on juggling, stilt walking, magic tricks, makeup, prop building, costume construction, pyrotechnics, unicycling, pantomime, improvisation, gag and character development, acrobatics and pratfalls—all that just for starters. But Smith said the main thing they were going to be trying to do was to stretch our imaginations. He gave this very nice pep talk, and then he introduced each member of the faculty—lots of whooping all around—and then he had us stand up one at a time and introduce ourselves, say where we came from, and tell why we'd decided to come here.

"The other students are all younger than I am. They come from all over, from places like Battle Creek, Michigan; Pullman, Washington; Oshkosh, Wisconsin; Upper Black Eddy, Pennsylvania; Mt. Desert Island, Maine; Atlanta, Georgia; and Venice, California—that fellow had only hours earlier completed a sixty-eight-hour transcontinental Venice-to-Venice bus run, so as to get here in time for the opening ceremonies. Some of them had great rationales for why they were here. The first kid got up and said, 'I want to be a clown because I want to freak out with a mass team.' Another guy said that it was because he got a lot of strange, crazy ideas in his head and he figured this was a way to get paid for them. One kid said it was because this was the only school that would take him. One of the women—about a fifth of the class are women—said she simply had no choice but to be a clown. I said I wanted to be a clown because they wouldn't let me ride my unicycle downtown where I worked. Another guy said he wanted to be a clown because he was sick of pulling teeth. That shut us all up. 'Cow teeth, that is,' he elaborated. So you can see I'm not the only one here with a curious résumé. Most of them are fresh out of college, or high school, or else have some sort of acting or theatrical background. But the guy they have me rooming with was an accountant with an insurance company in Connecticut for four years.

"So then Smith told us that on this one day only—and never again— we'd be offered an escorted tour of the back lot, out beyond the far hangar gates. We're never to go back there again, under any circumstances, because that's where they keep and train the wild animals all year round. And, sure enough, when we got back there, there they were— tigers and panthers and elephants and llamas and monkeys and cows—"

"Cows?" I asked.

"Yeah. A lady explained to me how they're trying to teach this group of cows to waltz. As we were walking around, taking it all in, one trainer came up to me and whispered, 'The real reason they don't let you back here is for fear you'll realize how similar the training regimens are.'

"We broke for lunch—today a catered affair, but from here on out strictly brown-bag. We got to know one another a little better. One fellow had the name Costello on his ID label, and I asked him if he was any relation. 'To Elvis, no,' he said. 'To Lou, yeah.' Turns out he's his great-grandson.

"After lunch, they had us doing all sorts of preliminary things: ID photos, incredibly detailed costume fittings, shoe fittings—we're each going to get a pair of those huge floppy shoes—and face plasterings. They took full plaster casts of our faces so as to be able, later, to mold perfectly fitted rubber noses.

"And between stations I kept coming back into the central arena. At one point, I was watching a group of the kids playing around with the bubble machine. They were miming baseball, and then football, and then golf. They were pirouetting as if in ballet. And gradually they devolved into a school of slow-motion fish, bobbing and floating in imaginary water, rippling their finlike arms, trying to mouth the bubbles, to open wide and swallow them whole. Suddenly I had this funny sensation, because for a moment it was exactly like being back in the savings-and-loan business all over again.

"It's incredible how well organized they've got everything over there. Unicycles lined up along the periphery, one beside another: three feet high, four feet, six feet; one that's actually five wheels, one on top of the next, so that the wheels mesh like gears; and one whose rim is made up entirely of shoes, one at the end of each spoke. Barrels of juggling pins. Stilts, low and tall and taller yet. All those portable shtick contraptions: the reducing machine, the washing machine, the food-vending wagon, the phony stove, the hollowed-out VW bug, the camera on a tripod with an eyeball lewdly ogling out, dangling at the end of a Slinky. Everything just sitting there, ready to be used, perfectly laid out, all of it close at hand, perfectly functional. Let me tell you, that place would put the High Bay back at TRW to shame."

About a week later, when I telephoned Isaacs again, I found him somewhat more subdued—though not much. "Some crazy people got off that bus last week," he remarked, with a tired sigh. "A lot of them are really good. There are some incredible jugglers, great stilt walkers, and several have all kinds of acting experience. It's pretty intimidating. It reminds me of my first days at MIT—how you might have been the brightest kid back in your high school class but now you were suddenly just like everybody else, if that, and how, in fact, for the first time in your life everybody else seemed a lot smarter than you. I imagine I'll get over it, but it's a little scary.

"We put on a variety show the other night—the faculty giving the students a chance to strut their stuff—and it was quite disconcerting, quite humbling. There were guys there eating fire, doing elaborate unicycle stunts, one guy juggling while he was handcuffed, a woman doing the equivalent of a competition-level gymnastics floor exercise. I didn't have any idea what I was going to do. Finally, I put in for thirty seconds with a piece I was calling 'A Very Cheap Bit.' Steve Smith has this line about how we should always remember that 'a cheap bit, well done, is a well-done cheap bit.' Well, this was about as cheap as you can get. I came into the ring, all decked out in white-face, rubbing my belly dolefully, as if I were really hungry, reaching into my pockets but extracting nothing—there was nothing there—and finally reaching into this virtually empty paper bag, poking all about, and eventually pulling out a single marshmallow. I then had all kinds of difficulty trying to get the thing into my mouth—my hand kept missing my face—till finally, in exasperation, I threw the marshmallow straight into the air— oh, twenty or thirty feet, so it disappeared into the darkness—and then, when it came plummeting back down, I managed to catch it perfectly in my open mouth. And I got a standing ovation—stole the show. It was great."

About a week after that call, I telephoned Isaacs once again, and this time he was decidedly more subdued. "I'm so sore," he said. "We all are. So incredibly tired. This place is like boot camp. They have us going fourteen hours a day, six days a week. You get up, stiff and sore from the previous day. The night before, you were too tired even to notice. It used to be you could hardly wait to get over there—the blocks passing by in the bus seemed endless—but now you're just desperately trying to squeeze in a few last moment of sleep and—bam!—you're already there. The first four hours in the morning, they have us doing acrobatics, stilt walking, juggling. By lunch—the first few days at lunchtime people were hopping about, showing off, experimenting with fresh turns; now lunchtime comes and it's like a landscape after battle: bodies strewn across the various mats, kids sprawled out sleeping or quietly moaning, massaging their strained ligaments. And then they have us up again, doing our routines—spitting water, falling off ladders, throwing pies, exploding little gunpowder-filled detonators off our backs, ducking hurled boards—all afternoon long and into the night. Being big. Big is something they keep emphasizing: how you have to be big, expansive, how your gestures have to play all the way back to the last row in Madison Square Garden, almost a quarter of a mile away. And then energy level: how your performance level has to be up, way up, from the moment you enter the arena till you march out with the finale, way up *and yet modulated,* under control, so you always still have someplace to go."

I asked Isaacs how he would compare Clown College with MIT now.

"Oh, there's no comparison," he said. "Clown College is much more demanding—physically, obviously, but mentally as well. At MIT, you had classes four hours a day, maybe, and you took notes. If you didn't understand something, you went up and asked. If you missed a class, you borrowed somebody else's notes. It was all relatively casual. Here there are no notes. They show you a stunt, how to do a front flip landing slam on your back, say, and you do it right away. It's impossible, but you do it. You do it again. One more time. And then they say, 'Now do it backward.' You're not scrawling notes across a piece of paper—it's your own body you're writing on. And it requires the utmost mental alertness. At MIT, you messed up a math problem: fine, cross it out and start over again. You can't stilt walk casually: it requires total concentration and centeredness, each time, all the time. At MIT, you messed up and you were only hurting yourself. Here others are depending on you every single second.

"And, in all this, college is obviously just a precursor of life in the circus itself. They're on the road three hundred and twenty-nine days, doing more than five hundred performances a year. Forget MIT. The level of concentration and alertness here beats anything at TRW or on the Street. It's like trying to rescue a satellite—only, all the time, every day, continuously. I'm sure if some of my friends back on the Street, busy trying to put together some deal or other, were to hear me talking like this, they'd say, 'What, are you kidding? That's just clowning.' But the alertness required is continuous. In finance, you take a break, you get help, change strategy—you make a mistake and you lose some money. With the circus, you make a mistake and you could break your neck, or, anyway, give yourself an injury whose effects would linger for years, or give someone else such an injury. It's fun—tremendous fun—but it's very serious work.

"And very dangerous. I don't think I ever realized how dangerous a place the circus can be—and not just for the lion tamers and the trapeze artists but, especially, for the clowns down there on the ground. The fifteen-foot-plank routine we were rehearsing today: the plank's standing there vertical, and then it gets released, it comes slicing through the air, and it's your job to position your body so it grazes just past you, close enough so you can react as if it cracked you straight in the face. Five inches too close and you've got a concussion. Five inches too far away and it's just not funny. Only one inch is funny.

"It's a science, but it's unlike any science I've ever been involved in before. At MIT, at TRW, one plus one equalled two, *every time*—that was the basis of the whole enterprise. On the Street, one plus one equalled two even if you were allowed to ignore the fact thanks to accounting procedures—those procedures, at any rate, were governed by strict mathematical relationships. Sometimes you didn't have the figures or the proper models, but had you had them they'd all have added up. Here, who knows what one plus one equals? Sometimes it equals nothing. Sometimes a thousand. It's the strangest thing. And yet the master clowns *do* know. They say *this* is funny, *that* is not. And, invariably, they're right. It's a knowledge—it's highly cerebral, even technical: it gets honed and honed and honed. Only, it's not analytical, and the kind of analytical thinking I've been used to up to now is almost entirely useless. Once in a while, I still find myself falling back into that old style of thinking. We were working on a stunt today where you fall onto a bunch of balloons and they momentarily cushion your fall as, one after another, they burst, and I was trying to figure out the physics involved—whether it was better for the balloons to be fully inflated or only partly so. It turns out medium is best, for various reasons. If we had a whiteboard I'd show you. But most of the time that kind of thinking is useless; in fact, it just gets in the way. You need a whole different kind of mental agility and conditioning—tied, of course, to a tremendous amount of physical conditioning as well.

"Clowns must be the most highly conditioned athletes in the world. Their season lasts the year round, and their bodies take tremendous punishment. We were mixing up cream pies today—they're whipped up out of soap flakes. Only lather from soap flakes gives the right consistency. You get that stuff in your eyes and it stings like hell. You're wearing three layers of costume, you're sweating, the makeup is melting into your eyes and making them sting all the more. And you're riding a unicycle. Backward. And sometimes, out on the road, they're doing that sort of thing three times a day."

The strange thing was, it sounded as if Isaacs couldn't wait. For all the moaning and groaning, he sounded as if he had found his heaven and never wanted to leave.

"Yeah," he remarked when I said as much. "Because, beyond all that, it's so much fun. It's so intensely focussed and yet so full of delight. And that's even before you get the audience. With the audience on top of all that . . ."

His voice drifted dreamily on. He spoke of the coming weeks, how on October 13th they would be mounting a gala graduation spectacular—a full-scale extravaganza performance, with family and friends cordially invited, highlighting both individual achievements and the integration of the troupe as a whole. Kenneth Feld, the son of the man who bought the circus back in 1967, and now his heir as the company's president, would be sitting up there in the bleachers. After the performance, Feld would offer apprenticeships to several of the graduates—if past years were any guide, however, to no more than about a third of them. The winners would get to perform with one of the circus's two travelling units over the coming year—a sort of graduate school following the college's undergraduate education. After that, if everything went well, they might even get offered regular positions. The competition was fierce, but fiercely sublimated, for one of the things Feld would be looking for, they were continually being told, was evidence of a sense of teamwork, of fellow-feeling.

"We think about it all the time in the back of our minds, I'm sure," Isaacs told me. "But, finally, you have to compete with yourself, and not with others. You have to reach for your own best.

"Oh, I almost forgot to tell you. Remember that variety show we did where I performed my Cheap Bit? Well, the other night, the faculty cancelled the video they'd scheduled for us and instead presented their own variety show—all the bits they do out on the road, truly an awesome display. And then one of them came out with a piece that was introduced as 'An Even Cheaper Bit'—so I got a little nervous. He started out just like me—the sad hungry clown, the near-empty bag, the marshmallow hurled into the sky. Only he hurled his much, much higher, all the way up almost to the rafters. I was getting set to be truly amazed when, suddenly, it turned out that he had a confederate up there in the rafters, and the guy dumped a barrelful of marshmallows—hundreds of them came falling out of the sky all around the stage, and the one he'd actually hurled landed a good twenty or thirty feet away from where he was standing. It was hilarious. I must say, I was sort of flattered."

Postscript (1998)

The graduation ceremony at Clown College consisted of a three-hour Saturday evening extravaganza in which the class showcased its cumulative shtick before an assembled multitude of friends, family, tourists, townspeople, and assorted Ringling organization executives. Gary displayed several of his turns, perhaps most winningly a bit called "Rocketman," in which, mounted astride roller skates with an elaborate propulsive device strapped to his back, he haplessly endeavored to achieve launch—to no avail. (He swore at the time that the per-

tinence of this particular routine to his earlier career hadn't even occurred to him.)

The next morning, the class members milled about, sore and anxious, as the Ringling executives convened a private meeting to cull
their picks. In my mind's eye, the ensuing scene played out like the
conclusion of a movie: the executives emerging from their colloquy,
the forty graduates bunched together on the sloping central bleacher
in an otherwise empty performance hanger, the head of the college
thanking them all before proceeding to reveal the names of the eight
finalists who were being offered paid apprenticeships with the circus
itself. At that point in my mind-movie, the scene cuts to a wide-angle
shot of the entire class as the names, one by one, begin to be pronounced. The camera hones in slowly, tighter and tighter, on Gary
himself—the fifth name, the sixth, the seventh—achieving a full-face
vantage at the very moment the final name is intoned.

Not his.

And of course this outcome must have been deflating and dispirit-
ing, except that in the film version unfurling across the interior screen
at my Cranium Cineplex, you'd also see (it would register fleetingly
across Gary's face), how, notwithstanding this setback, he'd achieved
a profound liberation: after all, whatever else, he wasn't likely to be returning to the trading floors on Wall Street anytime soon.

Maybe the reason I see this last scene as a movie is because, of
course, as soon as my piece appeared in the *New Yorker*, Hollywood
came courting—and indeed, within a few weeks Gary was in L.A., being
squired about, the subject of a tantalizingly imminent potential cine-
matic blockbuster. Which, however, likewise never quite came off (or,
as they say in Hollywood, "hasn't quite come off *quite yet.*")

In the years since, Gary has continued to steer clear of his former
haunts in the rocket lab and on the trading floor. He's been honing
his art in various ways, trying his hand at computer animatronics,
for example, and increasingly focusing on his photographic passion—
compiling a portfolio on, among other themes, life around the circus.

The other day I asked him how he was managing to make ends meet, and he referred to various odd commissions, among them one for the commercial real estate department at Merrill Lynch which had him roaming the city, compiling snaps of various buildings involved in upcoming pool transactions. In this, his latest metamorphosis—swear to Knipl!—Gary Isaacs had literally become a real estate photographer.

Afterword

The title of the current volume, *A Wanderer in the Perfect City,* derives, in the first instance, from the name I assigned the Ben Katchor/Julius Knipl piece when it originally appeared in the *New Yorker.* Whether that name was meant to apply primarily to Katchor or to Knipl was never entirely clear at the time—just as now I leave it to the reader to decide whether as a title for this entire collection it best frames the lives of my various dear subjects or rather my very own.

I will, however, note several uncanny convergences regarding the title as it applies to me. I wonder about the word "wander." Indeed, this book's title might easily have been *A* Wonderer *in the Perfect City.* If the original collection from which this book derives, *Shapinsky's Karma,* was filled, as the preface to the current volume still suggests, with "Passion Pieces," I gradually came to see the book itself as part of an ongoing series that I have collectively taken to calling "Passions and Wonders." The first installment in that series, as I've since come to understand, was my very first book, *Seeing Is Forgetting the Name of the Thing One Sees,* a biography of contemporary artist Robert Irwin (1982), a volume which launched out with the following story:

> During the early seventies, when Robert Irwin was on the road a lot, visiting art schools and chatting with students, he was proffered an honorary doctorate by the San Francisco Art Institute. The school's graduation ceremony that year took place in an outdoor courtyard on a sunny, breezy afternoon, sparkling

clear. Irwin approached the podium, and began, "I wasn't going to accept this degree, except it occurred to me that unless I did I wasn't going to be able to say that." He paused, waiting as the mild laughter eddied. "All I want to say," he continued, "is that the wonder is still there." Whereupon he simply walked away.

Subsequent volumes in the series included *David Hockney's Camera-works* (1986), the earlier version of this book (1988), and then, most recently, *Mr. Wilson's Cabinet of Wonder* (1995), a work of magic-realist nonfiction that endeavored to conjure David Wilson's marvelous Museum of Jurassic Technology in Culver City, California. As the epigraph for that book I enlisted Michael Faraday's electrifying insight that "Nothing is too wonderful to be true."

So why *not* call this book *A Wonderer in the Perfect City?* Because, in the end, I am every bit as drawn to the theme of *wandering*—of loss and exile, deracination and wanderlust. My most recent book (1998), a collection of three nonfiction novellas, bears the title *Calamities of Exile* and concerns the adventures of three expatriates from wildly various totalitarian regimes (Iraq, Czechoslovakia, and South Africa), each of whom tries to do the right thing with regard to the dictatorship continuing to hold sway back in his homeland—the thing you or I, too, might have done if only we were far more courageous than we are—only to end up thoroughly jammed and bollixed. That book, in turn, is dedicated to my four Viennese grandparents—their names and dates are listed—each of whom, I suddenly realized recently, were themselves forced into complicated exile at about the same age and point in their respective careers as I am now.

One of them, the modernist composer Ernst Toch, had enjoyed a truly illustrious career in Weimar Germany—his operas and concerti and chamber pieces performed by all the finest players—that is, before he was forced to flee in the face of the rising Nazi onslaught. ("I have my pencil" was the simple coded message he telegraphed my grandmother, once he had established a brief refuge in Paris, indicating that the coast was clear for her and their daughter to join him. As if that was going to be enough. As if a pencil was all he would ever need.) They eventually found their way to America, and though he enjoyed modest success here as a teacher and a film composer, he never regained his onetime audience, and, worse, for a long while he despaired over the possibility that he might have utterly squandered his native inspiration—indeed, he feared he had gone completely dry. Following the end of the war, however, and a shattering heart attack, his inspiration resurged, and he launched out upon the most prolific period of his entire life, composing, among other works, seven full symphonies across his final fifteen years. The third of these, in many ways the greatest (it was awarded the Pulitzer Prize), he often characterized as his musical autobiography, and to it he appended, as motto, lines from Goethe's *Sorrows of Young Werther:*

> Of course I am a wanderer, a pilgrim on this earth.
> But can you say that you are anything more?

Lines that for him somehow managed to accomplish a harmonic conflation of his beloved German and (wandering) Jewish traditions, and at the same time suggested how musical autobiography might itself transmute into a microcosm of universal human history.

And lines whose uncanny aptness, over forty years later, to this current venture of mine, likewise reduce me to—or rather, perhaps, raise up in me—a state of hushed wonder.